THE LENSES OF GENDER

Transforming the Debate on Sexual Inequality

Sandra Lipsitz Bem

YALE UNIVERSITY PRESS
NEW HAVEN AND LONDON

Published with assistance from the foundation established in memory of Philip Hamilton McMillan of the Class of 1894, Yale College.

"The Stranger" is reprinted from *Diving into the Wreck, Poems, 1971–1972*, by Adrienne Rich, by permission of the author and W. W. Norton & Company. Copyright © 1973 by W. W. Norton & Company. The lines from "Natural Resources" are reprinted from *The Fact of a Doorframe, Poems Selected and New, 1950–1984*, by Adrienne Rich, by permission of the author and W. W. Norton & Company. Copyright © 1984 by Adrienne Rich. Copyright © 1975, 1978 by W. W. Norton & Company. Copyright © 1981 by Adrienne Rich. Sigmund Freud's letter to an American mother is reprinted from *The Life and Work of Sigmund Freud* by Ernest Jones. Copyright © 1957 by Ernest Jones; copyright © renewed 1985 by Mervyn Jones. Reprinted by permission of Basic Books, a division of HarperCollins Publishers, Chatto & Windus, and the estate of the author. The figure in Chapter 4 is reprinted, by permission, from S. L. Bem, "Genital knowledge and gender constancy in preschool children," *Child Development*, 1989, *60*, 653–654. © The Society for Research in Child Development. Much of the preface is taken verbatim from S. L. Bem, "On the inadequacy of our sexual categories: A personal perspective," *Feminism and Psychology*, 1992, *2*, 435–437. I am grateful to *Feminism and Psychology* for allowing me to quote so freely from my earlier essay.

Set in Baskerville and Gill Sans type by Keystone Typesetting, Inc., Orwigsburg, Pennsylvania. Printed in the United States of America by Vail-Ballou Press, Binghamton, N.Y.

Library of Congress Cataloging-in-Publication Data
Bem, Sandra L.
The lenses of gender : transforming the debate on sexual inequality / Sandra Lipsitz Bem.
p. cm.
Includes bibliographical references and index.
ISBN 0-300-05676-1 (cloth)
      0-300-06163-3 (pbk.)
1. Sex role.   2. Sex differences (Psychology).   3. Sexism.   4. Equality.   5. Gender identity.   I. Title.
HQ1075.B45   1993
305.3—dc20   92-26345 CIP

A catalogue record for this book is available from the British Library.

The paper in this book meets the guidelines for permanence and durability of the Committee on Production Guidelines for Book Longevity of the Council on Library Resources.

10 9 8 7 6

CONTENTS

Preface vii

Acknowledgments xi

1
Introduction 1

2
Biological Essentialism 6

3
Androcentrism 39

4
Gender Polarization 80

5
The Construction of Gender Identity 133

6
Transforming the Debate on Sexual Inequality 176

CONTENTS

Notes   197

References   211

Index   239

feminist studies. At the same time, these three gender lenses also provide a coherent and accessible intellectual framework for organizing both the multidisciplinary knowledge that feminist scholars have accumulated and the intellectual and political debates that feminism has generated. I hope this framework will have special value for those who are unfamiliar with feminist scholarship or have not yet managed to construct such a framework for themselves.

This book, then, is broad ranging, reaching far beyond my expertise as a psychologist. The reason I have stepped outside the traditional boundaries of my discipline is that a more specialized book could not have explained the institutional, ideological, and psychological mechanisms that together keep the economic and political power of a society primarily in the hands of men.

The risks of writing such a book are these. Because I poach on the domains of other specialists, my rendition of their discourse may seem unoriginal; on some occasions, it may not even ring true to their ears. The rewards, however, are worth the risks. Not only do I finally have the opportunity to place my own previous research and theory in its proper setting. I also get to write the book that, as a younger feminist struggling to make sense of the oppression of women and the oppression of sexual minorities, I would have most wanted to have read.

PREFACE

I was recently asked to write a brief essay for *Feminism and Psychology* on "how my heterosexuality has contributed to my feminist politics." That essay turned out to be rather different from what the editors expected because although I have lived monogamously with a man I love for over twenty-seven years, I am not now and never have been a "heterosexual." But neither have I ever been a "lesbian" or a "bisexual." What I am—and have been for as long as I can remember—is someone whose sexuality and gender have never seemed to mesh with the available cultural categories, and *that*—rather than my presumed heterosexuality—is what has most profoundly informed not only my feminist politics but also the theoretical analysis of this book.

When I say that my sexuality does not mesh with the available cultural categories, I mean that the sex-of-partner dimension implicit in the three categories of heterosexual, homosexual, and bisexual seems irrelevant to my own particular pattern of erotic attractions and sexual experiences. Although some of the (very few) individuals to whom I have been attracted during my forty-eight years have been men and some have been women, what those individuals have in common has nothing to do with either their biological sex or mine—from which I conclude, not that I am attracted to both sexes, but that my sexuality is organized around dimensions other than sex.

Similarly, when I say that my gender does not mesh with the available cultural categories, I mean that since earliest childhood, my own particular blend of temperament and behavior has seemed to fall outside the categories of male and female, masculine and feminine; indeed, being female has never seemed a salient feature of my self-concept. Like being human, it is a fact, but a taken-for-granted background fact rather than a nucleus around which I have constructed my identity. (Being a feminist, on the other hand, is such a nucleus.)

Living in a heterosexual marriage and rearing two children have also contributed to my feminist politics by prompting me to theorize about, and experiment with, both egalitarian relationships and gender-liberated child-rearing. But it is still my subjective sense of being outside the categories of my culture that has most profoundly contributed to my feminist politics, because it has enabled me to see how cultural categories construct and constrain social reality by providing the historically specific conceptual framework through which we perceive our social world.

My ability to understand and to articulate this insight in the domain of gender and sexuality has evolved dramatically over the past twenty years. In the early 1970s, I focused almost exclusively on the concept of androgyny (from the Greek terms *andro,* meaning male, and *gyne,* meaning female) because that concept seemed to challenge the traditional categories of masculine and feminine as nothing before had ever done. By the late 1970s and early 1980s, however, I had begun to see that the concept of androgyny inevitably focuses so much more attention on the individual's being both masculine and feminine than on the culture's having created the concepts of masculinity and femininity in the first place that it can legitimately be said to reproduce precisely the gender polarization that it seeks to undercut. Accordingly, I moved on to the concept of gender schematicity because it enabled me to argue even more forcefully that masculinity and femininity are merely the constructions of a cultural schema—or lens—that polarizes gender.

Finally, in this book, I theorize the concept of the gender-polarizing lens more completely than I did before, and I expand the underlying insight into a comprehensive analysis of how gender lenses systemically perpetuate not only the oppression of women but the oppression of sexual minorities as well. Specifically, I now believe that there are actually *three* gender lenses embedded in the culture: gender polarization, androcentrism, and biological essentialism.

These three gender lenses provide the foundation for a theory of how biology, culture, and the individual psyche all interact in historical context to systemically reproduce male power. I hope this theory will constitute an original and integrative contribution to the literature in

ACKNOWLEDGMENTS

I have been writing this book in my mind for over twenty years and writing it on paper for almost five. Accordingly, there are a number of people, institutions, and sources of inspiration that I would now like to acknowledge.

First is the Rockefeller Foundation, whose fellowship from the Changing Gender Roles Program enabled me to spend the 1987–1988 academic year on leave at Harvard, where I could easily get myself the broad liberal-arts education I needed to write this book by browsing in the bookstores in the mornings and reading voraciously on everything from anthropology to sociobiology in the afternoons.

Next are the specific articles that opened my eyes to a new way of looking at social life. The first, Catharine MacKinnon's "Difference and Dominance," enabled me to see that the structure of my social world is indeed an affirmative action program for men. To this article I owe my current emphasis on the lens of androcentrism. The second, Richard Shweder's "Anthropology's Romantic Rebellion against the Enlightenment," is a more difficult choice to explain. Suffice it to say that this article introduced me to the concept of enculturation, which figures prominently in Chapter 5 and, even more important, provided me with an intellectual context for my work on schemas, or lenses, that was far more congenial than anything I had yet seen in psychology.

In addition, let me acknowledge my enormous debt of gratitude to the ever-expanding literature by feminist scholars on gender and sexuality. Twenty years ago, that literature did not exist, and this book could not have been written without it. Nor, I should add, could this book have been written without the regular biweekly meetings of the

ACKNOWLEDGMENTS

Cornell Women's Studies Study Group, which brought the multidisciplinary literature of feminist studies to my doorstep and helped me to feel comfortable with it.

Finally, there are the many individuals who helped to make this a better book than it would otherwise have been. Included here are those who graciously read early drafts and clarified my misunderstandings in their fields of expertise: Kathy Abrams, Joan Brumberg, Avshalom Caspi, Robert Connell, Richard Dietrich, Debbie Frable, Nellie Furman, Carolyn Heilbrun, Andy Hostetler, Itsy Hull, Mary Katzenstein, Isaac Kramnick, Bev Lipsitz, Will Provine, Elizabeth Adkins Regan, Glenn Schellenberg, and especially Sally McConnell Ginet and Daryl Bem. Also included here are all the talented and dedicated people at Yale University Press, especially my manuscript editor, Mary Pasti, who miraculously excised my verbal tics without modifying my voice.

In the field of psychology, academicians are so much more likely to write journal articles than books that this may prove to be the only book I ever write. Therefore, I would like to dedicate this book to the nine people who have meant the most to me in my life:

my grandmothers, Esther and Jennie, for their boundless and unconditional love

my mother, Lil, for her pride in her intelligence, her love of reading novels, and her honesty about much preferring her work outside the home (even as a secretary) to her work within the home

my father, Pete, for his obliviousness to the rhythms of masculinity

my sister, Bev, for sharing both a complicated family history with me and a lifetime of gender nonconformity

my children, Emily and Jeremy, for their wonderfully different ways of being nobody else's children but mine and Daryl's

my husband of twenty-eight years, Daryl, for being (like Charlotte in *Charlotte's Web*) both a good friend and a good writer

my youngest and newest friend, Beth, for enriching my life beyond measure.

I

INTRODUCTION

Throughout the history of Western culture, three beliefs about women and men have prevailed: that they have fundamentally different psychological and sexual natures, that men are inherently the dominant or superior sex, and that both male-female difference and male dominance are natural. Until the mid-nineteenth century, this naturalness was typically conceived in religious terms, as part of God's grand creation. Since then, it has typically been conceived in scientific terms, as part of biology's—or evolution's—grand creation.

Consequently, most Americans did not see any inconsistency between commitment to equality and denial of political rights to women until the appearance of the women's rights movement in the mid-nineteenth century. This first wave of feminist advocacy not only established women's basic political rights; it also made the inconsistency between ideology and the treatment of women widely visible for the first time in U.S. history.

Beginning in the 1960s, the second major wave of feminist advocacy raised social consciousness still further by exposing—and naming—the "sexism" in all policies and practices that explicitly discriminate on the basis of sex. This second feminist challenge gradually enabled people to see that restricting the number of women in professional schools or paying women less than men for equal work was not a natural requirement of a woman's biological and historical role as wife and mother but an illegitimate form of discrimination based on outmoded cultural stereotypes. Even political reactionaries began to espouse the principle of equal pay for equal work.

But as profound as the transformation of America's consciousness has been during the past 150 years, hidden assumptions about sex and gender remain embedded in cultural discourses, social institutions, and individual psyches that invisibly and systemically reproduce male power in generation after generation. I call these assumptions the lenses of gender. Not only do these lenses shape how people perceive, conceive, and discuss social reality, but because they are embedded in social institutions, they also shape the more material things—like unequal pay and inadequate day care—that constitute social reality itself.

The purpose of this book is to render those lenses visible rather than invisible, to enable us to look *at* the culture's gender lenses rather than *through* them, for it is only when Americans apprehend the more subtle and systemic ways in which the culture reproduces male power that they will finally comprehend the unfinished business of the feminist agenda.

The first lens embedded in cultural discourses, social institutions, and individual psyches is the lens of *androcentrism,* or male-centeredness. This is not just the historically crude perception that men are inherently superior to women but a more treacherous underpinning of that perception: a definition of males and male experience as a neutral standard or norm, and females and female experience as a sex-specific deviation from that norm. It is thus not that man is treated as superior and woman as inferior but that man is treated as human and woman as "other."

The second lens is the lens of *gender polarization*. Once again, this is not just the historically crude perception that women and men are fundamentally different from one another but the more subtle and insidious use of that perceived difference as an organizing principle for the social life of the culture. It is thus not simply that women and men are seen to be different but that this male-female difference is superimposed on so many aspects of the social world that a cultural connection is thereby forged between sex and virtually every other aspect of human experience, including modes of dress and social roles and even ways of expressing emotion and experiencing sexual desire.

Finally, the third lens is the lens of *biological essentialism,* which rationalizes and legitimizes both other lenses by treating them as the natural and inevitable consequences of the intrinsic biological natures of women and men. This is the lens that has secularized God's grand creation by substituting its scientific equivalent: evolution's grand creation. As we shall see, nothing in this book denies biological facts, but I do argue that these facts have no fixed meaning independent of the way that a culture interprets and uses them, nor any social implications independent of their historical and contemporary context.

The lenses of androcentrism, gender polarization, and biological essentialism systemically reproduce male power in two ways. First, the discourses and social institutions in which they are embedded automatically channel females and males into different and unequal life situations. Second, during enculturation, the individual gradually internalizes the cultural lenses and thereby becomes motivated to construct an identity that is consistent with them.

Not all males in U.S. society actually have power, of course, and the term *male power* should thus be construed narrowly as the power historically held by rich, white, heterosexual men, for it is they who originally set up and now primarily sustain the cultural discourses and social institutions of this nation. It is thus not women alone who are disadvantaged by the organization of U.S. society but poor people, people of color, and sexual minorities as well. Of these several other systemic oppressions, the oppression of lesbians and gay men so directly derives from the androcentric, gender-polarizing, and biologically essentialist definition of what it means to be a woman or a man that I have systematically integrated my analysis of this oppression into the structure of the book. Although the other oppressions that intersect with the oppression of women are mentioned explicitly in only the final chapter on social change, the applicability of the lens-based analysis of male power should be apparent throughout.

Similarly, I have drawn virtually all my specific examples from the history, culture, and contemporary context of the United States. But many of these examples are just as applicable to other countries that share the historical legacy of Western culture. Accordingly, I am suggesting more generally that the lenses of gender are embedded in cultural discourses, social institutions, and individual psyches in virtually all male-dominated societies. And *that* is about as universal as one can get!

The following three chapters introduce the three gender lenses and illustrate their pervasiveness in both the historical and contemporary discourses of Western culture. I begin with biological essentialism because Western culture has for so long analyzed almost all issues related to women and men in terms of biological difference that this cultural concern with biology must be laid to rest before I can go on with my story.

Accordingly, Chapter 2, on biological essentialism, documents and exposes the longstanding tendency of biological theorists to naturalize the social and economic inequalities between the sexes—to make them seem natural and inevitable rather than historically constructed and modifiable—which they do by overemphasizing biology and underemphasizing the historical and contemporary social context. The chapter then outlines a more interactionist, biohistorical, and biosocial account of sexual inequality.

Chapter 3 documents and exposes the lens of androcentrism in four of the most central discourses of Western culture: Judeo-Christian theology, ancient Greek philosophy, Freudian psychoanalytic theory, and the history of American equal rights law.

Chapter 4 examines the lens of gender polarization by documenting the way that the allied fields of medicine, sexology, psychiatry, and psychology have together given scientific and medical legitimacy not only to the cultural requirement that the sex of the body match the gender of the psyche but also to the cultural privileging of exclusive heterosexuality. It also discusses challenges to the scientific tradition (including my own work on androgyny and gender schema theory) that have helped to undermine gender polarization and considers a certain modern tradition within feminist theory, sometimes known as the "woman-centered" approach, that is itself gender polarizing.

In contrast to these first chapters, Chapter 5 focuses on the psychology of the individual. Specifically, it introduces my own "enculturated lens" theory of individual gender formation, which is an extension and elaboration of my earlier gender schema theory. This theory analyzes enculturation itself, or how androcentric and gender-polarizing social practices transfer the lenses of gender from the culture to the individual. It also analyzes the process of self-perception and self-construction, or how the individual who has internalized the culture's gender lenses *self*-constructs a gendered personality, a gendered body, an androcentric heterosexuality, and an abhorrence of homosexuality.

Because not all individuals become conventionally gendered, Chapter 5 also considers those who resist the gender lenses and thereby construct a gender-subversive identity. This group is wildly diverse, including lesbians, gay men, and bisexuals, as well as anyone whose way of living or being violates the androcentric, gender-polarizing, and biologically essentialist definition of a "real" woman or man.

Chapter 6, the final chapter of the book, articulates the most obvious pragmatic prescriptions that issue from the theoretical analysis of the book as a whole. Here I argue that because women in modern U.S. society are most insidiously disadvantaged by androcentric policies and practices that appear to be gender neutral, feminists must reframe the cultural debate on sexual inequality so that it focuses not on male-female difference but on how androcentric discourses and institutions transform male-female difference into female disadvantage. Finally, I argue for more than the abolition of androcentrism; I argue for the abolition of gender polarization as well. This book, then, is not only an exercise in deconstruction but also my own personal first draft of a blueprint for reconstruction.

2

BIOLOGICAL ESSENTIALISM

Whether science has ever been—or can ever be—fully objective is the subject of lively debate among feminist scholars.[1] Although challenging the objectivity of all scientific inquiry is not my intent here, I do argue that the biological accounts of male-female difference and male dominance that have emerged since the mid-nineteenth century have merely used the language of science, rather than the language of religion, to rationalize and legitimize the sexual status quo.[2]

My argument begins with two case studies from the nineteenth century, one concerning class and national origin, the other concerning the differences between women and men; it moves on to the two biological theories of sexual difference and dominance that have dominated the scientific literature since the 1970s, sociobiology and prenatal hormone theory; and it concludes with a proposal for a more interactionist account of sexual inequality, one that opens the door to social change even as it explains why women and men have historically played such different—and unequal—roles in virtually every society on earth.

BIOLOGICAL POLITICS

Class and National Origin

During many shameful periods in the history of science, biological theorizing has been used to naturalize, and thereby perpetuate, social inequality.[3] Perhaps the best known example in the United States was the claim that Africans were particularly well suited to slavery because of their "intrinsic race character" (Patterson, 1854, quoted in Fredrick-son, 1971).[4] Less well known but equally shameful was the claim that both the sterilization and the immigration laws that the government passed in the early 1900s were necessitated by the decline in American intelligence that would inevitably follow if either the unrestricted prop-agation or immigration of certain "defective strains" (Brigham, 1923, p. 210) was allowed to continue. In the context of sterilization, the defective strains that the United States didn't want polluting its popula-tion were mostly the inmates of publicly supported or charitable in-stitutions, that is, the poor. In the context of immigration, the defective strains were mostly the eastern and southern Europeans—especially the Italians, Poles, Russians, and Jews—who were just beginning to immigrate to this country in large numbers. Northern and western Europeans, in contrast, had been immigrating without restriction for years.

To keep these defective strains under control, the United States passed a whole series of sterilization and immigration laws between 1907 and 1924. The Supreme Court upheld the Virginia sterilization law in particular in *Buck v. Bell* (1927); that law was then quietly used until 1972 to sterilize over 7,500 men, women, and children in various mental health facilities. In 1924, the Congress passed the Johnson-Lodge Immigration Act, which limited the proportion of immigrants from each country to the proportion already present in the U.S. popu-lation in the 1890 census. This census, it should be noted, was taken before the shift in immigration from northern and western Europe to eastern and southern Europe. Not only did the 1890 quotas severely restrict the number of eastern and southern Europeans who could enter the country at the time, but fifteen to twenty years later, they also kept out thousands of European Jews who were trying desperately to escape extermination at the hands of the Nazis.

When these restrictive immigration laws were passed, one appar-ent moral justification for them was the legitimacy provided by that most modern of social science inventions, the IQ test. Originally devel-oped by Alfred Binet to identify French children in need of remedial help at school, once in the United States the IQ test quickly became a tool of the growing eugenics movement, because it was reconstrued as a measure of inborn intelligence. An educational problem could have been remedied; intelligence was presumably set at birth.

At the invitation of the U.S. Public Health Service, Henry Goddard began administering a very early version of the IQ test to the immigrants on Ellis Island in 1912. By 1917, the Stanford psychologist Lewis Terman had developed an Americanized version of Binet's IQ test, still known today as the Stanford-Binet test, and two special versions had further been developed for very large groups and "illiterates," respectively. By the time the United States entered the First World War, the stage was thus set for massive IQ testing of the approximately two million men drafted into the armed services.

On the basis of the original work with newly arrived immigrants on Ellis Island, Goddard preliminarily concluded that nearly 79 percent of Italians, 80 percent of Hungarians, 83 percent of Jews, and 87 percent of Russians were "feeble-minded" (1917, p. 252). On the basis of the army data, Carl Brigham more definitively concluded that there had, in fact, been "a gradual deterioration in the class of immigrants" who had come to this country "in each succeeding five year period since 1902" (1923, p. 111); furthermore, the more "Nordic blood" in a given period, the higher the level of intelligence (p. 162).

This totally invalid conclusion about Nordic blood and intelligence was based on a single correlation: overall, the earlier an immigrant had arrived in the United States prior to testing, the closer his IQ was to that of native-born Americans. Never mind that an earlier arrival was probably correlated with coming to the United States at a younger age, having a better command of the English language, attending American schools, and having more experience with standardized tests: those correlations were never computed. Never mind that an earlier arrival was probably correlated with a higher IQ for immigrants from each and every country of origin: those correlations were never computed either. In the words of Carl Brigham, then a psychology professor at Princeton University and later the secretary of the College Entrance Examination Board and the designer of the Scholastic Aptitude Test (SAT), the results indicate the "genuine intellectual superiority of the Nordic group" (p. 180).[5]

In recent years, scientists have engaged in a running battle about whether Brigham's army study played a significant role in the passage of the Johnson-Lodge Immigration Act, with Leon Kamin (1974) and Stephen Gould (1981) arguing that it did and with Mark Snyderman and Richard Herrnstein (1983) arguing that it did not. But regardless of its influence on the Congress, if any, the important point here is that

the psychologists of the period were as racist and biologically essentialist in the making of science as the politicians were in the making of law.

Sex

The second half of the nineteenth century was a time of great social up-
heaval in the United States.[6] Not only did the abolition movement, the
freeing of the slaves, and the granting of the vote to black men dramatically alter the relations between the races, but these same events spurred
feminists like Elizabeth Cady Stanton, Lucretia Mott, and Susan B.
Anthony to challenge the legal and social inequalities between the
sexes as well. As early as 1848, Stanton and Mott convened the first
women's rights conference in Seneca Falls, New York, where Stanton
demanded women's suffrage, along with a whole range of marriage
reforms. By 1869, when Stanton and Anthony founded the National
Women's Suffrage Association, there was thus the beginning of a full-
fledged women's rights movement in the United States, which was
already demanding not only the very same right to vote and to be
educated that men had but also the very same right to speak in public,
to own property, to practice law, and even to wear pants.

This feminist challenge was so threatening to the social order that
biological theorizing about women and men intensified in the 1870s,
thereby revealing how science is intertwined with cultural ideology.
The theories of four scientists, or groups of scientists, are noteworthy:
Edward Clarke, Herbert Spencer, Charles Darwin, and Patrick Geddes
and J. Arthur Thomson.

For centuries, physicians used the concept of "vital force" (C. E.
Rosenberg, 1976, p. 4) to explain such obvious individual differences
as why some people are better able than others to resist disease and
thrive in stressful environments. After the German physicist and phys-
iologist Hermann von Helmholtz measured the speed of a single nerve
impulse in 1852, it seemed reasonable to assume that this vital force
was some form of electrical energy and, concomitantly, that the nervous system was itself governed by the same conservation of energy
principle that was already known to govern heat, light, and electro-
magnetism. The conservation of energy principle—also known as the
first law of thermodynamics—states that the total amount of energy in
a system always remains constant because energy can be neither created nor destroyed.

The conservation of energy principle was used to naturalize a great number of nineteenth-century beliefs, including the belief that people should not indulge immoderately in any single activity lest they sap their limited complement of energy for other activities. Beginning with the publication of Edward Clarke's *Sex in Education* in 1873, the conservation of energy principle was used to naturalize the antifeminist belief that higher education was not a suitable activity for a woman.

Clarke's basic thesis was straightforward. The nervous system has a fixed amount of energy. Any energy spent on the development of one organ necessarily reduces the amount of energy available to other organs. Because education diverts a woman's energy from the development of her reproductive organs to the development of her brain, it is harmful to a woman's health. Education is especially harmful during menstruation, because a woman's reproductive organs normally require the most energy at that time.

The idea that education might be dangerous to a woman's reproductive system was voiced by several other noted writers of the late nineteenth and early twentieth centuries, including the British psychiatrist Henry Maudsley, the British philosopher Herbert Spencer, and the American psychologist G. Stanley Hall. Like Clarke, these writers were all reacting to at least two related social changes taking place in their countries: (1) increasing numbers of colleges and universities were opening their doors to women; and (2) the elite women educated in these institutions were giving birth to fewer offspring than their less educated counterparts. In the United States, this difference in fertility was exacerbated by the ever-growing number of immigrants, whose fertility rates were high—like those of the lower socioeconomic classes generally. At apparent risk in both countries were thus not only Victorian standards of womanly behavior but also what G. Stanley Hall later termed race suicide (Hall, 1904/1919, p. 606).

To make his argument against women's education, Edward Clarke misapplied to a woman's body what was essentially the first law of thermodynamics. To create a theory of evolution that would naturalize virtually every hierarchy in Victorian society, including the roles of women and men, Herbert Spencer (1852, 1873, 1876) inadvertently reversed what was essentially the second law of thermodynamics and combined that reversal with an optimistic reading of Malthus's (1798/1960) population theory. Spencer's theory of evolution may be all but forgotten today, but in the late nineteenth century, it was even more influential than Darwin's.

The second law of thermodynamics states that even though the total amount of energy in the universe always remains constant, that energy becomes less and less useful over time. Spencer argued, in contrast, that for biological and social systems alike, the "persistence of force"—or the conservation of energy—always and inevitably produces progress. More specifically, the persistence of force always and inevitably produces a shift from uniformity to specialization, as can be seen in both the evolution of humans from single-celled organisms and the evolution of a class- and sex-based division of labor from an undifferentiated social organization. To add credibility to his claim that evolution is inherently progressive, Spencer reinterpreted Malthus's population theory, arguing that the harshness of the struggle for existence amid scarce resources inevitably produces, not the misery and vice that Malthus predicted, but the survival of the fittest.

Applying this "progressive" theory of evolution to class and sex, Spencer concluded that the existence of a class- and sex-based division of labor in society is biologically ordained. He also concluded that biology has molded the classes and the sexes to fit their respective social roles, making men more competitive, for example, and women more nurturant. So nurturant and charitable has biology made women, in fact, that they must now be denied the right to vote, for they might interfere with the natural course of progress by giving state help to those who would otherwise be unable to survive in the struggle for existence. As this tortured argument against women's suffrage makes clear, Spencer was in the forefront of that conservative social movement known as Social Darwinism.

Today, Herbert Spencer is much less known for his evolutionary theory than for his use of evolutionary thinking to promote a conservative social agenda. Indeed, the political use of evolutionary thinking in the late nineteenth century should by rights be called Spencerism, because at least initially, it was Spencer's evolutionary theory that was put to political purposes, not Darwin's; moreover, Darwin himself was never much of a social or political activist. Still, it was Darwin whose theory and evidence gave scientific legitimacy to the conservative politics of the period, and it was also Darwin whose evolutionary theory survived the test of time.

Charles Darwin (1859/1952, 1871/1952) was much more interested in the evolution of animal and plant species than in the evolution of human social organization. Like Herbert Spencer, however, he, too, constructed a theory of evolution that naturalized the sexual inequalities inherent in Victorian society.

Darwin's evolutionary theory has three primary ingredients: endless variation among individuals, the "selection"—both "natural" and "sexual"—of certain variants, and the continued survival of only the selected variants. In natural selection, it is assumed that some variants are more successful than others in relation to the physical conditions of life; hence, those variants are more likely to survive and to produce offspring. In sexual selection, it is assumed that some variants are more successful than others in mating; hence, those variants are also more likely to produce offspring.

Although sexual inequality is not inherent in either of these two selection processes, Darwin's discussion almost always presupposes that the males of each species are subject to more selection than the females and that, as a result, the males of each species are also more highly evolved than the females. As Darwin himself put it, males are subject to more sexual selection than females because, among other things, they have to both "drive away or kill their rivals" and "excite or charm" their sexual partners (1871/1952, p. 594). Likewise, they are subject to more natural selection than females because, among other things, they have to "defend their females, as well as their young, from enemies of all kinds, and to hunt, for their joint subsistence. . . . [This] requires the aid of the higher mental faculties, namely, observation, reason, invention, or imagination. These various faculties will thus have been continually put to the test and selected during manhood" (p. 566).

The result of all this unequal selection among humans is that man can attain "a higher eminence, in whatever he takes up, than can woman—whether requiring deep thought, reason, or imagination, or merely the use of the senses and hands" (p. 566). Put somewhat differently, "man has ultimately become superior to woman"; and it is fortunate for women that men pass on their characteristics to their daughters, as well as to their sons, because "otherwise it is probable that man would have become as superior in mental endowment to woman, as the peacock is in ornamental plumage to the peahen" (p. 567).

Although Darwin was working on his theory of evolution at about the same time that Mendel was discovering the principles of genetics, and although modern evolutionary biology has adapted Darwin's original insights to accommodate those genetic principles, Darwin himself knew nothing at all about genes. In fact, he was a firm believer in the Lamarckian idea that an individual inherited from its parents all the characteristics that earlier generations had acquired during their lifetimes, which were somehow transmitted through their blood to the sperm and the egg.

In the last decade of the nineteenth century, when the German biologist August Weismann and others first suggested that an individual's life experiences did *not* affect the part of the sperm or egg that was related to heredity—which Weismann called the germ plasm—some scientists inferred that the differences between women and men could not have evolved historically, as Darwin had proposed. Consider, for example, Patrick Geddes and J. Arthur Thomson, who argued that if the germ plasm remains constant from generation to generation, then the difference between males and females must be as old as life itself and must also stem from differences in the sperm and egg themselves. And what ancient differences in the sperm and egg might there be? Well, as anyone can plainly see, the sperm and its metabolism are "katabolic," that is, "active, energetic, eager, passionate, and variable." The egg and its metabolism, on the other hand, are "anabolic," that is, "passive, conservative, sluggish, and stable" (1890, p. 270).

Forget about natural and sexual selection working slowly over time to select different characteristics in males and females, respectively. Forget about the all-too-liberal implication of Darwinian theory that sex differences might even be modified over time through the transmission of a new life experience, like higher education. As Geddes and Thomson so poetically put it in 1890, "What was decided among the prehistoric Protozoa cannot be annulled by an Act of Parliament" (p. 267).

As noted earlier, it was not for purely scientific reasons that so many scientists engaged in so much biological theorizing about women and men between 1870 and 1920. But as guilty as they were of naturalizing sexual inequality, it was never the scientists alone whose vision of social reality was distorted by biological essentialism. Quite the contrary. Seeing through this lens was so much a part of the cultural zeitgeist that even feminists like Stanton and Anthony fell back on the premise of inborn racial difference when they thought it might further their argument for female suffrage.

JUST-SO STORIES OF SOCIOBIOLOGY

The particular blend of antifeminist politics and biological theorizing that prevailed in the United States at the turn of the last century had begun to decline by 1920. Although many later scientists continued to find biological accounts of both sexual difference and sexual inequality more plausible than the evidence warranted, science was gradually becoming so much more grounded in well-controlled empirical research—and after the Nazi era, so much more aware of how a biological theory of group difference could be abused—that few of the truly major figures in biology were theorizing about any group difference, including the difference between women and men, between 1950 and 1970.

That period of biological quiescence came to an abrupt end in the late 1960s, when the civil rights and women's liberation movements again threatened the established social order, much as the abolition and women's rights movements had done a century earlier. One of the first biological challenges to the civil rights movement came in 1969, when Arthur Jensen argued against Headstart and other compensatory education programs in an article in the *Harvard Educational Review* entitled "How Much Can We Boost IQ and Scholastic Achievement?" One of the first biological challenges to the women's liberation movement came in 1970, when Lionel Tiger argued in an article entitled "The Possible Biological Origins of Sex Discrimination" that the exclusion of women from "the major political, economic and military decision-making processes of our time" results not from male chauvinism or from "a coercive process of socialization" but from a "genetically programmed behavioural propensity" for males to create bonds with one another. "These bonds are intrinsically related to political, economic, military, police, and other . . . power- and dominance-centered subsystems . . . [and] equal female colleagues—even one—could interfere with [them]" (pp. 33, 36).

Although several other writers in this period also naturalized the inequalities of sex, race, and class in their biological theories, the bombshell came in 1975, when Edward O. Wilson of Harvard declared, in effect, that both human social behavior and human social organization were encoded in the genes. The title of Wilson's book, *Sociobiology: The New Synthesis,* was a play on Julian Huxley's earlier *Evolution: The Mod-*

ern Synthesis. The title alone revealed the scale of Wilson's ambition. Just as Huxley had synthesized Darwinian evolution and modern genetics, so Wilson would now subsume the humanities and social sciences within biology.

Wilson's *Sociobiology* keyed in to the ongoing cultural debate over men's and women's roles with a whole new evolutionary perspective on the origins of sexual difference and sexual inequality. Apart from theorizing about the sexes, however, Wilson so masterfully expanded on an earlier conceptual breakthrough by W. D. Hamilton (1964) that his theory almost instantly became the most prominent and the most controversial biological theory of human social life in the twentieth century.

Since the time of Darwin, evolutionary theory had been plagued by the unsolved problem of how a behavior like altruism could continue to exist in a species if the altruists themselves did not reproduce. The problem was salient to entomologists like Wilson because many social insect species contain precisely this anomalous group of altruists who tirelessly work for the good of the group but who are sterile and hence unable to pass on their altruistic genes. As late as 1962, evolutionary theorists like V. C. Wynne-Edwards were still trying to explain the persistence of insect altruism with a variant of one of Darwin's ideas about how natural selection might operate at the level of the group rather than at the level of the individual. But the theory was not adequate, so evolution remained at the periphery of biological theorizing about social behavior.

The solution to this longstanding problem, as set forth by Hamilton in 1964, was not group selection but kin selection. True, the altruists themselves do not reproduce, but their siblings do; and as Hamilton showed mathematically, those siblings share an even higher proportion of the altruists' genes than the altruists' own offspring would. To the extent that insect altruists help their kin to survive and reproduce, they are helping their own genes to survive and reproduce. Hamilton's mathematics, it should be noted, applies to social insects, not human beings.

This solution to the problem of altruism explicitly shifted the focus of natural selection from the individual to the gene. A century earlier, Darwin had argued that evolution selects whatever traits foster individual survival or individual ability to reproduce. In contrast, Hamilton said that evolution selects whatever traits foster the ability of the genes to reproduce. According to this model, individuals might sometimes be altruistic, but their genes are always selfish.

By positing the gene as the target of natural selection, Wilson constructed a theory of genetic evolution that could apply to a dazzling array of behaviors and species, including human beings. Wilson elaborated on his analysis of human beings in a full-length book entitled *On Human Nature* in 1978. About the same time, four other scientists working within Wilson's framework also published sociobiological analyses of human behavior; they included David Barash (*The Whisperings Within*, 1979), Richard Dawkins (*The Selfish Gene*, 1976), John MacKinnon (*The Ape within Us*, 1978), and Donald Symons (*The Evolution of Human Sexuality*, 1979). The aspects of sociobiology, or of the controversy surrounding sociobiology, that do not relate directly to sexual difference and sexual inequality are beyond the scope of this book. As will become clear, however, the problems with the sociobiological analysis of the sexes apply to the whole of the sociobiological analysis of human behavior.

Sexual Difference and Sexual Inequality

The sociobiological analysis of both sexual difference and sexual inequality is based on the simple fact that the number of offspring a male can produce is biologically limited only by the number of fertile females that he can manage to inseminate, whereas a female can produce only a limited number of offspring in her lifetime—a maximum of about twenty in the case of humans. In the days when evolution was still thought to operate on traits that benefited the species as a whole, the different reproductive capacity of the sexes was seen as far less important than their shared interest in the survival of the species. But now that evolution was thought to operate only at the level of the genes, that very same sex difference in reproductive capacity suddenly seemed all important. As Wilson himself put it in 1978,

> During the full period of time it takes to bring a fetus to term,
> . . . one male can fertilize many females but a female can be
> fertilized by only one male. Thus if males are able to court one
> female after another, some will be big winners and others will
> be absolute losers, while virtually all healthy females will suc-
> ceed in being fertilized. It pays males to be aggressive, hasty,

fickle, and undiscriminating. In theory it is more profitable for females to be coy, to hold back until they can identify males with the best genes. In species that rear young, it is also important for the females to select males who are more likely to stay with them after insemination. Human beings obey this biological principle faithfully. (Pp. 124–125)

Wilson's "conflict of interest between the sexes" (p. 124) is described even more baldly by David Barash in *The Whisperings Within*:

Sperm are cheap. Eggs are expensive. . . . For males, reproduction is easy, a small amount of time, a small amount of semen, and the potential evolutionary return is very great if offspring are produced. On the other hand, a female who makes a "bad" choice may be in real evolutionary trouble. If fertilization occurs, a baby is begun, and the ensuing process is not only inexorable but immensely demanding. . . . The evolutionary mechanism should be clear. Genes that allow females to accept the sorts of mates who make lesser contributions to their reproductive success will leave fewer copies of themselves than will genes that influence the females to be more selective. Accordingly, genes inducing selectivity will increase at the expense of those that are less discriminating. For males, a very different strategy applies. The maximum advantage goes to individuals with fewer inhibitions. A genetically influenced tendency to "play fast and loose"—"love 'em and leave 'em"—may well reflect more biological reality than most of us care to admit. (P. 48)

In fairness to Wilson, it should be noted that his discussion of human evolution included the speculation that humans and a few other primates like the marmosets and the gibbons may have evolved under conditions that actually made it reproductively more advantageous for males to pair-bond with females and to cooperate in the rearing of young than to seek additional mates.

But other sociobiologists must have found the hypothesized conflict between the sexes to be much more compelling than the factors tempering that conflict because the consequences they extrapolated from it were truly extraordinary. On the male side, for example, sociobiologists offered up sexual promiscuity, rape, the abandonment of mates and children, intermale aggression, an intolerance for female infidelity, the sequestering of females, the killing of stepchildren, and universal male dominance. On the female side, they offered up the coy holding back of sex, the careful selection of sexual partners, the investment of time and energy in parental care, the preference for at least serial monogamy, and the deceiving of males with respect to paternity.

The sociobiological reasoning in all these cases was straightforward. Males are sexually promiscuous, they rape, and they abandon mates and offspring because these behaviors enable them to maximize the number of females they can inseminate and thus to maximize the reproduction of their own genes. They are aggressive toward other males (especially during the breeding season if they are not human) because they are in competition with those males for the scarce reproductive resources of females. They are intolerant of female infidelity, and they sequester females whenever possible to ensure that those scarce female resources are used to reproduce their own genes and not someone else's. They kill stepchildren to ensure that any investment they do make in parental care will benefit their genes and their genes alone. And finally, they are universally dominant over females because their reproductive strategies so highly select them for that particular trait.

Females, in contrast, withhold their sexual favors until they have found the best sexual partner because that strategy enables them to invest their scarce reproductive resources in both the best males and the best offspring. They invest far more time and energy in parental care than males do because they cannot so easily replace the offspring in whom they have already invested nine months of pregnancy. They prefer at least serial monogamy to promiscuity because that is the social organization that gets males to invest the most time and energy in the survival of female genes. And finally, they sometimes lie about paternity because that behavior, too, gets some male—even if not the father—to help them in the reproduction of their genes.

Not surprisingly, this sociobiological analysis of sexual difference and sexual inequality has generated enormous controversy, with feminists like Ruth Bleier (1984), Anne Fausto-Sterling (1985), and Janet Sayers (1982) seeing it as nothing more than the twentieth-century version of science stepping in to naturalize the status quo and with sociobiologists defending it as neither politically conservative nor biologically essentialist. David Barash, the sociobiologist who may be more criticized by feminist scholars than any other for his discussion of rape, explains that his "intent has been only to explore the evolutionary biology of male-female differences, not to espouse any particular social, political or ethical philosophy. Evolution simply *is*—or, better yet, evolution *does*. It says nothing whatever about what ought to be. . . . Furthermore, the inclinations predicted by sociobiology are just that: inclinations. They are not certainties" (1979, p. 70).

Critiques of Sociobiology

Sociobiologists begin their analysis of human behavior with what they construe to be the universal aspects of human social life and human social organization.[7] In developing a theory of those universals, they focus on evolutionary and genetic factors, rather than cultural or historical factors, because they rightly see any purely environmental explanation as inadequate. One such explanation of sexual difference and dominance that is "common in social science," according to David Barash, and which sociobiology rejects outright, is that "boys act as they do because such behavior is taught to them, and the same for girls." Barash concedes that

> we do do a great deal to inculcate gender identity among our children. Girls are more likely to be given dolls to play with, and boys . . . airplanes. . . . But as an all-encompassing explanation for male-female differences, early social experience is simply insufficient. If we are to believe that there are no real male-female differences in behavior, and that such differences as we see are simply a result of the differential experiences that society provides little boys and little girls, we must also explain why such differences are promulgated independently by every society on earth. (1979, pp. 71–72)

From the sociobiological point of view, the reason for this cross-cultural universality is clear. During our evolutionary prehistory, the males with more aggressive, dominant, and sexually promiscuous genes were able to leave many more copies of themselves, as were the females with more sexually selective and maternal genes. As a result of this evolutionary selection, genetic differences between the sexes that are directly related to behavior now exist in every culture, and these universal genetic differences ultimately explain why boys and girls are everywhere treated differently.

It is not only the universality of sexual difference and dominance that sociobiologists seek to explain with this model. They also seek to explain every other aspect of human behavior construed to be universal—including aggression, altruism, territoriality, xenophobia, and war. In every case, however, the reasoning is the same. Evolutionary selection enables certain behaviorally specific genes to leave many more copies of themselves than other behaviorally specific genes; as a result, the human species now has a genetic makeup that predisposes it to behave in more or less the same way in all cultures.

Critics of sociobiology have attacked at least three major aspects of this explanatory model. First, they have attacked the empirical claim of universality, arguing that in almost every instance, sociobiologists have distorted the human and the animal evidence, and in some cases, even the plant evidence, in order to create the appearance of many more human universals than may actually exist. Second, they have attacked the empirical base for the genetic claims of sociobiology, arguing that no evidence as yet exists for any link between human genes and the kinds of human behaviors that sociobiologists are trying to explain. And finally, they have attacked the nature of sociobiological reasoning itself, arguing that in the absence of any empirical evidence for the kinds of behaviorally specific genes that sociobiologists have postulated, the whole sociobiological enterprise becomes an exercise in tautological reasoning. To paraphrase Ruth Bleier:

> Having selected a certain animal or human behavior, sociobiology makes it a *premise* that that behavior has a genetic basis; it then constructs a speculative story to explain how that behavior could have served to maximize the reproductive success of the individual, and could thereby have also been selected during the course of evolution, *if* it were genetically based; this *conjecture* then becomes evidence for the *premise* that the behavior is genetically based. (1984, p. 17)

Precisely this circularity has led at least one set of critics to liken the evolutionary reasoning of sociobiology to the just-so stories of Rudyard Kipling that were so popular during the nineteenth century (Lewontin, Rose & Kamin, 1984, p. 258).

Although I agree with all three of these earlier critiques, my own critique of sociobiology focuses less on the empirical question of whether behaviorally specific genes and human universals exist than on the more conceptual question of how sociobiology theorizes the interaction between biology and culture—and what role that theorizing gives to cultural invention. Sociobiologists have constructed what they consider to be a theory of biology and culture working together to create human universals. That theory, however, is so unimaginative about how biology and culture interact that it ends up treating culture and history almost as epiphenomena.

The sociobiological model of the interaction between biology and culture is easy to explain. Behaviorally specific genes provide genetically programmed predispositions for humans in all cultures to behave in particular ways. Those universal predispositions are differentially shaped by the social practices of different cultures, however. Put somewhat differently, culture adds a surface, or phenotypic, variability on top of what is a deeper, or genotypic, universality. In discussing how very little room biology allegedly allows for social change, E. O. Wilson argues that, like it or not, human cultures have but "three choices" (1978, p. 132). They can exaggerate genetic predispositions, they can fight against them, or they can leave them alone.

In fact, however, cultural invention can so radically transform the situational context of human life that the human organism can be liberated from what had earlier seemed to be its intrinsic biological limitations. Consider but three examples.

1   As a biological species, human beings require food and water on a daily basis, which once meant that it was part of universal human nature to live as survivalists. But now human beings have invented agricultural techniques for producing food, and storage and refrigeration techniques for preserving food, which means that it is no longer part of universal human nature to live as survivalists.

2   As a biological species, human beings are susceptible to infection from many bacteria, which once meant that it was part of universal human nature to die routinely from infection. But now human beings have invented antibiotics to fight infection, which means that it is no longer part of universal human nature to die routinely from infection.

3   As a biological species, human beings do not have wings, which once meant that it was part of universal human nature to be un-

able to fly. But now human beings have invented airplanes, which means that it is no longer part of universal human nature to be unable to fly.

As dramatically liberating as these three examples of technological innovation clearly are, the general principle that they illustrate is so mundane and noncontroversial that even sociobiologists would unhesitatingly endorse it. Simply put, the impact of any biological feature depends in every instance on how that biological feature interacts with the environment in which it is situated. That is why there is a technical distinction between a genotype and a phenotype in the first place. That is also why biologists never specify a one-to-one correspondence between biology and behavior but always specify a norm, or range, of reaction. More specifically, they say that in Environment 1, a given biological feature will produce Behavior A, but in Environment 2, that same biological feature will produce Behavior B.

Ironically, sociobiologists massively underestimate the contributions of culture and history to this interaction, not only because they pay too little attention to culture and history but because they also pay too little attention to what is arguably the most distinctively human feature of human biology: the ability of human beings to transform their environments through cultural invention and thereby to transform themselves. Just like the human capacity for language, this human capacity for cultural invention is a product of the evolution of the human brain.

Minimizing how the human brain has itself evolved leads sociobiologists to misconstrue the human organism as a being whose way of relating to the world is heavily constrained by genetic predispositions for specific behaviors, rather than as a being whose way of relating to the world is much more loosely constrained by a less specific set of genetic programs. It also leads sociobiologists to grossly underestimate how radically different the situational context of human life could be in different historical eras.

As noted earlier, sociobiologists are especially concerned with the universals of human social life and human social organization because they see these universals as the product of biology alone. If there is any single moral to my critique of sociobiology, however, it is that even universals are the product of an interaction between biology and culture. Accordingly, when trying to explain the emergence of a true human universal across time and place, scientists had better look for a constant in history and culture, as well as a constant in biology, because it is the interaction between those two constants that has produced that universal, not the constant in biology alone.

PRENATAL HORMONE THEORY

Long before sociobiologists came up with their own particular just-so story about the differential evolution of male and female genes, less fanciful biopsychologists offered a hormonal theory about the differential development in utero of male and female brains.[8] This prenatal hormone theory was an extrapolation of what was already known in the late 1940s about the differential development in utero of male and female bodies (Jost, 1953).

By the late 1940s, biopsychologists had established that regardless of their genetic sex, all mammalian embryos initially have the rudimentary tissue required for both male and female genitalia, as well as for both male and female reproductive organs. They had also established that what fashions this hermaphroditic embryo into either a male or a female body is the presence or absence of testosterone during a critical prenatal period. An embryo will thus develop into a male body if testosterone is present during this critical period; it will develop into a female body if testosterone is absent; and it will develop into a partly male and partly female—or pseudohermaphroditic—body if testosterone is present but either in the wrong amount or for the wrong period of time.

A decade later, this observation about male and female bodies becoming physically differentiated during a critical prenatal period was expanded into the theory of hormonally induced brain organization (Phoenix et al., 1959). According to this theory, prenatal hormones not only shape mammalian bodies into a male or female pattern during the critical period of sexual differentiation; they also irreversibly organize mammalian brains into a male or female pattern, and these hormonally organized brains, in turn, organize mammalian hormone function and mammalian behavior into a male or female pattern.

The evidence for this prenatal hormone theory is now extensive. In every mammalian species that has been comprehensively examined to date—including guinea pigs, rats, mice, hamsters, dogs, sheep, ferrets, voles, rabbits, and rhesus monkeys but excluding humans—prenatal hormones have been shown to have some kind of permanent organizing effect on sexually dimorphic behaviors directly related to copulation, such as mounting and positioning one's body for penile penetration (Baum, 1979). In some of these mammalian species, prenatal hormones have also been shown to have a permanent organizing effect on sexually dimorphic behaviors not directly related to copulation, such as aggression and activity level (Beatty, 1979; Meaney, 1988), as well as on the cyclicity of hormone production—which is directly controlled by the hypothalamic portion of the brain in many species. Finally, in an even smaller number of species, prenatal hormones have been shown to have a permanent organizing effect on the structures of certain neurons within the brain itself (Arnold & Gorski, 1984; Feder, 1984).

In spite of the abundance of animal evidence supporting the prenatal hormone theory, there are at least two empirical reasons for thinking that this theory would not pertain to human beings as much as it does to other species.

1 Although prenatal hormones do shape the human body into a male or female pattern, they do not have any permanent effect on the cyclicity of hormone production in either humans or other primates (Karsch, Dierschke & Knobil, 1973; Kuhlin & Reiter, 1976; Goy & Resko, 1972; Valdés et al., 1979; Knobil et al., 1980). Breaking the link between the shaping of the body and the organizing of hormone function calls into question whether the functioning of the primate brain is even affected by prenatal hormones.

2 Even among rats, some of the effects of prenatal hormones on adult behavior are now known to be partially mediated not by a hormonally organized brain but by a social interaction pattern evoked by the male or female body of the young. To give but one example, male rat pups give off an odor different from that of female rat pups, and the additional anogenital licking that this odor evokes from their mothers is at least partially responsible for the higher rates of mounting behavior among male adults than among female adults (C. L. Moore, 1984). If sex differences are sometimes mediated by social interaction even among rats, they are even more likely to be mediated by social interaction among humans, whose social life is much more complex.[9]

But however much reason there was to doubt the human applicability of the prenatal hormone theory, the animal evidence was so provocative—and the habit of looking at human sex differences biolog-ically was so ingrained—that many studies were undertaken to test the prenatal model in humans. In addition, the results of those studies were widely seen as providing support for the prenatal model, even though they really didn't.

Two human studies are especially famous, and both are subject to many alternative interpretations: the Money and Ehrhardt study, which purports to show that prenatal testosterone in genetic females masculinizes the brain and thereby produces "tomboyism," and the Imperato-McGinley study, which purports to show that the prenatal masculinization of the fetal brain by testosterone is so directly related to the development of a male gender identity that for certain individ-uals, it can overcome even the experience of being reared as a female.

In contrast to all the animal studies on the prenatal hormone the-ory, which directly manipulate the level of a fetus's prenatal hormones and then measure the effect of that manipulation on later behavior, the human studies merely examine the effects on later behavior of unusual hormone conditions that a fetus happens to have experienced. In all cases, these unusual hormone conditions have either occurred natu-rally or are the side effect of some medical procedure that the mother underwent while pregnant, usually to save her pregnancy.

The Money and Ehrhardt Study

John Money and Anke Ehrhardt (1972) studied twenty-five genetic females who were exposed to abnormally high levels of testosterone in utero. Fifteen of these girls had a genetic disorder that caused their adrenal glands to malfunction, producing too few adrenocorticoids and too much adrenal testosterone. Ten of these girls had mothers who received progestins during pregnancy, a treatment now known to mas-culinize the external genitalia of girls. The fifteen girls with the adre-nogenital syndrome (AGS) required cortisone treatment throughout their lives for their adrenal glands to function properly. All twenty-five girls had such male-looking genitalia that each required at least one surgery in order to look more like a girl. In many cases, several sur-geries were required—including the cutting back of the clitoris, the conversion of the scrotum to labia, and the fashioning of a vagina—which sometimes brought the date of the last surgery well into adoles-cence.

At the time of the study, these twenty-five girls were between the ages of five and sixteen. For purposes of comparison, a control group of twenty-five medically normal girls was also studied. The girls in the control group were of the same age and socioeconomic background as the fetally masculinized girls.

On the basis of interviews with both the girls and their mothers, Money and Ehrhardt found that the fetally masculinized girls were more "tomboyish" than the normal girls. That is, they had a pattern of more intense energy expenditure in play; they had a higher preference for boys as playmates, for boys' toys, for boys' clothes, and for outdoor play and athletics; they had a lesser interest in dolls, in infant care, and in marriage; and they had a greater interest in a career. In their much-cited book, *Man and Woman, Boy and Girl,* Money and Ehrhardt concluded that the most likely explanation for this higher level of tomboyism was "a masculinizing effect on the fetal brain" (1972, p. 103).

In fact, at least three alternative explanations are even more likely.

1 Cortisone is a potent drug known to raise both activity level in general and the level of rough outdoor play in particular. The fifteen AGS girls may thus have become more "tomboyish" not because testosterone masculinized their fetal brains but because their lifelong cortisone therapy raised their activity level.

2 Because of either their continuing need for surgery or their continuing cortisone therapy or both, all twenty-five of the fetally masculinized girls were, in a sense, chronically ill during some portion of their childhood. This is especially true of the AGS girls who experienced the "salt-loss" form of the condition, which is associated with frequent hospitalization during the early years of life. Because all chronically ill children have to deal with a sense of inadequacy and a sense of uncertainty about the future and because some chronically ill children compensate for these feelings by developing a kind of bustling self-assurance, the possibility exists that the so-called tomboyism of the fetally masculinized girls resulted not from any masculinization of their brains but from their psychological reaction to the experience of being chronically ill.

Support for this alternative hypothesis is available in a recent study in which a group of normal healthy girls between the ages of seven and seventeen was compared with three groups of chronically ill girls: AGS girls with salt loss, AGS girls without salt loss, and diabetic girls—who were chronically ill during childhood but had normal hormones in utero (Slijper, 1984). Not only were all three groups of chronically ill girls more "boyish" than healthy girls on a test of their interests and values; in addition, the sicker AGS girls (those with salt loss) were significantly more boyish than the less sick AGS girls.

3   Finally, and perhaps most important, the girls' tomboyism may have resulted from the psychological impact on the girls and their parents of the girls' having masculinized genitalia. Among other things, for example, both the girls and their parents may have doubted what sex the girls actually were; they may also have wondered whether the girls' personalities had been altered along with their genitalia, whether the girls would ever be able to have children, and whether the girls would ever be able to find anyone to marry them. With all of this gender-related uncertainty, it would not be the least bit surprising if the parents of the fetally masculinized girls and the parents of the normal girls treated their daughters differently. Nor would it be surprising if the fetally masculinized girls themselves developed a somewhat different self-concept from that of the normal girls—and hence selected a somewhat different pattern of activities and friends.

Although several recent studies have tried to control for even these psychological effects of a girl's having masculinized genitalia, the "tomboy" experiments to date provide very little support for the theory that prenatal hormones differentially organize male and female brains.[10]

The Imperato-McGinley Study

In contrast to Money and Ehrhardt, who studied girls with prenatally masculinized bodies, Julianne Imperato-McGinley and her colleagues (1979a, 1979b) studied boys with prenatally feminized bodies. More specifically, they studied eighteen genetic males living in the Dominican Republic who were suffering from a rare enzyme deficiency that prevented their prenatal testosterone from masculinizing their genitalia during the critical period in utero but did not later prevent their adolescent testosterone from masculinizing either their genitalia or their secondary sex characteristics at puberty. As a result of this enzyme deficiency, these boys not only looked like girls but were raised as girls from birth to puberty, when they finally began to look more like the boys they were genetically.

In spite of being reared as girls, sixteen of these eighteen genetic males allegedly changed their self-definition from female to male sometime after their physical masculinization at puberty. On the basis of this psychological change, Imperato-McGinley and her colleagues concluded that biology rather than environment is critical to the evolution of a male gender identity. "Just as the development of the male . . . [body] is [normally] induced by androgens at a critical period in utero, the formation of a male gender identity is also an induced state with androgens acting on the brain at critical periods (in utero, neonatally, and puberty)" (1979b, p. 644).

Imperato-McGinley and her colleagues clearly believe that the feminized boys in their study switched at puberty from a female gender identity to a male gender identity because their high level of prenatal testosterone had already masculinized their brains, and their high level of pubertal testosterone was allowing that dormant masculinity to finally express itself psychologically. Their pubertal testosterone was accomplishing this by masculinizing their brains still further and by masculinizing their bodies as well.

This purely biological hypothesis has, however, an obvious interactionist alternative. Perhaps the brains of these individuals were never masculinized at all; perhaps when their bodies began to be masculinized at puberty, both they and the others in their community began to believe that some kind of male identity would be much more appropriate than any kind of female identity. If so, the switch from female to male did not necessarily happen overnight or without conflict; nor was it necessarily a switch from one unambiguous gender identity to another unambiguous gender identity. Rather, the implication is that whatever the precise nature of the switch, (1) it was initiated by the masculinization of the body rather than by the masculinization of the brain, and (2) it was mediated by the reactions of both the self and others to that physical masculinization.

Imperato-McGinley and her colleagues did not gather the kind of detailed cultural or psychological information that would allow us to evaluate the importance of this biocultural interaction in the context of their sample of boys. Consistent with this interactionist interpretation, however, is the very detailed description by an anthropologist and a biologist of the process by which a group of Sambian boys in Papua, New Guinea, with the same enzyme deficiency made their switch from female to male. In the words of these two authors, "Sambian subjects who switched from the female to male role did so only under the greatest external public pressure. Once exposed, they had 'no place to hide,' and no public in which to continue to pose as 'female.' . . . *Only the failure of their own bodies to fulfill their social destiny as sex-assigned females seemed to have caused these individuals to change*" (Herdt & Davidson, 1988, p. 53).

As even this brief discussion of the literature makes clear, the fundamental conceptual problem with the prenatal hormone theory is strikingly similar to the fundamental conceptual problem discussed earlier with respect to sociobiology. In both cases, the importance of the individual's situational context is massively underestimated, and the importance of the individual's biology is massively overestimated. To put it somewhat differently, the interaction between situation and biology is insufficiently theorized; hence, the theorists jump too quickly to the conclusion that either sexual difference or sexual inequality is the product of biology alone.

This failure to theorize biology in context has fostered wild and premature speculation about the existence of profound differences between the sexes in the biology of their genes and their brains; ironically, it has also hampered theorizing about the consequences, in context, of the more mundane and indisputable bodily differences between the sexes—including, for example, that only women bear children and breastfeed or that men, on average, are bigger and stronger. I propose an interactionist theory of sexual difference and sexual inequality, a theory that works—in context—with the bodily differences known to exist, rather than with other differences only hypothesized to exist.

AN ALTERNATIVE HYPOTHESIS:
THE BODY IN CONTEXT

To account for sexual difference and sexual inequality, two separate kinds of questions need to be addressed, one having to do with social organization and the other with individual behavior and psychology. The first question is, Why have women and men, as groups, played such different and unequal roles in virtually every society on earth? Why, in other words, have both a sexual division of labor and an institutionalized system of male political power been the norm throughout human history? The second question is, Why do women and men, as individuals, have the differing behavioral predispositions that they seem to have even in modern societies? Why, for example, are men more physically aggressive and women more nurturant toward children?

A debate now going on in anthropology has a bearing on the first, social organization question. At issue is whether certain early hunting-and-gathering societies managed to develop a sexual division of labor without also developing an institutionalized system of male political power.[11] One part of my mind listens hopefully to this debate and is cheered by the possibility that the exercise of seeking an alternative explanation for gender universals may be beside the point. Another part of my mind doesn't quite believe it, however, and neither will the general reader, because those egalitarian hunter-gatherer societies (even if they once existed) cannot wipe away the consistent pattern of sexual difference and dominance that not only appears to exist across time and place but that a theory like sociobiology appears to so elegantly explain.

Given this consistent pattern of sexual difference and dominance, I will accept the premise of gender universals for the sake of argument and will proceed to offer the best biohistorical account of those universals that I can come up with at the present time. This account is not set in cement; it is, rather, one example of what a biohistorical account might look like.

The Sexual Universals of Human Social Organization

I said earlier that any serious attempt to explain a human universal across time and place would have to theorize a biohistorical interaction between a constant in human biology and a constant in human history and culture. Accordingly, my biohistorical account will attempt to explain the sexual universals of human social organization by situating both male and female bodies in what has been, for almost all of human history, a universal environment.

This account proceeds as follows. Once upon a time, there were certain indisputable and universal differences between men's and women's bodies, with only women being able to become pregnant and to breastfeed and with men, on average, being bigger and stronger. Once upon a time, there were also certain indisputable and universal features of the environment, with all cultures everywhere having no effective means of controlling fertility, no digestible substitutes for mother's milk, few technological instruments for extending the strength of the human body, and little work that did not place a premium on physical strength.

In that sociohistorical context, the bodily differences between the sexes made it likely that most women would be either pregnant or breastfeeding during most of the years from menarche to menopause. They also made it likely that the society would develop a division of labor based on sex, with women everywhere being primarily responsible for the care of infants and children and with men everywhere being primarily responsible for the physical defense of the group and, where relevant, for hunting. Women would be primarily responsible for childcare—and for whatever else they could do simultaneously—because they would always have children either in them or on them. Men would be primarily responsible for defense and for hunting both because they were bigger and stronger and also because they did not have their mobility limited by the continuous presence of children.

In addition to developing a sex-based division of labor, the great majority of human societies also developed an institutionalized system of male political power. Although the reason for this is not clear, one possibility is that if a nontechnological society typically assigns the males rather than the females to defend the group, then that role assignment may lead those warrior-males to see themselves—and to be seen by others—as the most important and powerful members of the group. If so, they might then be in a position to easily take control over the decisions of the group, beginning with such matters of physical security as where the group can safely live and when the group can safely move. Still another possibility is that because the females in a nontechnological society are so continuously occupied with babies and children, as well as with all the other productive activities that they can do simultaneously, the males may simply have more opportunity than the females to institutionalize whatever levers of power they have—including the "brute" power that comes directly from their size and strength.

Although this once-universal environment may seem too far in the past to explain today's gender universals, the critical features of that environment were in place even in U.S. society as recently as 150 years ago, and they are still in place today in many societies that are not technologically advanced. To explain the consistency across time and place of both the sexual division of labor and the institutionalization of male political power, there is thus no need for anyone to postulate that males and females are differently programmed by their genes or their brains. It is sufficient to postulate that the indisputable and universal differences between male and female bodies have interacted for almost all of human history with the indisputable and universal features of a nontechnological environment.

But this biohistorical alternative then raises the question that is almost always presented as the ultimate challenge to modern feminism: If cultural invention has now so transformed the situational context of human life that the bodily differences between the sexes are no longer as functionally significant as they once were, then why do males and females continue to play such different—and unequal—roles in even a modern technological society, which has not only effective control over fertility and digestible substitutes for mother's milk but little or no labor for which the sex of the laborer is truly decisive? There are both short and long answers to this question, both of them historical.

The long answer is spelled out in Chapters 2 through 6 of this book, which together explain how and why the sexual division of labor and the institutionalization of male political power have been reproduced in generation after generation by cultures whose discourses and social institutions have been organized for centuries—and continue to be organized—around the three lenses of androcentrism, gender polarization, and biological essentialism.

The short answer is that once instituted, the sexual division of labor and the system of male political dominance gave rise to a whole network of cultural beliefs and social practices, which came to have a life and a history of their own. Modern technology may have so changed the situational context of human life that those beliefs and practices would not now emerge de novo, but modern technology did not and could not instantly eliminate the inertia produced by all of that cultural and political history.

Consider but one example of this modern paradox. Although modern technology has so transformed the functional significance of male and female biology that, for the first time in human history, very few activities cannot be done, and done well, by women and men alike, many cultural institutions in the United States continue to make it extremely difficult for any individual to simultaneously be both a parent and a worker in the paid labor force; these institutions include the lack of pregnancy leave, the absence of day-care facilities, the mismatch between the school day and the workday, the unavailability of part-time work, and the geographical separation between the workplace and the home, which began at the time of the industrial revolution and increased dramatically with the move to the suburbs that followed World War II.

Although nothing inherent in most of these cultural institutions says that women, rather than men, must forgo full-time work outside the home in order to care for children, given both the biological fact of female pregnancy and the biocultural history of female childcare, that outcome is all but guaranteed in any two-parent family that can afford to have but one parent working outside the home for money. As a modern technological society, the United States may thus have made it possible for women to have as few or as many children as they wish. What the United States has not yet done, however, is to construct a cultural environment in which those women who decide to have even one child can easily step outside the role of childcare.

This discussion of recent historical factors that interact with biology highlights a critical point. Even though a particular biohistorical interaction may have originally set up the pattern of male political dominance, the earliest biohistorical origins of male political dominance (whatever they were) are now irrelevant. Today, the institutionalized pattern of male political dominance that is a reality in almost every known society is maintained and reproduced by contemporary cultural institutions that interact with biology in the here and now. It is thus not the biohistorical origins of male dominance that we need to analyze; it is these contemporary cultural institutions that we need to analyze *and alter* if the longstanding pattern of male political dominance is ever to be eradicated.

The Sexual Differences of Individual Psychology

In trying to explain the sexual universals of human social organization, the constant in human history and culture that seemed most important to me was the universal absence of modern technology, which was here hypothesized to interact with male and female bodies to universally produce a sexual division of labor and an institutionalized system of male political dominance. In contrast, the constants in human history and culture that seem most important for explaining the sexual differences of individual behavior and psychology are the sexual division of labor and the institutionalized system of male political dominance, which—once created by the interaction of biology and history—then programmed such differing life experiences for males and females, respectively, that male and female were thereby transformed into "masculine" and "feminine."

Although psychological gendering will be much more fully discussed in Chapter 5, here I would simply like to illustrate how the sexual division of labor could itself produce two of the sexually differentiated behaviors that are frequently discussed in terms of biology: physical aggression and "maternal" responsiveness to infants and children.

In their encyclopedic review of the human sex differences literature, Eleanor Maccoby and Carol Jacklin conclude that of all the social behaviors yet investigated empirically, biological factors are most clearly implicated for the sex difference in physical aggression. Maccoby and Jacklin base this conclusion on what they take to be four scientifically established facts.

> (1) Males are more aggressive than females in all human societies for which evidence is available. (2) The sex differences are found early in life, at a time when there is no evidence that differential socialization pressures have been brought to bear by adults to "shape" aggression differently in the two sexes. . . . (3) Similar sex differences are found in man and subhuman primates. (4) Aggression is related to levels of sex hormones, and can be changed by experimental administrations of these hormones. (1974, pp. 242–243)

According to a recent review by Anne Fausto-Sterling (1985), however, at least three of these four arguments are much weaker than Maccoby and Jacklin originally supposed. With respect to the child development data, for example, it now appears that the earliest human sex differences in both physical aggression and rough-and-tumble play could just as well have been caused by the differential treatment of boys and girls as by biology: even in Maccoby and Jacklin's own literature review, parents were already handling their sons more roughly than their daughters by three weeks of age. With respect to the nonhuman primate data, it now appears that there is a sex difference in physical aggression only among some primate species, not all; and even for those species, the sex difference is present only in some environments.

And finally, with respect to the link between physical aggression and hormones, it now appears that although very good evidence supports the claim that testosterone is causally related to physical aggression in rats and mice, no good evidence yet supports the claim that testosterone is causally related to physical aggression in humans or other primates.

Although Fausto-Sterling challenges even Maccoby and Jacklin's final claim about the human sex difference in physical aggression being cross-culturally universal, this claim seems to me to be at least as strong now as it was when it was made. But I also think that one does not need to theorize a direct link from biology to brain to behavior in order to explain it. Quite the contrary. One can theorize that the sexual division of labor itself produces this universal sex difference in aggression by assigning males to the role of warrior and females to the role of caregiver.

Assigning males, but not females, to the role of warrior could produce the sex difference in physical aggression by having males and males alone spend their time—not just during adulthood but during childhood and adolescence as well—in activities that are directly related to fighting or killing, such as testing their physical strength or proving their physical courage. By the same token, assigning females, but not males, to the role of caregiver could also produce the sex difference in physical aggression by having females and females alone spend their time in one of the few activities that has been shown to reduce aggression: taking care of infants and young children (Barry, Bacon & Child, 1957; Ember, 1973; Whiting & Edwards, 1988).

Consistent with this analysis of physical aggression, I further postulate that women are everywhere more psychologically predisposed to care for infants and children than men are, not primarily because they have female genes or female hormones or even a developing baby inside their bodies, but because the sexual division of labor has everywhere assigned women, and women alone, to the role of caregiver; and that role assignment has given women and girls, but not men and boys, the kinds of social experiences with babies and children that foster the development of what is usually called maternal motivation but that I prefer to call parental motivation. Consistent with this hypothesis are the results of two very well controlled studies on how contact with babies itself fosters parental behavior in adults, the first study done with rats and the second, with humans.

In the rat study (Rosenblatt, 1967; see also Rosenblatt & Siegel,

1981), the investigators placed five newborn rats in a cage along with a single adult rat and then measured how much the adult rat engaged in four different parental behaviors: retrieving the babies, crouching over the babies, licking the babies, and building a nest for the babies. The adult rats were either fully normal males and females complete with all their circulating hormones or males and females with no circulating hormones because their testes, their ovaries, or their pituitary gland had been surgically removed. None of the female adults had ever given birth.

The results were compelling. Although none of the male or female adults began to engage in any of the parental behaviors as soon after being exposed to the babies as a normal mother does after giving birth, all of the male and female adults eventually engaged in all four of the parental behaviors; in addition, there were no differences between the adults as a function of either sex or the presence of hormones. This study unequivocally demonstrates that although something about the experience of birth surely speeds up the onset of parental behavior in birthing mothers, even in rats, the simple experience of having contact with babies, or being given responsibility for babies, is ultimately sufficient to motivate males and females alike to engage in a whole array of parental behaviors usually seen only in mothers.

In the human study (Leifer et al., 1972; see also Leiderman, 1981; Myers, 1984), mothers who had just given birth to premature babies were randomly divided into two groups. One group, the "contact" group, was allowed to interact with, feed, and generally take care of their own babies during the four to eight weeks that the babies were still in the hospital. The other group, the "no-contact" group, was allowed no such contact until the babies had reached a normal birth weight and had been placed in the discharge nursery. At the time this study was done, no contact was standard procedure in almost all U.S. hospitals.

To determine whether contact affected the overall level of a mother's attachment or commitment or bonding to her baby, each mother was observed three times while she was feeding, diapering, or bathing her baby. The first time was at the mother's fifth visit to the discharge nursery; the second time was at home a week after the baby's discharge from the hospital; and the third time was in the clinic a month after the baby's discharge from the hospital. In follow-up research, many of the mother-baby pairs were also observed when the baby was twelve months old, twenty-one months old, and between five and eight years old. During the initial three observations, two aspects of the mother's behavior were of special interest: (1) the mother's skill at caretaking, as measured by such things as how well she could stimulate the baby to feed, keep the nipple full of milk, and provide head support; and (2) the mother's level of attachment or attentiveness to the baby, as measured by such things as how much she looked at the baby, smiled at the baby, talked to the baby, caressed the baby, maintained eye contact with the baby, and held the baby close to her own body.

The results of this study were clear. Although all differences between contact and no-contact mothers were gone by the time the baby was twenty-one months old, and although an initial difference in caretaking skill was also gone by just one week after the baby's discharge from the hospital, even when the babies were twelve months old, the contact mothers were still showing signs of being more attached to their babies than the no-contact mothers.

Taken together, the rat and the premature baby studies support the hypothesis that women and girls are everywhere more motivated to take care of infants and children than men and boys, not because of any "maternal instinct," but because the sexual division of labor always places women and girls in the contact condition and men and boys in the no-contact condition.[12]

BEYOND THE BODY

The question remains: Do I really believe that there are no biological differences between the sexes beside the obvious differences in their anatomy and physiology? Here I am an agnostic. For all I know, Alan Alda's (1975) argument may contain a kernel of truth: men may be more physically aggressive than women because they are suffering from prenatal "testosterone poisoning." Alice Rossi's (1977, 1985) argument may have some truth to it, too: women may be more maternal than men because of their female hormones. And even Camilla Benbow's (1988) argument may have some validity: males may be better at higher mathematics than females because they have some special biological ability to reason mathematically.

But about three related issues I am not at all agnostic, nor am I likely to become agnostic, even if it should turn out that human males and females differ biologically with respect to any number of specific abilities or predispositions.

1   There would be so much overlap between the sexes in all of these abilities and predispositions that the differences would pale into insignificance next to the bigger and more obvious differences between male and female bodies. No matter how many sex differences are someday shown to have a biological component, that knowledge will thus add little or nothing to our understanding of why women and men have universally played such different—and unequal—roles in virtually every society on earth.

2   These biological differences would be so poorly matched to the requirements of the jobs that women and men currently hold in American society that they would again add little or nothing to our understanding of why women and men hold the different—and unequal—positions that they do. So yes, women might turn out to be more biologically nurturant than men on the average, but that should make them psychiatrists, not secretaries. And yes, men might also turn out to have a higher aptitude for mathematics than women on the average, but that would not explain why so many more women have a high aptitude for mathematics than have careers requiring one. Stated more generally, no matter what subtle biological differences there may someday prove to be between women and men on the average, those differences will never justify the sexual inequality that has, for centuries, been a feature of human social life.

3   No matter how many subtle biological differences between the sexes there may someday prove to be, both the size and the significance of those biological differences will depend, in every single instance, on the situational context in which women and men live their lives. The feature of the situational context that was consistently emphasized in this chapter was the historically universal absence of modern technology. As least as important in the development of sexual difference and sexual inequality, however, is the male-centeredness that has resulted, in every single culture, from the institutionalization of male political power. That feature of the environment is discussed next.

3

ANDROCENTRISM

In 1963, when Betty Friedan first wrote in *The Feminine Mystique* about "the problem that has no name" (p. 10)—that is, the problem of full-time American homemakers in their mid-thirties suddenly discovering when their last child goes off to school that they have no sense of identity apart from being either Bob's wife or Mary's mother and no sense of purpose or direction for the remaining four decades of their life span—she touched a sensitive nerve in millions of women who weren't satisfied with their lives but who couldn't yet articulate either the depth or the source of their dissatisfaction. After all, they were living the perfect middle-class life in this, the most perfect society in the history of the world. If that wasn't satisfying, then obviously something must be wrong with them.

This sense that the United States was the best of all possible worlds changed dramatically during the late 1960s, when the rage against involvement in the Vietnam War, the riots in the black ghettos of major cities, the student rebellions on college campuses, and the police suppression of the protesters at the Democratic National Convention all exposed the hidden underbelly of American society to the light. Born during these fiery days of self-criticism was what the media called the women's liberation movement and what the activists themselves called radical feminism.

The activists in this movement were not the selfless homemakers that Friedan had talked about in *The Feminine Mystique,* however. They were, if anything, the daughters of those homemakers, who were determined not to repeat their mothers' mistakes by sacrificing themselves for the sake of either husbands or children. In many cases, they were also university students protesting the Vietnam War, who dis-covered for themselves just how ubiquitous male dominance was when their male comrades-in-arms relegated them to the task of preparing the food while they—the menfolk—planned revolutionary strategy. For many of these young women, the discovery that male dominance was alive and well even among the most radical of the male student activists was what ultimately led them to realize that as egalitarian as America might appear, at a deeper level it was still a "patriarchy."[1]

As Kate Millett wrote in *Sexual Politics*, the book that made *pa-triarchy* a household word among feminists, "Our society, like all other historical civilizations, is a patriarchy. The fact is evident at once if one recalls that the military, industry, technology, universities, science, po-litical office, and finance—in short, every avenue of power within the society, including the coercive force of the police, is entirely in male hands" (1969, pp. 34–35). Or, as Adrienne Rich later wrote in *Of Woman Born*,

> Patriarchy is the power of the fathers: a familial-social, ideo-logical, political system in which men—by force, direct pres-sure, or through ritual, tradition, law and language, customs, etiquette, education, and the division of labor, determine what part women shall or shall not play, and in which the female is everywhere subsumed under the male. It does not necessarily imply that no woman has power, or that all women in a given culture may not have certain powers. . . . Under patriarchy, I may live in *purdah* or drive a truck; . . . I may become a heredi-tary or elected head of state or wash the underwear of a mil-lionaire's wife; I may serve my husband his early-morning cof-fee within the clay walls of a Berber village or march in an academic procession; whatever my status or situation, my de-rived economic class, or my sexual preference, I live under the power of the fathers, and I have access only to so much of privilege or influence as the patriarchy is willing to accede to me, and only for so long as I will pay the price for male ap-proval. (1976, pp. 40–41)

Although the concept of patriarchy makes much clearer than the more generic concept of sexism which sex holds the power in society, the concept of androcentrism, or male-centeredness, is even more use-ful. It goes beyond telling *who* is in power to tell *how* their power is culturally and psychologically reproduced. As already noted in Chapter 1, androcentrism is the privileging of male experience and the "otherizing" of female experience; that is, males and male experience are treated as a neutral standard or norm for the culture or the species as a whole, and females and female experience are treated as a sex-specific deviation from that allegedly universal standard.

The concept of androcentrism was first articulated in the early twentieth century by Charlotte Perkins Gilman, who wrote in *The Man-Made World or Our Androcentric Culture* that

> all our human scheme of things rests on the same tacit assumption; man being held the human type; woman a sort of accompaniment and subordinate assistant, merely essential to the making of people. She has held always the place of a preposition in relation to man. She has always been considered above him or below him, before him, behind him, beside him, a wholly relative existence—"Sydney's sister," "Pembroke's mother"—but never by any chance Sydney or Pembroke herself.

Gilman went on: "What we see immediately around us, what we are born into and grow up with, . . . we assume to be the order of nature," but "what we have all this time called 'human nature' . . . was in great part only male nature." Her conclusion: "Our androcentric culture is so shown to have been, and still to be, a masculine culture in excess, and therefore undesirable" (1911/1971, pp. 20–22).

Without using the term *androcentrism*, Simone de Beauvoir brilliantly elaborated on the concept and integrated it into a theory of sexual inequality. In *The Second Sex*, which was originally published in France in 1949, she said that the historical relationship of men and women is not best represented as a relationship between dominance and subordination, between high and low status, or even between positive and negative. No, in all male-dominated cultures,

> man represents both the positive and the neutral, as is indicated by the common use of *man* to designate human beings in general; whereas woman represents only the negative, defined by limiting criteria, without reciprocity. . . . It amounts to this: just as for the ancients there was an absolute vertical with reference to which the oblique was defined, so there is an absolute

human type, the masculine. Woman has ovaries, a uterus; these peculiarities imprison her in her subjectivity, circumscribe her within the limits of her own nature. It is often said that she thinks with her glands. Man superbly ignores the fact that his anatomy also includes glands, such as the testicles, and that they secrete hormones. He thinks of his body as a direct and normal connection with the world, which he believes he apprehends objectively, whereas he regards the body of woman as a hindrance, a prison, weighed down by everything peculiar to it. . . . Thus humanity is male and man defines woman not in herself but as relative to him; she is not regarded as an autonomous being. . . . She is the incidental, the inessential as opposed to the essential. He is the Subject, he is the Absolute—she is the Other. (1952, pp. xv–xvi)[2]

As I see it, the central image underlying the concept of androcentrism is males at the center of the universe looking out at reality from behind their own eyes and describing what they see from an egocentric—or androcentric—point of view. They divide reality into self and other and define everything categorized as other—including women—in relation to themselves. In thus defining the other, they do at least two related things simultaneously.

First, they define everything they see in terms of its similarity to, or its dissimilarity from, themselves. They take their own being and experience to be the reference point or the standard for the culture—or the species—as a whole, and they take everyone else's being and experience to be merely an inferior departure or deviation from the standard that they themselves set.

Second, they define everything they see in terms of the meaning or the functional significance that it has for them personally rather than defining it in its own terms. Through the centuries, woman in particular has most often been defined either in terms of her domestic and reproductive functions within a male-dominated household or in terms of her power to stimulate and satisfy the male's sexual appetite.

In the final two chapters of this book, I shall analyze not only how the institutionalization of the androcentric lens has shaped the psyches of individual women and men but also how it has structurally transformed male-female difference into female disadvantage. In this chapter, in contrast, I shall document the pervasiveness of the androcentric lens in Western culture by analyzing four central cultural discourses: Judeo-Christian theology, ancient Greek philosophy, Freudian psycho-analytic theory, and the history of the U.S. equal rights law. I begin with Judeo-Christian theology because, in addition to being a fundamental underpinning of contemporary Western thought, it is also a powerful case study of how those seeking power must sometimes suppress alter-native perspectives if they are to shape the cultural discourse in their own image.

JUDEO-CHRISTIAN THEOLOGY

History

Judaism and Christianity were established as major religions in the Middle East between the seventeenth and the fifth centuries B.C. and between the first and the fourth centuries A.D., respectively.[3] Although most people are familiar with these two historical periods as they are described in the Old and New Testaments, very few know how or why or when the testaments came to be written. This history is important to the analysis of androcentrism because it involves the replacement of a goddess with a god and also the defining of woman as the other. That is, it constitutes "the genesis of two of the guiding symbols of Western male dominance—the patriarchal, decidedly masculine God and the sexual, inferior female who tempts the male from the path of righ-teousness" (Sanday, 1981, p. 215).

The Jewish religious experience began in the sixteenth or seven-teenth century B.C., when Abraham reportedly made the first covenant with the god of Israel, typically called Yahweh. For the next four hun-dred years or so, Yahweh was primarily the god of the Hebrew tribe known as Judah, but the other Hebrew tribes worshiped him as well— along with many other gods and goddesses, including Asherah, who was the prototype for the creation-goddess of all the ancient Middle Eastern peoples. The only rituals uniting the Hebrew tribes at this time were male circumcision and the prohibition against human sacrifice, as embodied in the story of Isaac.

After a long period of enslavement in Egypt, the Hebrew tribes were freed in the thirteenth century B.C., at which time they left Egypt for Canaan under the leadership of Moses. Because the Exodus narra-tive so clearly emphasizes Moses' receiving of the Ten Commandments from Yahweh and Moses' anger at the Hebrews for their continuing fascination with other deities, as symbolized by the golden calf, scholars have generally regarded Moses as the founder of Jewish monotheism. Even after arriving in Canaan, however, the Hebrew tribes continued to worship gods and goddesses besides Yahweh. In fact, as they shifted from seminomadic pastoralism to sedentary farming, they became increasingly involved with those particular gods and goddesses who could supposedly enhance the fertility of the soil—especially Baal, the son of Asherah, and his consort, Anath.

Sometime after 1100 B.C., the Hebrew tribes in Canaan united politically to defend themselves against their common enemies, beginning with the Philistines. The monarchy they formed had three successive kings: Saul, who ruled until 1004 B.C.; David, who ruled until 965 B.C.; and David's son Solomon, who ruled until 922 B.C. (these dates are approximate). David in particular created the Jewish national state and made Jerusalem its capital. Because he had previously been the king of Judah, the new Jewish state came to be dominated by Judean ideas, including the belief that Yahweh was the one and only true god.

After Solomon's death in 922 B.C., the Jewish state split into the two kingdoms of Israel and Judah. Judah survived for almost four hundred years, ending only when the Babylonians destroyed Jerusalem and its temple in 586 B.C. Israel survived for only two hundred years, ending when the Assyrians captured its capital, Samaria, in 722 B.C. During the early part of its history, and especially during the reign of King Ahab and his foreign-born wife, Jezebel, the cult of Asherah and Baal spread within the kingdom. It was finally suppressed in 852 B.C., however, after a political coup and the assassination of some four hundred priests.

The splitting apart of the Jewish national state was an obvious threat to the ascendancy of Yahweh as the one and only true god. At that critical moment, therefore, the Judean prophet whom scholars now call the Yahwist took it upon himself to write a history of the Hebrew people that would be consistent with the monotheistic tradition of Moses. This history was later elaborated by many other writers, including a group known as the Priestly writers, and it was finally fused into the Pentateuch—also known as the Five Books of Moses—and canonized as a sacred text by the prophets Ezra and Nehemiah in approximately 450 B.C.

To control the Hebrews' continuing tendencies in non-Yahwist directions, the Yahwist wrote a most unusual creation story. Rather than telling of a power struggle between male and female deities, as most other ancient Middle Eastern creation stories did, he denied the existence of any gods or goddesses besides Yahweh and attributed to Yahweh many of the feats and accomplishments that had earlier been credited in oral narratives to other deities—including the creation of life itself. Given the prolonged ideological struggle of the Yahweh cult against the worship of other deities—the creation-goddess Asherah among them—some modern scholars now see the Yahwist's very masculine representation of God and his very negative representation of Eve, not to mention his total exclusion of women from all of the covenants that Yahweh made with Israel, as part of his mission to depose the creation-goddess once and for all.

Although the Yahwist's representations were later tempered a little by the Priestly writers, they basically went unchallenged until the first through the fourth centuries A.D., when several groups of early Christians, now known as the Gnostics, elaborated on some of the Priestly verses in a way that more orthodox Christians considered highly heretical. Picking up on the Priestly verse that reads, "In the image of God He created him: male and female He created them" (Genesis 1:27), as well as on other Priestly verses, the Gnostics constructed a representation of both God and human nature that included masculine and feminine elements; they also constructed a representation of Eve as Adam's adviser. Consistent with this more positive representation of Eve, the Gnostics actually permitted women to be priests.

But none of these was the worst of the Gnostic heresies. Fascinated by the question of how such an imperfect universe could have been created by a perfect god, many Gnostics reached the truly heretical conclusion that the god of the Hebrews must himself be an imperfect emanation from a Primal Source, and they represented that Primal Source dualistically as both male and female.

Because the ideas of the Gnostics so fundamentally challenged the absolute monotheism and the absolute maleness of the Jewish God, whom all Christians now took to be the father of Jesus Christ, the Gnostic texts were excluded from the select list of twenty-six that were canonized as the New Testament. Like all the other documents condemned as heretical when Christianity became an officially approved religion in the fourth century A.D., they were also burned and their possession made a criminal offense. The only reason that scholars now know about these texts and the particular ideological struggle within early Christianity that they represent is because some survived, hidden in clay pots for over 1,600 years: an Arab peasant found them in Egypt in 1945. Given what is now known about this early period, however, a number of scholars have recently come to see many documents in the New Testament—especially Paul's pronouncements on women—as part of a renewed and systematic effort to expunge from the Judeo-Christian tradition all vestiges of female participation in the priesthood and all vestiges of feminine symbolism in the divine.

The Biblical Definition of Woman

With this brief historical survey as our backdrop, we are now ready to analyze the androcentrism in some of the most important biblical verses defining woman. Earlier, I defined androcentrism as the privileging of males, male experience, and the male perspective, which leads to defining woman as the other.[4] I also suggested that in defining woman as the other, man has traditionally focused on three aspects of woman's relationship to him: (1) her difference from, and her inferiority to, the universal standard or norm that he sees himself as naturally representing; (2) her domestic and reproductive function within the family or household that he sees himself as naturally heading; and (3) her ability to stimulate and to satisfy his own sexual appetite, which he finds both exciting and threatening.

All but one of these ideas are present in the biblical story of the creation. Not only is Adam explicitly given the power to name—that is, define—every single creature on earth, including woman, from his own perspective, but only Adam is unambiguously said to be created in God's image. Eve, in contrast, is an inferior departure from this godly standard, a secondary being created merely to be a helper to Adam; she is not a namer herself:

> Then God said, "Let us make man in our image, after our likeness; and let them have dominion over the fish of the sea, and over the birds of the air, and over the cattle, and over all the earth, and over every creeping thing that creeps upon the earth." So God created man in his own image, in the image of God he created him; male and female he created them. (Genesis 1:26–27)

> Then the Lord God said, "It is not good that the man should be alone; I will make him a helper fit for him." So out of the

ground the Lord God formed every beast of the field and every bird of the air, and brought them to the man to see what he would call them; and whatever the man called every living creature, that was its name. The man gave names to all cattle, and to the birds of the air, and to every beast of the field; but for the man there was not found a helper fit for him. So the Lord God caused a deep sleep to fall upon the man, and while he slept took one of his ribs and closed up its place with flesh; and the rib which the Lord God had taken from the man he made into a woman and brought her to the man. Then the man said, "This at last is bone of my bones and flesh of my flesh; she shall be called Woman, because she was taken out of Man." (Genesis 2:18–23)

The story of Adam and Eve's fall from grace accentuates these several themes and also introduces the definition of woman as a sexual temptress. The fall from grace begins with Eve's being persuaded by the serpent to eat from the forbidden tree of knowledge. Although the biblical verses do not explain why the serpent approaches Eve, rather than Adam, John Phillips says in his richly documented study of the Eve myth that biblical interpreters through the ages have been "nearly unanimous" in supposing that "the serpent, being shrewd, recognizes that she is the weaker of the two humans." And why is she the weaker? Because she is "a less than perfect approximation of her Creator; inferior not only to him, but to Adam as well . . . a dilution in power, rational faculties, self-control, piety, and moral strength" (1984, p. 57). The serpent's choice thus emphasizes the definition of woman as an inferior departure from the male standard.

The definition of woman as a sexual temptress who lures man to do what he would otherwise eschew is suggested by Adam's transgressing along with Eve. Although the reason for Adam's transgression is not provided in the biblical verses, interpreters through the ages have frequently attributed his transgression to Eve's evil seductiveness. John Phillips summarizes this sexual explanation as follows: "Having been seduced because of her weakness, she is able to seduce her husband because she is filled with the power of the Devil." As "the special instrument of Satan's will," she possesses "a heightened sexuality that inevitably lures" Adam to destroy the state of paradise (p. 64).

And finally, the definition of woman in terms of her domestic and reproductive functions within the male-dominated family is accentuated by the punishment she receives for her transgression. Having been created to be man's helper, now she is even more subordinated, and even more defined in terms of her childbearing function, than before she ate the forbidden fruit from the tree of knowledge: "To the woman he said, 'I will greatly multiply your pain in childbearing; in pain you shall bring forth children, yet your desire shall be for your husband, and he shall rule over you'" (Genesis 3:16).

The question remains: Apart from Eve's disobedience to God, what exactly was the nature of her transgression? What, in other words, does the eating of the forbidden fruit symbolize? Biblical interpreters have offered the following three answers, among others.

1   Eating the forbidden fruit symbolizes carnal sexuality. This interpretation is consistent with Adam and Eve's perception, after eating the fruit, that they are naked. Because Eve was attracted to the fruit in the first place and then tempted Adam, it is also consistent with the definition of woman as a sexually dangerous being.

2   That Eve in particular ate the forbidden fruit symbolizes both her—and woman's—insufficient obedience not only to God but to man as well. This interpretation was suggested in the sixteenth century by Protestant reformers like Martin Luther and John Calvin, who rejected "the sexual tendentiousness surrounding the fall of humanity as so much Jewish fable and Popish nonsense" (Phillips, 1984, p. 99). Consistent with this view is the specific punishment given to Eve for her transgression.

3   That Eve in particular ate the forbidden fruit also symbolizes her—and woman's—vanity in supposing that she might conceivably be "like God," as the serpent put it. Consistent with this view is the whole history of the ideological struggle between the monotheistic believers in Yahweh and the polytheistic believers in other deities besides Yahweh, including the creation-goddess. Given this struggle, it is easy to imagine that by punishing Eve so severely for seeking to emulate the divine, the Yahwist was deposing the creation-goddess symbolically, much as he had earlier deposed her materially by removing her from the cast of characters present at the creation.

I have here considered the Eve of Genesis, along with the Eve in the standard biblical interpretations of Genesis, because as Phillips has so aptly put it, Eve's story is "at the heart of the concept of Woman in Western civilization." As "Everywoman," she is "a living part of the cultural and social histories of the people touched by her characterization. . . . To follow the path of Eve is to discover much about the identity that has been imposed upon women in Western civilization. If one would understand Woman, one must come to terms with Eve" (1984, p. xiii).

But it is not just the story of Eve that one must come to terms with. Western thought in general, and the Western concept of woman in particular, are also based on a philosophical and political tradition that has its roots in ancient Greece.

ANCIENT GREEK PHILOSOPHY

Historians generally regard the ancient Greeks as the founders of Western civilization.[5] Not only did they establish the traditions of individual freedom and justice that are so fundamental to democracy but their art, philosophy, and science served as the basis for much of Western thought and culture. Consider how many aspects of American culture are Greek in origin, including not only the very concept of a citizen in a democracy but also the Socratic method, the Hippocratic oath, the Euclidian geometry, the theory of the Oedipus complex, and even the Olympic Games—first held in the Stadium of Olympia in western Greece in 776 B.C.

In addition to all these well-known positive contributions, however, the ancient Greeks also founded a tradition of misogyny that has helped to shape the conception of woman to the present day. This tradition dates back to at least the eighth century B.C., when the Greek poet Hesiod recorded the story of Pandora.

According to Greek mythology, Pandora was the first woman on earth, created under orders from Zeus in order to punish Prometheus for stealing fire from heaven and giving it to men. Because Zeus's intent was to create an evil being that all men would find desirable, Pandora was created in the image of the goddesses, who each gave her some special gift, like beauty or grace, to enhance her attractiveness—hence her name, Pandora, which means "all gift."

Pandora was given a box—some versions say a vase—which she was warned never to open. After her marriage to Prometheus's brother, her curiosity got the better of her, and she opened it, unintentionally letting loose all the vices, sins, diseases, and troubles imprisoned therein. When she slammed the box closed, the only thing trapped inside was hope. In the ancient Greek tradition, just as in the ancient Judeo-Christian tradition, the first woman on earth was thus held responsible for the fall of humanity from a state of paradise.

Hesiod lived and wrote not very long after Homer. In contrast, most of the well-known Greek writers lived in the fourth and fifth centuries B.C., including Sophocles (who wrote the Oedipus tragedy), Socrates (who was Plato's teacher), Plato (who was Aristotle's teacher), and Aristotle himself. Of these, the two with the most to say about the nature and function of woman were Plato and Aristotle, who defined woman in much the same way that the androcentric writers of the Judeo-Christian tradition had also defined her: (1) as an inferior departure from the male standard and (2) as a subordinate within the male-dominated family whose specialized functions were to provide legitimate heirs, rear young children, and perform various domestic chores. (In addition to being androcentric, this definition was completely class bound, with female slaves not even included in the category of woman.)

Completely missing from the writings of Plato and Aristotle, however, was the definition of woman as a sexual temptress who either lures man to do evil deeds (as in the case of Adam and Eve) or weakens him (as in the case of Sampson and Delilah). This gap in the androcentric conception of woman probably relates to the homoeroticism of ancient Greek culture. To men like Plato and Aristotle, women were not the center of either their affective lives or their sexual desires; even though defined androcentrically, women were thus not defined in terms of male sexuality.

Plato

Plato's conception of woman as inferior to man is clearly communicated by his own creation myth. Human nature is of two kinds, with men as "the superior race." The original creation actually contained no women at all, just men, each with a soul assigned to a star. Of these original men,

> he who lived well during his appointed time was to return and dwell in his native star, and there he would have a blessed and congenial existence. But if he failed in attaining this, at the second birth he would pass into a woman, and if, when in that

state of being, he did not desist from evil, he would continually
be changed into some brute who resembled him in the evil
nature which he had acquired. (*Timaeus*, 42)

According to this creation myth, woman is created from man—just as
she was in the Old Testament. Even worse, she is created from those
men "who were cowards or led unrighteous lives" (90) during their first
existence on earth. And out of what are the brutish lower animals
created? Why, from those souls who continued to be wicked even during their lives as women—which places women midway in goodness
and rationality between men and beasts.

Because Plato was essentially a social critic and a visionary, much of
his writing consists of prescriptions for life in two hypothetical types of
cities: the ideal city, where all property is owned communally by an elite
group of guardians who—because they have no private or vested interests—are able to make the best decisions for the city as a whole, and the
second-best city, where property is not held in common. Plato eliminated the institution of private property from his ideal city because he
believed that private property generates the kind of possessiveness that
leads not only to the "excessive love of self" (*Laws*, V, 731) but also to
the political degeneration of the polity. In so doing, moreover, he eliminated the private household, the private family, the private child, and
the private wife!

As we might expect, the elimination of all these traditional forms
led to a revolutionary restructuring of social life. To produce the best
offspring for the social collective, male and female guardians who were
well matched eugenically were brought together by the state in tempo-
rary, but sacred, unions. To prevent those same men and women from
treating the offspring they produced as theirs rather than the collective's, all infants were taken away from the women who bore them
immediately after birth and raised communally; hence no woman—or
man—ever had any way of knowing which child in the collective was
hers or his.

As noted earlier, the ancient Greek definition of woman was already missing one traditional androcentric element: the definition of
woman as a sexual temptress. When Plato eliminated the private family, the private child, and the private wife, it lost yet another traditional
androcentric element: the definition of woman as a subordinate within
the male-dominated family. This second gap not only left intact the

definition of woman as an inferior departure from the male standard; it also left the woman herself with no role or function apart from pregnancy and lactation, because almost everything else was done by men or slaves.

In this extraordinary social context, Plato envisioned an extraordinary new role for women. Specifically, he argued that in the ideal city, women would not only be persons in their own right; they would also play precisely the same role that the male guardians would play. Plato was serious about this identity of male and female roles, requiring that women participate fully in the military, for example, and that men participate fully in communal child-rearing.

In anticipation of the ridicule that this proposal would surely bring, Plato argued at length that once removed from the traditional role of private wife, and once given the same education and training as men, women would be capable of performing the full range of activities and functions that men performed. On average, they would still perform somewhat less outstandingly than men because the male sex has all "gifts and qualities in a higher degree than the female." Although "all the pursuits of men are the pursuits of women also, . . . in all of them a woman is inferior to a man" (*Republic,* V, 455). We have heard this many times before, of course.

Plato had strong reservations about the institution of private property, but he believed that few human beings were virtuous enough or rational enough to hold their property in common. Accordingly, the institution of private property continues to exist in his second-best city. As he saw it, however, the institution of private property necessitates the existence of legitimate heirs, and the need for legitimate heirs in its turn necessitates the institution of private wives.

In the context of Plato's prescriptions for life in the second-best city, we finally see his androcentric conception of woman as a subordinate within the male-dominated family. For here, not only are women denied the most basic civil and legal rights, including the right to own property, the right to inherit, and the right to give evidence in a court of law, but they are segregated and secluded within the household, where they carry out their three primary functions: attending to domestic chores, bearing children, and looking after infants. Within the context of childcare, moreover, their function does not extend to anything so intellectual as giving the children their lessons; that educational role—like virtually all public roles—is reserved for men.

Although Plato does give lip service to women's citizenship even in his second-best city, in fact, their status as private wives defines them as little more than a specialized category of private property, as Plato himself acknowledges when he laments that "women and children and houses and all other things are [still] the private property of individuals" (*Laws*, VII, 807). Consistent with this categorization, women— like all other kinds of property, including servants and children—can legally be given away by their male relatives; that is, they have no choice about whom they will marry.

Plato may have been unable to think of a woman as a person in her own right in the context of a culture where both private property and the private family were intact. He was, nevertheless, the first male writer in the history of the Western world to have seriously wondered whether males and females might be similar enough in their natures to play similar roles in society. And for that singular achievement, he deserves a certain amount of credit. For Aristotle, in contrast, the very idea that women and men could be that similar was out of the question.[6]

Aristotle

Because Aristotle was more of a scientist than a social critic or a visionary, he was less interested in how things might be different than in "why the world and its constituent parts are, and must be, the way they are" (Okin, 1979, p. 73). His answer to this question was teleological. Just as the maple sapling has a specific purpose or potential that it does—and should—fulfill by becoming a maple tree, so, too, does every living thing have a specific purpose or function that it should fulfill during the course of its existence. As he explained in a commentary on why women and slaves should always be distinguished from one another, "Nature . . . is not niggardly, like the smith who fashions the Delphian knife for many uses; she makes each thing for a single use, and every instrument is best made when intended for one and not for many uses" (*Politics*, I, 2, 1252b).

This is not to say that each thing can be considered in isolation. On the contrary. The world is a unified structure whose constituent parts are organized hierarchically. Hence there is a natural and orderly relation among the parts, with some being higher or superior and with others being lower or inferior. Aristotle is explicit about the basis for this ranking and the differing functions of the higher and lower ranks:

"In the world both of nature and of art the inferior always exists for the sake of the better or superior, and the better or superior is that which has a rational principle" (*Politics,* VII, 14, 1333a). In other words, those beings who are capable of reason or deliberative thought are at the top of the hierarchy, and the general function of everything and everyone else is to help them in the fulfillment of their specific destiny.

The question for us is where in this hierarchy women are positioned relative to men and why they are so positioned. According to Aristotle, "the male is such in virtue of a certain capacity and the female is such in virtue of an incapacity" (*Generation of Animals,* IV, 1, 766a); that is, "we must look upon the female character as being a sort of natural deficiency" (IV, 6, 775a), an impotent or "mutilated" male (II, 3, 737a), whose "deliberative faculty" is "without authority" (*Politics,* I, 13, 1260a). True, she does exist as "a natural necessity" among all those beings who reproduce sexually, but she is born of the same circumstances at conception that also produce deformed children and other "monstrosit[ies]." She is thus one of those cases in which "Nature has in a way departed from the type." Indeed, she is the "first departure" from type (*Generation,* IV, 3, 767b). If this doesn't qualify as a textbook example of a woman's being androcentrically defined as an inferior departure from the male standard, I don't know what would qualify.

What follows from a woman's natural inferiority is that she exists for the sake of her superiors. Like a slave, her general purpose in life is to enable her male betters to live the most rational, deliberative, and well-ordered life that they possibly can. In contrast to the slave, however, who serves this general function by doing menial labor, the woman serves it by doing those things that Aristotle sees as part of her unique nature: namely, caring for children and maintaining the stability of the household. The household is itself a hierarchy, of course, with father having authority over son, master over slave, and husband over wife.

A Conflicted Legacy

Implicit in even this brief discussion of Plato and Aristotle are two themes that the ancient Greeks themselves did not find conflictive but which later cultures have had trouble reconciling. The first theme concerns hierarchy, status, and natural difference. Here, the collective is seen as naturally having a hierarchical structure; a person is seen as naturally having a level of virtue that determines his or her status within the hierarchy; and lower persons are seen as naturally serving the interests of higher persons. The second theme concerns reason, equality, and democracy. Here, rational thought and discussion— rather than obedience to authority—are seen as the highest virtues, and all citizens of the polity are supposed to participate fully and equally in the political process, with no citizen having any priority over any other citizen.

The ancient Greeks took their notion of natural hierarchy so for granted that they applied their notion of democracy and equality only to the elite group at the top of the hierarchy. By the time of the Enlightenment, two millennia later, however, the individual had come to have so much more priority than the collective that the intellectual elite— which included Thomas Hobbes, René Descartes, and John Locke, among others—placed much less emphasis on the collective's having any kind of a natural structure and much more emphasis on the individual's having certain natural and inalienable rights. Grounding the Enlightenment in the universalistic language of natural rights made it unnatural for individuals to be ruled without their consent. It also made all individuals inherently equal in nature, thereby demolishing in one theoretical stroke the ancient Greek rationale for giving some individuals more political rights than others.[7]

But as theoretically inconsistent with the universalistic language of natural and inalienable rights as it was, the ancient Greek assumption that natural differences justify political inequalities nevertheless managed to insinuate itself into the writings of all the Enlightenment theorists, as well as the constitutions of all the modern democracies in the world. In the U.S. Constitution, for example, that most basic of all political rights—the right to vote—was not only denied to women and to blacks but also to white men who were not property owners.

Because of his impassioned arguments against all forms of political inequality among men, Jean Jacques Rousseau is often regarded as the only Enlightenment theorist who transcended the ancient Greek assumption that natural differences justify political inequality. But not only did Rousseau never once acknowledge the relevance of his arguments to the subordination of women; even worse, he argued that because women can use their sexual attractiveness to men to "establish their empire, and put in power the sex that ought to obey" (1755/1952, p. 346), men must subjugate women in all other spheres of life if they are to preserve a balance of power. What he did, then, was to argue against the political equality of women by resurrecting that ancient Judeo-Christian definition of a woman as an evil sexual temptress.[8]

The political philosopher Arlene Saxonhouse has written that "the tension we find in much of the contemporary debate about the place of women in society arises from a conflict between the egalitarian assumptions of liberalism" on which the American political system "has been built, and the practices of patriarchal and sexual differentiation out of which our society has grown" (1985, pp. 6–7). What I hope is now clear is that in America, both the emphasis on reason and democracy and the androcentric exclusion of women from the public sphere (which will be documented below) have derived, at least in part, from the ancient Greeks.

Whereas the two androcentric discourses discussed thus far date back thousands of years, the next androcentric discourse to be discussed dates back less than a hundred years. In spite of being so new, this third discourse has so radically altered the way human nature is conceptualized in modern Western culture that it must be seen as a major building block of the modern Western definition of woman.

FREUDIAN PSYCHOANALYTIC THEORY

Freud

Up to this point, we have seen two different categories of explanation for why women and men have such different and unequal natures. One argument is that when human beings were first created, the two sexes were given their different and unequal natures—by God in the context of Judeo-Christian theology or by nature itself in the context of ancient Greek philosophy. The second argument is that the two sexes gradually developed their different and unequal natures during the course of biological evolution. In sharp contrast to both of these arguments is the psychoanalytic explanation developed by Sigmund Freud in the early 1900s. The argument here is that women and men develop their different and unequal natures during the course of their psychological development as children.

Three aspects of this psychosexual development are especially important. (1) Even in the context of normal psychological development, the child is necessarily confronted with so many thoughts and feelings that are psychologically threatening that development always involves the repression of some of this painful material into the unconscious. (2) Sexual material in particular is most often repressed into the unconscious because sexuality (or sensuality) dominates not only the child's but even the infant's early experience. (3) Different aspects of the child's sexuality are salient during different stages of his or her psychosexual development. During the "oral" stage, for example, the child's sexuality is primarily focused on the act of sucking. During the "anal" stage, it is primarily focused on the withholding and expelling of feces. And during the "phallic" stage, it is primarily focused on the fondling of the genitalia.[9]

According to Freud, it is during the phallic stage, which lasts from approximately age three to age six, that the child normally develops a feeling of sexual attraction toward the parent of the other sex and an awareness that the two sexes have different sorts of genitalia. This discovery of genital difference has drastically different consequences for the psychosexual development of the two sexes.

For the boy, "whose own penis is such a proud possession" (1924/ 1959, p. 271), the sight of a girl's genitalia fills him with either a "horror of the mutilated creature or triumphant contempt for her" (1925/ 1959, p. 191). In addition, it convinces him of the very real risk to his own penis—which has already been threatened with castration on numerous occasions or which he has already imagined to be threatened— because of his masturbation or because of his sexual interest in his mother or both. All of this is much more painful and threatening than the little boy can possibly bear, so he represses his sexual feelings for his mother, identifies with his father, and—through that process of identification—not only resolves his Oedipus complex but also develops normal masculinity and a strong superego.

For the girl, in contrast, who has so far been "a little man," happily engaged in masturbation with her "penis-equivalent," the discovery of genital difference arouses, not the dread of castration, but the desire for the "superior organ" (1933/1964, p. 104; 1925/1959, p. 195). Freud describes the critical moment as an epiphany: having but once noticed the penis "of a brother or playmate, strikingly visible and of large proportions," the little girl "makes her judgment and her decision in a flash. She has seen it and knows that she is without it and wants to have it." In other words, the little girl instantly falls "a victim to envy for the penis" (pp. 190–191). Freud does not see this envy as abnormal in any way. Quite the contrary. In a girl, penis envy paves the way to normal femininity, just as in a boy, castration anxiety paves the way to normal masculinity.

To be more specific, there are at least six normal and natural psychological consequences of a girl's penis envy, all of which are a part of her developing femininity. First, as soon as "she becomes aware of the wound to her narcissism, she develops, like a scar, a sense of inferiority." Second, when she has "passed beyond her first attempt at explaining her lack of a penis as being a punishment personal to herself and has realized that that sexual character is a universal one, she begins to share the contempt felt by men for a sex which is the lesser in so important a respect." Third, "even after penis-envy has abandoned its true object, it continues to exist . . . in the character-trait of jealousy." Fourth, the girl "gives up her affectionate relation to her mother," whom she almost always considers "responsible for her lack of a penis." Fifth, because of the "sense of humiliation" she feels over the "inferiority of the clitoris," she gives up her clitoral masturbation, thereby making "room for the development of her [vaginal] femininity." Finally, "she gives up her wish for a penis and puts in place of it a wish for a child" (pp. 192–195).

At this point, says Freud, "the girl has turned into a little woman" (p. 195). This little woman will be especially happy, however, if the baby she now wishes for turns out to be a little boy "who brings the longed-for penis with him" (1933/1964, p. 113).

Unfortunately, a girl's "discovery that she is castrated" does not always send her down this path to "normal femininity" (p. 114). In some cases, the girl's "self-love" is so "mortified by the comparison with the boy's far superior equipment" that she "represses a good part of her sexual trends," which leads to "sexual inhibition or to neurosis" (pp. 111–112). In other cases, the girl develops a "powerful masculinity complex" (p. 114). By this, Freud means that she "refuse[s] to accept the fact of being castrated," "harden[s] herself in the conviction that she *does* possess a penis," and subsequently "behave[s] as though she were a man" (1925/1959, pp. 191–192). The "essence of this process," according to Freud, is that she avoids "the wave of passivity . . . which opens the way to the turn toward femininity." The most extreme outcome of such a masculinity complex is "manifest homosexuality" (1933/1964, p. 115), but there are many less extreme outcomes as well—including the rejection of the traditional role of wife and mother and the desire "to carry on an intellectual profession" (p. 111).

Embedded in this discussion of a girl's psychosexual development are the same three androcentric definitions of a woman that carried forward in the Judeo-Christian and ancient Greek traditions. In keeping with the more scientific conception of sex in the twentieth century, however, the definition of a woman in terms of male sexuality has been greatly modernized.

Because Darwin's theory of evolution made sex a natural activity critical to the development of the species and an explicitly male-directed activity at that, the Judeo-Christian conception of a woman as a sexual temptress who actively initiates sexual activity to lure men to their doom could not be incorporated into a post-Darwinian scientific theory like Freud's. What Freud proffered instead was thus the much more modern definition of a woman as the object—rather than the temptress—of the male sexual appetite. Specifically, he posited a "passive" and "masochistic" woman (p. 102) whose sexual gratification finally comes to be situated—after a tortuous process of psychosexual development—not in her "masculine" clitoris, which is where it was originally, but in her "truly feminine" vagina (p. 104), which is exactly where it can best serve the male's sexuality.

Although there is no dramatic change in Freud's definition of a woman in terms of her domestic and reproductive function within a male-dominated household, there is a dramatic change in the meta-theory underlying this definition. Whereas the ancient traditions found it difficult to conceive of a woman as anything other than a wife and a mother, Freud treated other possibilities as eminently real. To undermine their viability, however, he distinguished theoretically between "normal femininity" and the "masculinity complex" (p. 111), thereby defining any woman who wishes to be something other than a wife and mother as psychologically pathological.

This is not to say that Freud completely abandoned the idea that a woman's nature ill suits her for activities outside the home. He saw women as naturally having "less capacity for sublimating their instincts than men" (p. 119), and this ability to transform the instincts was precisely what was required for cultural achievement outside the home.

This brings us to Freud's definition of a woman as an inferior departure from the male standard, which is beautifully embodied in his twin concepts of male castration anxiety and female penis envy, both of which presuppose a priori that the female genitalia are merely an already-castrated or mutilated version of the male genitalia. A woman's inferiority to the male standard is not limited to the body alone, however. As Freud himself put it: "In the absence of fear of castration the chief motive is lacking [in girls] which leads boys to surmount the Oedipus Complex. . . . In these circumstances the formation of the super-ego must suffer; it cannot attain the strength and independence which give it its cultural significance" (p. 114).

In Freud's view, the child's perspective on reality, and not the adult's, is privileged because it is almost always as a child that the adult originally finds most of the material in his or her unconscious to be painful or threatening. Accordingly, it is the child through whom Freud says that the female body is an inferior departure from the male standard. Situating the androcentric lens within the mind of every child, both male and female, was a brilliant stroke. Not only did it naturalize the female's inferiority by making it instantly recognizable to the very young child of either sex; it also naturalized the androcentric lens by putting it in the mind of the human child rather than the mind of the male theorist.

Feminist Reactions to Freud

Over the years, there have been at least three varieties of feminist reaction to Freud's androcentric analysis of psychosexual development. The first reaction came from certain of his contemporaries, like Ernest Jones, Karen Horney, and Melanie Klein, who found his analysis of women to be "unduly phallo-centric" (Jones, 1927/1961, p. 438). According to these theorists, a girl's femininity "develops progressively," not from a phallocentric process of psychosexual development, but "from the promptings of an instinctual [female] constitution" (Jones, 1935/1961, p. 495).[10]

This emphasis on the distinctive biological attributes of women as well as men was later elaborated by Erik Erikson (1968), who argued that the foundation of female identity is not the absence of a penis but the presence of a uterus. More specifically, Erikson argued that just as the male psyche is mainly organized around what the penis has always symbolized—"what man can make, whether it helps to build or to destroy" (p. 262)—so the female psyche is mainly organized around what the uterus or the "inner space" has always symbolized, "a biological, psychological, and ethical commitment to take care of human infancy" (p. 266). Although not nearly so biologically essentialist as Erikson himself, two French psychoanalysts who also treat the body as a metaphor for the nature of male and female identity are Luce Irigaray (1985, 1991) and Michele Montrelay (1977).

The second variety of feminist reaction came from non-psychoanalytic believers in social constructionism. According to these theorists, virtually all psychological sex differences result from some combination of cultural conditioning and life in a male-dominated society. Insofar as women do envy men, they envy them their power and status, not their penises.

In keeping with this line of reasoning, Kate Millett criticized Freud for having made "a major and rather foolish confusion between biology and culture, anatomy and status" and for also having "spurned an excellent opportunity" to study "the effect of male-supremacist culture on the ego development of the young female, preferring instead to sanctify her oppression in terms of the inevitable law of 'biology.'" As Millett herself saw the situation,

> Girls are fully cognizant of male supremacy long before they see their brother's penis. It is so much a part of their culture, so entirely present in the favoritism of school and family, in the image of each sex presented to them by all media, religion, and in every model of the adult world they perceive, that to associate it with a boy's distinguishing genital would, since they have learned a thousand other distinguishing sexual marks by now, be either redundant or irrelevant. Confronted with so much concrete evidence of the male's superior status, sensing on all sides the depreciation in which they are held, girls envy not the penis, but only what the penis gives one social pretensions to. (1969, pp. 264–265)

Two other feminist theorists who made much the same point were Betty Friedan (1963) and Eva Figes (1970).

Ironically, the third and most recent variety of feminist reaction to Freud praises him for creating precisely what Millett accused him of not creating: a theory of how female sexuality and the female unconscious are shaped—or misshaped—by a patriarchal culture.[11] These feminist psychoanalysts emphasize Freud's fundamental premise that masculinity and femininity are made, not born. In addition, they follow the French psychoanalyst Jacques Lacan in viewing the penis as psychologically important to children because of the privileged role given to the phallus as a symbol within patriarchal society. For these theorists, the Oedipus complex is thus not primarily a natural or biological phenomenon; rather, it is a cultural phenomenon "marking the entry of the child into . . . the Symbolic Order" (Sayers, 1982, p. 135). In the words of the British psychoanalyst Juliet Mitchell, whose 1974 book *Psychoanalysis and Feminism* was the first to introduce this perspective to an English-speaking audience: "Psychoanalysis is not a recommendation *for* a patriarchal society, but an analysis *of* one" (p. xiii). "The myth that Freud rewrote as the Oedipus complex epitomizes man's [and woman's] entry into culture itself. . . . It is specific to nothing but patriarchy" (p. 377).

What follows from psychoanalytic theory, according to Mitchell, is thus not that the patriarchal order should continue to be reproduced within every person's unconscious; what follows is that patriarchy itself should be overthrown.

But regardless of whether this most recent rereading of Freud is consistent with his original intentions, one thing is beyond dispute. Since psychoanalytic theory was originally presented in the early 1900s, its legacy has not been the suggestion that patriarchy oppresses women and should therefore be overthrown. On the contrary. Like the Judeo-Christian and ancient Greek traditions before it, it has provided yet another language in which to define woman from an androcentric perspective.

AMERICAN EQUAL RIGHTS LAW

Of the three androcentric definitions of a woman thus far traced through Judeo-Christian theology, ancient Greek philosophy, and Freudian psychoanalytic theory, two—the definition of a woman in terms of her domestic and reproductive function within a male-dominated household and the definition of a woman in terms of her departure from a male standard—are deeply embedded in the history of American equal rights law. In contrast, the third androcentric definition of a woman in terms of her ability to stimulate and to satisfy the male sexual appetite is embedded in the history of American rape law, which is beyond the scope of this book.[12]

From the Colonial Period to the Civil War

Beginning as early as the colonial period, the legal status granted to American women was strongly influenced by two aspects of English common law: the doctrine of coverture, under which a woman's legal identity is submerged into that of her husband, and the doctrine of family privacy, under which the family and the home are held to be immune from legal interference.[13] These doctrines were articulated by William Blackstone in his *Commentaries on the Laws of England* (1765–1769/1979). On the doctrine of family privacy, Blackstone wrote:

> Crimes and misdemeanors are a breach and a violation of . . . public rights and duties, owing to the whole community, considered as a community, in its social aggregate capacity. . . . Private vices . . . are not, cannot be, the object of any municipal law. . . . Thus the vice of drunkenness, if committed privately and alone, is beyond the knowledge and of course beyond the reach of human tribunals: but if committed publicly, in the face of the world, its evil example makes it liable to temporal censures. (Vol. 4, pp. 41–42)

On the doctrine of coverture, Blackstone was even more explicit. "By marriage," he wrote, "the husband and wife are one person in law: that is, the very being or legal existence of the woman is suspended during the marriage, or at least is incorporated and consolidated into that of the husband; under whose wing, protection, and cover, she performs everything" (Vol. 1, p. 430).

Although neither principle was rigidly or consistently followed during the colonial period—owing primarily to the scarcity of labor in general and women in particular—both were closely followed in the critical decades after the revolutionary war, when the new United States was busily compiling its laws into national and state constitutions. As a result, these new constitutions excluded women from participation in the public sphere by denying them many of the rights explicitly granted to their white male counterparts, including the right to vote, the right to hold or sell property, the right to execute contracts, the right to conduct business, the right to sue, and the right to have legal guardianship over their children. In addition, they isolated women within the privacy of the male-dominated family, where not only did the husband have the legal right to physically chastise his wife for any disobedience but the wife also had little in the way of legal protection if the husband abused his power over her or failed to fulfill his duties toward her in any way.

Excluding women from the public sphere but giving them no legal protection in the private sphere was seriously challenged for the first time when sixty-eight women and thirty-two men signed the Declaration of Sentiments and Resolutions at the Seneca Falls convention in 1848. Built on the model of the Declaration of Independence, this radical document demanded not only that women be granted all of the rights previously denied to them in the public domain, including the right to vote, but also demanded that women be granted complete equality in marriage.

Although the Seneca Falls convention is generally regarded as the official beginning of the women's rights movement in the United States, the women who organized that convention had long been active in the antislavery movement; in fact, their experience as abolitionists was responsible for their growing commitment to women's rights. Their experience as abolitionists affected them in at least two ways: it sensitized them to the similarities between the legal status of slaves and the legal status of married women, which motivated them to work simultaneously for both the abolition of slavery and the abolition of female subordination, and it showed them how vehemently opposed to women's rights the majority of their male abolitionist colleagues were, which convinced them of the need to form a separate women's rights movement.

The opposition of the male abolitionists was highlighted at the World Anti-Slavery Convention of 1840, when the official female delegates to the convention were denied the right to be seated. Among the many unseated women were Lucretia Mott, who was herself a delegate, and Elizabeth Cady Stanton, who attended as the wife of a seated male delegate. Although the two women had never previously met, they apparently talked for hours about the injustice of female subordination generally and about the irony of female subordination within the abolition movement itself. The Seneca Falls convention grew out of that discussion.

History did not work itself out as these early feminists would have most liked, of course. When Abraham Lincoln issued the Emancipation Proclamation on January 1, 1863, he made no mention of any similarity between the institution of slavery and the institution of male-dominated marriage. Even more important, when the Fourteenth and Fifteenth amendments to the Constitution were ratified in 1868 and 1870, the former merely specified that the states could not deny the right to vote to any "male" citizen over the age of twenty-one, and the latter merely specified that no citizen could be denied the right to vote on account of "race, color, or previous condition of servitude." In other words, there was no mention of sex discrimination.

While these two amendments were being drafted, feminists fought long and hard to get the word *male* eliminated from the Fourteenth Amendment and the word *sex* added to the list of protected categories specified in the Fifteenth Amendment. Having failed on both counts, their next move was to argue in the courts that—despite the absence of any language specifically referring to women—these amendments guaranteed the rights of citizenship to *all* American citizens, including women. That strategy failed. And the reason it failed is that for the full one hundred years between 1870 and 1970, an all-male Supreme Court androcentrically defined women not in terms of their role as citizens but in terms of their domestic and reproductive functions within a male-dominated household.

From the Civil War to the Civil Rights Era

Prior to the ratification of the Fourteenth and Fifteenth amendments, the U.S. Constitution offered feminists no grounds for challenging laws that assigned rights, duties, or privileges on the basis of sex.[14] Although the case against such laws would have been much easier to make if feminists had managed to get either "male" eliminated from the Fourteenth Amendment or "sex" added to the Fifteenth, the Fourteenth Amendment did include one section that was worded so generically as to seem applicable to both sexes. That section served as the basis for the unsuccessful challenge to sex discrimination in the nineteenth century and, a hundred years later, as the basis for the successful challenge to sex discrimination in the twentieth century. The full text of this section reads:

> All persons born or naturalized in the United States, and subject to the jurisdiction thereof, are citizens of the United States and of the state wherein they reside. No state shall make or enforce any law which shall abridge the privileges or immu-

nities of citizens of the United States, nor shall any state de-
prive any person of life, liberty, or property, without due process of law; nor deny to any person within its jurisdiction the
equal protection of the laws.

Note the famous "equal protection" clause at the end. In the 130 years
since the Fourteenth Amendment was passed, this clause has been the
grounds for almost all constitutional challenges to discriminatory laws,
including those that discriminate against blacks and other minorities.

This is not to say that the equal protection clause has always been
broadly interpreted to apply to women. On the contrary. Until 1971,
the Court consistently refused to extend the protection of the Fourteenth Amendment to women, arguing—in the spirit of what has come
to be called judicial conservatism—that the Court, as part of the ap-
pointed judiciary, does not have the constitutional authority to create
what would essentially be new law. That lies within the purview of the
elected legislature. The Court has only the much narrower authority to
judge whether an existing law is constitutional.

This judicial conservatism is evident in four important decisions
that the Court made in the first decade after the Fourteenth Amendment was ratified. In the first case—which had nothing to do with
women's rights—the Court "doubt[ed] very much whether any action
of a state not directed by way of discrimination against the negroes as a
class, or on account of their race, will be held to come within the purview of this provision" (*Slaughter-House*, 1873).[15] The second decision,
announced just one day after the *Slaughter-House* decision, upheld an
Illinois law that rendered women ineligible to practice law within that
state. Here, the Court did little more than assert that "the opinion just
delivered in the *Slaughter-House Cases* renders elaborate argument in
the present case unnecessary" (*Bradwell v. Illinois*, 1873). The third
decision upheld a Missouri law that gave the right to vote to men alone.
Although here the Court conceded that the law in question might be
"wrong," it explicitly denied having the power "to make the alteration"
being requested. "If the law is wrong, it ought to be changed, but the
power for that is not with us" (*Minor v. Happersett*, 1875). And finally,
the fourth decision struck down a West Virginia law that excluded
blacks from serving on juries. The Court ruled that although a state
could no longer confine its selection of jurors to whites, it could still
"confine [its] selection to males" (*Struader v. West Virginia*, 1879).[16]

Judicial conservatism was only a small part of the story. In concert with the larger society in which they lived, the nine male Supreme Court justices androcentrically defined women in terms of their domestic and reproductive functions within a male-dominated household; and that androcentrism was at least partially responsible for the Court's persistent refusal to grant women, as citizens, the "equal protection of the laws." The Court's androcentrism can be seen clearly in two famous cases: *Bradwell v. Illinois* (1873) and *Muller v. Oregon* (1908).

Bradwell v. Illinois, which was cited earlier, upheld an Illinois law that rendered women ineligible to practice law in that state. Although the majority opinion in *Bradwell* was argued on grounds of judicial conservatism, Justice Joseph Bradley presented another argument in a concurring opinion. According to him, the feminist claim in this case "assumes that it is one of the privileges and immunities of women as citizens to engage in any and every profession, occupation, or employment in civil life." Not clear, however, is whether "this has ever been established as one of the fundamental privileges and immunities of the sex." Bradley continues:

> On the contrary, the civil law, as well as nature herself, has always recognized a wide difference in the respective spheres and destinies of man and woman. Man is, or should be, woman's protector and defender. The natural and proper timidity and delicacy which belongs to the female sex evidently unfits it for many of the occupations of civil life. The constitution of the family organization, which is founded in the divine ordinance, as well as in the nature of things, indicates the domestic sphere as that which properly belongs to the domain and functions of womanhood. The harmony, not to say identity, of interests and views which belong, or should belong, to the family institution is repugnant to the idea of a woman adopting a distinct and independent career from that of her husband. So firmly fixed was this sentiment in the founders of the common law that it became a maxim of that system of jurisprudence that a woman had no legal existence separate from her husband, who was regarded as her head and representative in the social state. . . . The paramount destiny and mission of woman are to fulfill the noble and benign offices of wife and mother. This is the law of the Creator.

Justice Bradley eloquently expressed the "separate spheres" ideology that constituted the nineteenth-century version of defining women in terms of their domestic and reproductive function within a male-dominated household. That ideology subtly shifted in the twentieth century to an emphasis on women's reproductive difference.

With the advent of industrialization and urbanization in the mid-nineteenth century, working-class women and men alike found themselves working up to thirteen hours a day, seven days a week, in crowded and unsafe working conditions. In response to the immorality of this exploitation and the lobbying of the emerging labor movement, states began to pass "protective legislation" limiting, among other things, the number of hours per day or week that an employee could legally work. This protective legislation was dealt a critical blow in *Lochner v. New York* (1905) when the Supreme Court ruled that limiting an employee's hours constituted "an illegal interference with the rights of individuals . . . to make contracts regarding labor upon such terms as they may think best."[17] Just three years later, however, another protective legislation case reached the Supreme Court, this one involving an Oregon law that limited a woman's working day to a maximum of ten hours. Here, in *Muller v. Oregon* (1908), the Court upheld the protective legislation, arguing that a woman's biological difference placed her "in a class by herself." The Court reasoned as follows:

> That woman's physical structure and the performance of maternal functions place her at a disadvantage in the struggle for subsistence is obvious. This is especially true when the burdens of motherhood are upon her. Even when they are not, by abundant testimony of the medical fraternity, continuance for a long time on her feet at work, repeating this from day to day, tends to injurious effects upon the body, and, as healthy mothers are essential to vigorous offspring, the physical well-being of woman becomes an object of public interest and care in order to preserve the strength and vigor of the race.
>
> Still again, history discloses the fact that woman has always been dependent upon man. He established his control at the outset by superior physical strength, and this control in various forms, with diminishing intensity, has continued to the present. As minors, though not to the same extent, she has been looked upon in the courts as needing special care that her

rights may be preserved. Education was long denied her, and while now the doors of the schoolroom are opened and her opportunities for acquiring knowledge are great, yet even with that and the consequent increase of capacity for business affairs it is still true that in the struggle for subsistence she is not an equal competitor with her brother. . . . Differentiated by these matters from the other sex, she is properly placed in a class by herself, and legislation designed for her protection may be sustained, even when like legislation is not necessary for men, and could not be sustained. . . .

The limitations which this statute places upon her contractual powers, upon her right to agree with her employer as to the time she shall labor, are not imposed solely for her benefit, but also largely for the benefit of all. Many words cannot make this plainer. The two sexes differ in structure of body, in the functions to be performed by each, in the amount of physical strength, in the capacity for long continued labor, particularly when done standing, the influence of vigorous health upon the future well-being of the race, the self-reliance which enables one to assert full rights, and in the capacity to maintain the struggle for existence. This difference justifies a difference in legislation. . . . For these reasons, and without questioning in any respect the decision in *Lochner v. New York,* . . . the judgment of the Supreme Court of Oregon is affirmed.

The impact of this precedent-setting decision was both immediate and long lasting. With respect to the history of labor in America, not only did *Muller* bring the reformist effort to get more humane working conditions for everyone to an almost complete standstill; it also made it impossible for women even to compete for jobs that paid a living wage. With respect to the history of women's rights in America, not only did the decision split the women's rights movement over the appropriateness of emphasizing woman's biological difference; even more important, it provided a whole new rationale for assigning rights, duties, and privileges on the basis of sex. For all practical purposes, the decision thus eliminated any possibility that the Court would overturn such laws in the foreseeable future—which is why, for over sixty years thereafter, the Court upheld virtually every single case of sex discrimination that came before it, in each case citing *Muller* as binding precedent (Baer,

1978, p. 66). Early in this sixty-year period, the many laws denying women the right to vote were finally overturned. But it was not the Court that overturned these laws; it was the Nineteenth Amendment to the Constitution, which was ratified in 1920.

The Modern Equality Era I: Challenging the Definition of Woman as Wife and Mother

With a completely new set of justices and a completely transformed America, the Court finally put aside its judicial and its social conservatism in 1954, when it ruled in *Brown v. Board of Education* that racially segregated schools were "inherently unequal" and therefore violated the equal protection clause of the Fourteenth Amendment.[18] This landmark ruling ushered in the civil rights movement—which, in turn, ushered in the modern women's movement—and just as important, it led to the development of the Court's equal protection analysis, which was ultimately applied not only to blacks but to women as well.

With respect to blacks, what the Court concluded was that although the equal protection clause does normally allow the government to have the widest possible discretion in making distinctions between people if those distinctions are "rationally related" to some legitimate government objective (for example, distinguishing between people with good and bad vision when issuing driver's licenses), racial classifications "must be viewed in light of the historical fact that the central purpose of the Fourteenth Amendment was to eliminate racial discrimination emanating from official sources in the States. This strong policy renders racial classifications 'constitutionally suspect,' and subject to the 'most rigid scrutiny.'" In the absence of any overriding statutory purpose, every racial classification is thus "reduced to an invidious discrimination forbidden by the Equal Protection Clause" (*McLaughlin v. Florida,* 1964). In practice, this policy of subjecting racial classifications to the strictest judicial scrutiny is barely distinguishable from an outright prohibition. Rarely if ever do blanket classifications survive it.[19]

With respect to women, the Court has been much less definitive. Although it did conclude in *Reed v. Reed* (1971) that women are covered by the equal protection clause of the Fourteenth Amendment—and hence, in this case, that a state could not automatically favor a male over a female when appointing an administrator for the estate of someone who has died without a will—a majority of the Court has never been willing to assert that classifications based on sex should be treated in exactly the same way as classifications based on race; hence there has never been a binding precedent establishing sex as an inherently suspect category subject to strict judicial scrutiny.

The closest the Court ever came to the establishment of such a precedent was in *Frontiero v. Richardson* (1973). In overturning a law that automatically gave dependents' benefits to the spouses of all male members of the armed services while simultaneously requiring female members of the armed services to demonstrate that their spouses were dependent on them for over half of their support, four of the five concurring justices wrote as follows:

> At the outset, appellants contend that classifications based upon sex, like classifications based upon race, alienage, and national origin, are inherently suspect and must therefore be subjected to close judicial scrutiny. We agree and, indeed, find at least implicit support for such an approach in our unanimous decision only last Term in *Reed v. Reed*.
>
> There can be no doubt that our Nation has had a long and unfortunate history of sex discrimination. Traditionally, such discrimination was rationalized by an attitude of "romantic paternalism" which, in practical effect, put women, not on a pedestal, but in a cage. . . .
>
> As a result of notions such as these, our statute books gradually became laden with gross, stereotyped distinctions between the sexes and, indeed, throughout much of the 19th century the position of women in our society was, in many respects, comparable to that of blacks under the pre–Civil War slave codes. Neither slaves nor women could hold office, serve on juries, or bring suit in their own names, and married women traditionally were denied the legal capacity to hold or convey property or to serve as legal guardians of their own children.
>
> It is true, of course, that the position of women in America has improved markedly in recent decades. Nevertheless, it can hardly be doubted that, in part because of the high visibility of the sex characteristic, women still face pervasive, although at

times more subtle, discrimination in our educational institutions, in the job market and, perhaps most conspicuously, in the political arena. . . .

Moreover, since sex, like race and national origin, is an immutable characteristic determined solely by the accident of birth, the imposition of special disabilities upon the members of a particular sex would seem to violate "the basic concept of our system that legal burdens should bear some relationship to individual responsibility. . . ." And what differentiates sex from such nonsuspect statutes as intelligence or physical disability, and aligns it with the recognized suspect criteria, is that the sex characteristic frequently bears no relation to ability to perform or contribute to society. As a result, statutory distinctions between the sexes often have the effect of invidiously relegating the entire class of females to inferior status without regard to the actual capabilities of its individual members. . . .

With these considerations in mind, we can only conclude that classifications based upon sex, like classifications based upon race, alienage, or national origin, are inherently suspect, and must therefore be subjected to strict judicial scrutiny.

Had but one more justice agreed with this reasoning, it would have been treated as a binding precedent. Because a majority did not endorse it, however, the Court gradually evolved a much more lenient standard of scrutiny, described in *Craig v. Boren* (1976): "Classifications by gender must serve important governmental objectives and must be substantially related to achievement of those objectives."

Although this "substantial relationship" standard is clearly more stringent than the "rational relationship" standard that the Court applies to nonproblematic classifications, it is nowhere near the "strict scrutiny" standard that feminists had hoped for when the Court finally ruled, in *Reed v. Reed* (1971), that sex was "a classification subject to scrutiny under the Equal Protection Clause." Accordingly, it became all the more important to feminists that the equal rights amendment to the U.S. Constitution be passed and ratified.

The feminist reasoning here was as follows: by explicitly asserting that "equality of rights under the law shall not be denied or abridged by the United States or by any State on account of sex," the equal rights amendment would mandate, once and for all, that any classification based on sex must be subject to the strictest possible judicial scrutiny. This, ironically, was precisely what Justices Lewis Powell and Harry Blackmun had argued in *Frontiero v. Richardson* when they dissented from the plurality's "strict scrutiny" argument on the grounds of judicial conservatism.

Once again, however, history did not work out as the feminists would have liked. Although the equal rights amendment was finally passed by both the House and the Senate in 1970—after being introduced at every single session of Congress since 1923—it fell three states short of the thirty-eight that were required for ratification and did not become the law of the land.

The fundamental problem with the recent women's rights rulings of the Supreme Court, however, is not that they apply too lenient a standard of judicial review to explicit sex classifications, although they do that, too. The fundamental problem is that they give equality only to those few women who manage to be in the same situation as men while denying equality to those many women who are in a different situation from men. In other words, they androcentrically take the male as the standard and judge a woman worthy of equality only if she matches that male standard.

The Modern Equality Era II: Unwittingly Perpetuating the Male Standard

The fundamental principle underlying the Court's equal protection analysis has always been that "people who are similarly situated in fact must be similarly treated by the law" (Taub & Schneider, 1982, p. 130); that is, "like cases must be treated alike" (Lindgren & Taub, 1988, p. 41). Until the 1970s, however, the Court so completely emphasized the differences between women and men that the two sexes seemed more unlike than like.

To get the Court to realize that its equal protection analysis should apply to sex as well as to race, the Women's Rights Project of the American Civil Liberties Union brought a series of cases to the Court in the 1970s in which similarly situated (or even identically situated) women and men were being differently treated by the law because of archaic and outmoded assumptions about the roles of men and women. So that women would not seem to be the only ones victimized by these discriminatory laws, the ACLU tended to select cases that involved issues, like dependency benefits, that could hurt both women and men, rather

than issues, like pregnancy discrimination, where the harm fell disproportionately on women. As often as not, the plaintiffs in these cases
were men.[20]

The ACLU's strategy so beautifully matched the Court's equal protection analysis and so perfectly challenged the Court's stereotyped
views of women that the Court was quickly persuaded to bring sex
within the purview of the Fourteenth Amendment. By the end of the
1970s, the Court had thus overturned a whole slew of laws discriminating between women and men who were similarly situated. (Overturning these laws was made easier for the Court by the congressional
passage of the Equal Pay Act in 1963 and the Civil Rights Act in 1964.)

But as effective as the ACLU's strategy was, however, it obscured the
fact that the great majority of American men and women were *not*
similarly situated. It also obscured the fact that the Court's equal protection analysis would itself have to be modified if the majority of
American women were ever to be granted complete equality.

The problem with the Court's equal protection analysis is most
evident in its rulings on whether pregnancy can be excluded from the
disabilities covered by an employer's disability insurance package.[21]
The Court has ruled on this issue twice, deciding in *Geduldig v. Aiello*
(1974) that such an exclusion was not a violation of the equal protection clause of the Fourteenth Amendment and later deciding in *General
Electric Co. v. Gilbert* (1976) that such an exclusion was not a violation of
Title VII of the Civil Rights Act of 1964, either. Although the Congress
effectively reversed these two decisions when it enacted the Pregnancy
Discrimination Act in 1978, the Court's reasoning so perfectly illus-
trates both the inadequacy of the Court's equal protection analysis and
the continuing readiness of the Court to take the male situation as the
standard that it is worth discussing in some detail.

In *Geduldig v. Aiello*, the Court reasoned that the exclusion of pregnancy from a disability insurance program does not amount to "invidious discrimination" under the equal protection clause because it does
not involve "discrimination based upon gender as such." The Court
conceded:

> While it is true that only women can become pregnant, it does
> not follow that every legislative classification concerning preg-
> nancy is a sex-based classification like those considered in
> *Reed* . . . and *Frontiero*. . . . The lack of identity between the

excluded disability and gender . . . becomes clear upon the most cursory analysis. The program divides potential recipients into two groups—pregnant women and nonpregnant persons. While the first group is exclusively female, the second includes members of both sexes. The fiscal and actuarial benefits of the program thus accrue to members of both sexes.

According to the Court, the neutrality of the pregnancy exclusion can be seen in yet another way: "There is no risk from which men are protected and women are not. Likewise, there is no risk from which women are protected and men are not."

The Court expanded on this reasoning in *General Electric Co. v. Gilbert*. "Pregnancy-related disabilities constitute an *additional* risk, unique to women," the Court wrote, "and the failure to compensate them for this risk does not destroy the presumed parity of the benefits" that accrue to women and men alike.

Because the Court treated women and men who were similarly situated with respect to their current condition of pregnancy in exactly the same way, its reasoning in *Geduldig* and *Gilbert* was consistent with the model of equal protection that had been used since at least the 1920s: people who are similarly situated in fact must be similarly treated by the law. But a deeper examination of the Court's reasoning makes it clear how little equality such a model could ever provide for the great majority of American women, who are not now and never have been "similarly situated in fact."

The problem with the Court's reasoning goes beyond the presupposition that women and men are similarly situated with respect to pregnancy; the Court also androcentrically defines whatever is male as the standard and whatever is female as something "additional" or "extra." In their dissenting opinion to *Geduldig*, Justices William Brennan, William Douglas, and Thurgood Marshall came within millimeters of exposing this androcentrism. They wrote that

> by singling out for less favorable treatment a gender-linked disability peculiar to women, the State has created a double standard for disability compensation: a limitation is imposed upon the disabilities for which women workers may recover, while men receive full compensation for all disabilities suffered, including those that affect only or primarily their sex, such as prostatectomies, circumcision, hemophilia, and gout.

In effect, one set of rules is applied to females and another to males. Such dissimilar treatment of men and women, on the basis of physical characteristics inextricably linked to one sex, inevitably constitutes sex discrimination.

Justice John Stevens came even closer to exposing the Court's androcentrism when he argued in his dissent from *General Electric* that

> it is not accurate to describe the program as dividing "potential recipients into two groups—pregnant women and nonpregnant persons." . . . The classification is between persons who face a risk of pregnancy and those who do not. . . . By definition, such a rule discriminates on the basis of sex; for it is the capacity to become pregnant which primarily differentiates the female from the male. . . .
>
> Nor is it accurate to state that under the plan "[t]here is no risk from which men are protected and women are not." . . . If the word "risk" is used narrowly, men are protected against the risks associated with a prostate operation whereas women are not. If the word is used more broadly to describe the risk of uncompensated employment caused by physical disability, men receive total protection . . . against that risk whereas women receive only partial protection.

What is going on in these pregnancy cases should be apparent. Like the ancient Judeo-Christian theologians and the early Greek philosophers and Freud himself, the Court is androcentrically defining the male body as the standard human body; hence it sees nothing unusual or inappropriate about giving that standard human body full insurance coverage for each and every condition that might befall it. Consistent with this androcentric perspective, the Court is also defining equal protection as the granting to women of every conceivable benefit that this standard human body might require—which, of course, does not include disability coverage for pregnancy.

Had the Court had even the slightest sensitivity to the meaning of androcentrism, there are at least two truly gender-neutral standards that it would have considered instead. In set-theory terms, these are the *intersection* of male and female bodies, which would narrowly cover only those conditions that befall both men and women, and the *union* of male and female bodies, which would broadly cover all those conditions that befall men and women separately. In fact, the Court was so blind to the meaning of androcentrism that it saw nothing the least bit amiss when, in the name of equal protection, it granted a whole package of special benefits to men and men alone.

What keeps even nonpregnant women from being similarly situated to men in the *Geduldig* and *Gilbert* cases is their biological capacity to become pregnant. What keeps women from being similarly situated to men in most cases, however, is not their biology but their gendered life experience—their female biography—in a society that consistently denies them access to economic and political resources. Three examples will further illustrate both the reality of women's different situation and the androcentrism of the Court's similarly situated model.

Consider first the case of *Personnel Administrator of Massachusetts v. Feeney* (1979), in which the Supreme Court ruled that although women were "overwhelmingly" disadvantaged by a state law mandating a lifetime preference for qualified veterans over qualified nonveterans in the filling of civil service positions, such a law did not violate the equal protection clause of the Fourteenth Amendment, the reason being in part that because "the statute has always been neutral as to gender," the distinction "is, as it seems to be, quite simply between veterans and nonveterans, not between men and women." As far as the Court's equal protection analysis is concerned, it is thus an irrelevant aspect of history that so many fewer women than men are in the privileged situation of being veterans.

Consider next the case of *A.F.S.C.M.E. v. Washington* (1985), in which the U.S. Court of Appeals for the Ninth Circuit ruled that although the reliance on prevailing market rates to set salaries for state employees did create "a wage disparity of about twenty percent" between women's jobs and men's jobs that a state-commissioned survey had found to be "of comparable worth" to the employer, that disparity was not a violation of Title VII of the Civil Rights Act, the reason being in part that

> the State did not create the market disparity and has not been shown to have been motivated by impermissible sex-based considerations in setting salaries. . . . Neither law nor logic deems the free market system a suspect enterprise. Economic reality is that the value of a particular job to an employer is but one factor influencing the rate of compensation for that job. Other

considerations may include the availability of workers willing to do the job and the effectiveness of collective bargaining in a particular industry. . . . Title VII does not obligate . . . [a state] to eliminate an economic inequality which it did not create. . . . Absent a showing of discriminatory motive, which has not been made here, the law does not permit the federal courts to interfere in the market based system for the compensation of . . . employees.

As far as the Court is concerned, it is thus an irrelevant aspect of history that the market has almost never been "free" for women but has been constrained by both unions and the law itself, as we saw earlier in *Bradwell v. Illinois* and *Muller v. Oregon.* It is also an irrelevant aspect of history that women have been concentrated in a tiny number of predominantly female occupations, where the wages are depressed, in part, because of the longstanding devaluation of women workers in U.S. culture. This devaluation of women's work *on account of sex* can be seen most clearly in nursing, where wages continue to be well below the worth of the job despite critically high demand and critically short supply.[22]

Consider, finally, the many, many cases in which women who have been either full-time or part-time homemakers during most of their adult lives are awarded little in the way of financial support at the time of divorce, the reason being in part that since the early 1970s, no-fault divorce rulings have usually presumed women to be as capable of self-sufficiency after divorce as men are. As gender neutral as this presumption may be in principle, its impact over the last twenty years has been to produce a 10–15 percent *rise* in the standard of living for divorced husbands and a 30 percent *decline* in the standard of living for divorced wives and the minor children living in their households.[23]

Both the cause of this post-divorce disparity and its relation to the Supreme Court's equal protection analysis should be clear. Awarding minimal financial support to divorced women ignores the different situations of the majority of women and men in the United States. At the time of divorce, not only are women more likely than men to have custodial responsibility for any minor children; they are also more likely than men to be without the education, credentials, skills, and history of continuous full-time employment needed to get anywhere near as high-paying a job as their husbands already have. In the context of such strikingly different male and female situations, the last thing most divorced women need is an equal protection model that gives equality only to those few women lucky enough to be in a situation similar to their husband's.

What is going on in all three of these cases should be clear. Just as in the pregnancy cases, insurance benefits were organized around the male body, so, too, in these cases are economic benefits organized around the male biography. Organizing benefits androcentrically is precisely what men in power have done since time immemorial. Put somewhat differently, they have used their position of public power to create cultural discourses and social institutions that automatically privilege male experience and otherize female experience.

4

GENDER
POLARIZATION

Even many feminists commonly assume that if androcentrism and biological essentialism were both eliminated, only sexual difference would remain. In fact, what would remain is gender polarization, the ubiquitous organization of social life around the distinction between male and female. Social life is so linked to this distinction that the all-encompassing division between masculine and feminine would still pervade virtually every aspect of human experience, including not just modes of dress and social roles but ways of expressing emotion and experiencing sexual desire.

Nor is it only social life that is dichotomously organized around the male-female distinction. Gender polarization also superimposes a male-female dichotomy on the biological continuum of genes, chromosomes, hormones, and reproductive physiology that constitutes sex itself, which means that gender polarization, and not biology, is the reason that people perceive even the existence of two—and only two—sexes (Kessler & McKenna, 1978). Consistent with this constructivist view of sex are the facts that not all cultures categorize humans into two and only two sexes (see Martin & Voorhies, 1975, on "supernumerary sexes") and that every biological correlate of sex from chromosomes to facial hair is much less bimodally distributed in the human population as a whole than it would appear to be in the highly gender-managed U.S. society.

Gender polarization operates in two related ways. First, it defines mutually exclusive scripts for being male and female.[1] Second, it defines any person or behavior that deviates from these scripts as problematic—as unnatural or immoral from a religious perspective or as biologically anomalous or psychologically pathological from a scientific perspective. Taken together, the effect of these two processes is to construct and to naturalize a gender-polarizing link between the sex of one's body and the character of one's psyche and one's sexuality.

Although many American institutions contribute to gender polarization—including religion, law, education, and the mass media—this chapter, like Chapter 2, focuses on the way that nineteenth- and twentieth-century scientists have done so. Since the second half of the nineteenth century, the allied fields of medicine, sexology, psychiatry, and psychology have together given scientific and medical legitimacy not only to the cultural requirement that the sex of the body match the gender of the psyche but also to the cultural value given to exclusive heterosexuality. This privileging of exclusive heterosexuality is a special case of gender polarization known today as heterosexism.

The mid to late nineteenth century was a time of social disruption in England and parts of Europe, as well as in the United States. At the heart of the disruption were two different threats to the sex and gender order. The first, which we discussed earlier, was the feminist demand for women's rights. The second came from changes in the patterning of sexual behavior.[2]

As John D'Emilio and Estelle Freedman vividly describe it in their 1988 history of sexuality in America, the urbanization and commercialization of American life during the late eighteenth and early nineteenth centuries brought a dramatic shift in the meaning and social organization of sexuality. Whereas sexual relations had earlier been mostly limited to the marriage bed by the surveillance of tightly knit village communities, by the mid to late nineteenth century, a thriving business in prostitution, as well as the beginnings of a predominantly male homosexual culture, had developed within the urban areas of America; by a somewhat earlier period, these had also developed within the urban areas of Europe. Although many different aspects of these sexual developments could be emphasized, what seems significant here is that because they occurred at about the same time as the feminist demand for women's rights, they helped to create the feeling that the whole sex and gender fabric of nineteenth-century Western society was coming apart at the seams. At issue, after all, was more than the rights of women. At issue was the political, social, psychological, and even sexual meaning of being male or female.

Not surprisingly, conservative social reformers, social scientists, and physicians began to focus an extraordinary amount of their attention on the nature of women and men and the meaning of sexuality. The conservative social reformers mounted a political battle against anything and everything that facilitated non-procreative sexual behavior, including prostitution, homosexuality, masturbation, abortion, and birth control. The social scientists and the physicians abounded with theories about the biological origins of male-female difference and the biological—and pathological—nature of gender deviation. This chapter presents the scientific tradition of gender polarization and its derivative in the context of sexuality, heterosexism, that began with this nineteenth-century theorizing about gender deviation.

SEXUAL INVERSION

Odd as it may seem in the twentieth century, the explosion of theorizing about gender deviation in the late nineteenth century was not yet organized around homosexuality per se but on what was then seen as the biological and psychological pathology of anyone who deviated from the traditional gender scripts, including not only those we would today call homosexuals, bisexuals, and lesbians but feminists as well.[3] One reason feminists and sexual minorities were diagnosed as having the very same condition or disease is that in the nineteenth century, sexual orientation was not yet conceptualized as a distinct and separate aspect of a person's psyche. Any individual with cross-gender desires, whether sexual or nonsexual, was seen as but another instance of what psychiatrists, physicians, and sexologists defined as "sexual inversion." This new category of pathology was conceptualized "not as homosexuality, but as . . . a complete exchange of gender identity of which erotic behavior was but one small part" (D'Emilio & Freedman, 1988, p. 226).

This late nineteenth-century emphasis on the inversion of gender identity is readily apparent in the language of the major theorists. As early as 1870, for example, the German psychiatrist Karl Westphal described a female patient with "contrary sexual feelings" as "fond of boys' games" and liking "to dress as a boy" (quoted in Greenberg, 1988, p. 380). About the same time, another prolific German psychiatrist,

Karl Heinrich Ulrichs, described "Uranians" (his term for male inverts) as having "a feminine soul enclosed in a male body" (quoted in Marshall, 1981, p. 142). Picking up on both Westphal's and Ulrichs's notions, the most influential theorist of the period, Richard Krafft-Ebing, noted that in cases where the "peculiar sex instinct" is fully developed, "feeling, thought, will, and the whole character" correspond with it (quoted in Greenberg, 1988, p. 414).

Although all three of these early theorists happened to be German, many nineteenth-century theorists outside Germany also considered the totality of sexual inversion, the American neurologist George Beard among them. Beard wrote in 1884 that when "sex is perverted," individuals "hate the opposite sex, and love their own; men become women, and women men, in their tastes, conduct, character, feelings, and behavior" (quoted in Greenberg, 1988, p. 380). This totalizing focus on gender identity rather than on sex-of-partner preference sometimes produced distinctions that would no longer be made today. For example, whenever it was discovered about a particular married couple that instead of being a man and a woman, they were actually two women—one of whom dressed and passed as a man—the doctors of the day all but ignored the "wife," whom they seemed to regard as the passive, and gender-normal, victim of an inverted "husband" (Greenberg, 1988, p. 382).

The distinction between the true female invert and her gender-normal victim is explicit in sexologists' analyses of the kinds of women who were allegedly participating in the feminist movement of the day. On the one hand, there were the core members of the movement, "who do not altogether represent their sex." They were "mannish in temperament" and "homogenic"; they found children "more or less a bore" and "man's sex-passion . . . a mere impertinence" (Carpenter, 1896, quoted in Jeffreys, 1985, p. 107). On the other hand, there were the "spurious imitations" of these mannish inverts (Ellis, 1897, quoted in Jeffreys, 1985, p. 108), who were drawn toward feminism not by their own inherent masculinity but by the intelligence and the influence of the female inverts with whom they came into contact. That these female inverts had so much power over their gender-normal counterparts was itself "due to the fact that the congenital anomaly occurs with special frequency in women of high intelligence who, voluntarily or involuntarily, influence others" (p. 108).[4]

Nineteenth-century sexologists came up with a variety of explanations to account for the sexual inversion that they thought they were seeing. Although the earliest of these explanations treated inversion as an acquired disease resulting from masturbation, the later explanations treated it as a biological condition. According to the most influential of these, it was a less evolved form of human development, it was one aspect of a family's biological deterioration after generations of excess and vice, or it was some kind of intermediate—or third—sex.

By the end of the century, sexologists had set forth numerous hypotheses about the biological mechanism that might produce an intermediate sex—including a quite modern one by Karl Ulrichs about the brain's having failed to sexually differentiate in utero despite the body's having done so successfully. Sexologists had also set forth numerous taxonomies for describing the many intermediate sexes—or sex types—that at least some of them saw in the population at large. Although these taxonomies differed in a variety of ways, they shared the underlying assumption that the inversion of sexual desire was not a biological or psychological phenomenon in and of itself but an intermediate point on a continuum whose end point was a fully developed male or female psyche within the body of the opposite sex.

The historian Lawrence Birken (1988) has recently suggested that when nineteenth-century scientists and physicians began to conceptualize the male-female distinction in terms of a quantitative spectrum of biologically differentiated types, rather than in terms of an absolute dichotomy between two unrelated forms, they were taking a gigantic, if inadvertent, step forward in the depolarization of males and females. Although perhaps true in the long run, at the time the biological and psychological pathologizing of anything and everything that did not fit the male and female cultural scripts was a gigantic step backward. It was a move toward naturalizing a sex and gender order that was increasingly threatened by social change.

In 1895, the French writer M. A. Raffalovich signaled the coming of a new era in sexology when he criticized the then-popular theories of male sexual inversion. "The inverts," he wrote, "are not at all content with the old explanation of the feminine soul in the masculine body. Some of them are more masculine than other men and are attracted to their own sex in proportion to the resemblance. They say . . . that similarity is a passion comparable to that excited by sexual dissimilarity" (quoted in Birken, 1988, pp. 105–106). Although it would be twenty years before Freud developed a theory of sexual desire based on similarity—or narcissism—rather than on dissimilarity, within just two or three years after Raffalovich's article, several sexologists, including Havelock Ellis and John Symonds in England and Magnus Hirschfeld in Germany, took the first steps in that direction when they treated the object of *sexual* desire as a phenomenon in its own right, rather than as an aspect of gender identity. Although splitting off sexuality from the other aspects of a person's gender was much slower in coming for women than for men, and although it is not an absolute and total separation even today, the initial moves toward separation are evident in the turn-of-the-century writings of Havelock Ellis, who has been called one of the first post-Victorian "sexual enthusiasts" (Robinson, 1976) because of his effort to extend the range of acceptable sexual behavior far beyond the procreative.[5]

In the context of same-sex sexuality in particular, Ellis tried to make inverts seem almost as normal with respect to gender as everyone else. To this gender-normalizing end, he rejected outright "the vulgar error which confuses the typical invert with the painted and petticoated creatures who appear in police courts from time to time" (Ellis & Symonds, 1897/1975, p. 120). He also theorized the existence of two completely distinct empirical phenomena: sexual inversion, which he reconceptualized as the biological (or "congenital") turning of the sexual instinct toward persons of the same sex—this is what we today call homosexuality—and sexo-aesthetic inversion, or eonism (Ellis, 1928), which he conceptualized as a nonsexual phenomenon with various manifestations. Eonists could just want to wear the clothing of the opposite sex or, at the other extreme, could so identify with the opposite sex psychologically that they felt as though they were in the wrong body.

Although Ellis's theoretical distinction between sexual inversion and eonism anticipated the two main branches of twentieth-century sexology (one on homosexuality as a sexual orientation per se and the other on the gender—or the masculinity-femininity—of the individual psyche), his writing about sexual inverts themselves was not nearly so free of the nineteenth-century concern with the totality of inversion as his theoretical writings portended. In describing male sexual inverts, Ellis wrote that "there is a distinctly general, though not universal, tendency" for them "to approach the feminine type, either in psychic disposition or physical constitution or both." In fact, "although the invert himself may stoutly affirm his masculinity, and although . . . [his] femininity may not be very obvious, its wide prevalence may be asserted with considerable assurance, and by no means only among the small minority of inverts who take an exclusively passive role, though in these it is usually most marked" (Ellis & Symonds, 1897/1974, p. 119).

This statement might seem at first glance to be completely at odds with the claim that Ellis was trying to dissociate homosexuality from the other aspects of inversion, but when taken together with his insistence that "the typical invert" is not "the painted or petticoated creature who appears in police courts," it seems likely that the particular aspect of inversion that Ellis was most trying to dissociate from male homosexuality was cross-dressing. This dissociation was also important to Magnus Hirschfeld, who isolated the phenomenon and gave it a name—transvestism—in 1910.

Ellis's inability to rid himself of the nineteenth-century assumption that sexuality is but an aspect of gender identity shows up even more clearly in his discussion of female inverts. According to Ellis, the chief characteristic of the sexually inverted woman is "a certain degree of masculinity." There is even "a very pronounced tendency among sexually inverted women to adopt male attire when practicable. In such cases male garments are not usually regarded as desirable chiefly on account of practical convenience, nor even in order to make an impression on other women, but because the wearer feels more at home in them" (Ellis & Symonds, 1897/1975, pp. 94–95).

Why was he unable—especially in the case of women—to separate even cross-dressing from homosexuality? The answer is historical. Because women were conceptualized in both nineteenth-century culture and nineteenth-century science and medicine as completely lacking in sexual motivation until and unless they were stimulated by men, autonomous female sexuality was inconceivable except as inherently masculine.[6]

This view of autonomous female sexuality as masculine is present even in Freud's analysis of homosexuality, which was far more radical than Ellis's analysis. Even though Freud went sufficiently beyond what he called character inversion to insist, in 1905, that "in men the most complete mental masculinity can be combined with inversion" (p. 8), he argued that in inverted women, "masculine characteristics, both physical and mental," are exhibited "with peculiar frequency," as is the desire "for femininity in their sexual objects" (p. 11). Thus, "it is only in inverted women that character-inversion . . . can be looked for with any regularity" (p. 8).

But regardless of whether Ellis and Freud fully distinguished female homosexuality from the totality of female inversion, there can be no doubt about the fact that, over time, both the culture and the scientific and medical establishment came to view inversion as more a pathology of sexual desire than a pathology of gender. This conceptual shift from gender to sex was helped along by changing social realities, including the breakdown of the separate male and female spheres and the increasing sexualization of Western culture. This sexualization had many causes and many facets: the growing availability of birth control; the development of a consumer economy and an advertising industry that relied on sex and sexual allure to sell consumer products; the invention of the automobile, which apparently gave young people of a certain class so much more sexual opportunity than they had before that at least one conservative commentator was troubled enough to call it "a house of prostitution on wheels" (quoted in D'Emilio & Freedman, 1988, p. 257); and the Freudian expansion of the meaning of sex to encompass even such things as what the tiniest infants did and felt.

In the context of this cultural sexualization, it was probably inevitable that what in the nineteenth century had been a single tradition of theory and research on the pathology of inversion would become, in the twentieth century, two separate traditions of theory and research, one on homosexuality as a sexual orientation and the other on the gender—or the masculinity-femininity—of the individual psyche.[7] Although this conceptual bifurcation may have made it easier for a few early twentieth-century advocates of homosexuality, like Magnus Hirschfeld, to argue that same-sex sexuality should no longer be treated as pathological, it did absolutely nothing to challenge the long-standing collaboration of science and culture in polarizing gender. For this reason, the two twentieth-century traditions that grew out of the inversion concept continued to legitimize not only the privileging of exclusive heterosexuality but also the cultural requirement that the sex of the body match the gender of the psyche.

HOMOSEXUALITY

Freud

The twentieth-century tradition of research on homosexuality as a sexual orientation began—as did so much else in psychology and psychiatry—with the psychoanalytic theory of Sigmund Freud. This tradition paid so much more attention to males than to females that even my own discussion of it must necessarily reflect that androcentric bias.

Although Freud's followers eventually made psychoanalytic theory the century's most powerful scientific instrument for privileging heterosexuality by pathologizing homosexuality, Freud's own analysis of homosexuality was so deeply Darwinian that it contained the seeds of a scientific challenge to the heterosexism of Western culture.[8] Fundamentally, the theory of evolution maintains that the species inhabiting the planet today are biohistorical constructions that have developed over time through the interaction of biology and environment. What Darwin held to be true for the phylogenetic development of species, Freud held to be true for the ontogenetic development of psyches, including the development of what Freud called an individual's sexual "object choice" (Freud, 1905/1962, p. 11). Just as Darwin de-privileged homo sapiens by considering it, like all other species, a biohistorical construction that had evolved from earlier forms of life, so, too, did Freud de-privilege heterosexuality by arguing that it, like homosexuality, was merely one possible outcome of a child's psychosexual development.

Freud's most important discussion of homosexuality occurs in his *Three Essays on the Theory of Sexuality,* first published in 1905. These essays constituted his major theoretical statement on the development of sexuality in infants and children.[9] Two specific details of his developmental theory are especially relevant to his de-privileging of heterosexuality. First, the "sexual instinct" that children bring into the world is "at first without an object." In other words, the sexual instinct is initially so "auto-erotic" and so "polymorphously perverse" that it can readily attach itself to any object or activity that gives the infant physical pleasure (pp. 98–100). Second, the sexual instinct "finds a sexual object" only after a lengthy process of psychosexual development (p. 73). Given the polymorphous perversity of the initial instinct, moreover, that psychosexual process necessarily involves both the progressive focusing of the individual on just one subset of all possible sexual objects and the progressive exclusion—or repression into the unconscious—of all other sexual objects.

These notions share the underlying assumption that "the sexual instinct and the sexual object are merely soldered together" during the course of the child's psychosexual development—"a fact which we have been in danger of overlooking in consequence of the uniformity of the normal picture, where the object appears to form part and parcel of the instinct." As Freud was himself aware, to "loosen the bond that exists in our thoughts between instinct and object" (p. 14) has the radical effect of transforming heterosexuality from a natural phenomenon requiring no explanation at all to a phenomenon requiring just as much explanation as homosexuality.

Freud argued that heterosexuality and homosexuality were products of the same process of psychosexual development in a lengthy footnote that he added to *Three Essays* in a 1915 revision. A portion of that footnote reads as follows:

> Psycho-analytic research is most decidedly opposed to any attempt at separating off homosexuals from the rest of mankind as a group of a special character. By studying sexual excitations other than those that are manifestly displayed, it has been found that all human beings are capable of making a homosexual object-choice and have in fact made one in their unconscious. . . . Psycho-analysis considers that a choice of an object independently of its sex—freedom to range equally over male and female objects—as it is found in childhood, in primitive states of society and early periods of history, is the original basis from which, as a result of restriction in one direction or the other, both the normal and the inverted types develop. Thus from the point of view of psycho-analysis the exclusive sexual interest felt by men for women is also a problem that needs elucidating and is not a self-evident fact based upon an attraction that is ultimately of a chemical nature. (1905/1962, pp. 11–12)

Freud reemphasized that homosexuality and heterosexuality were but differing outcomes of the same psychosexual process when he pessimistically discussed the prospects for the psychoanalytic cure of a homosexual woman in 1920. "One must remember," he wrote, "that normal sexuality also depends upon a restriction in the choice of object; in general, to undertake to convert a fully developed homosexual into a heterosexual is not much more promising than to do the reverse" (p. 207). The reason for his pessimistic prognosis was simple: The task to be carried out does "not consist in resolving a neurotic conflict but in converting one variety of the genital organization of sexuality into the other." This is "never any easy matter" (p. 206).

Although Freud's loosening of the bond between instinct and object unquestionably constituted a scientific challenge to the privileging of heterosexuality, that challenge was significantly blunted by his continuing to privilege reproductive sexuality as the "final, normal shape" of psychosexual development. Whereas "the sexual instinct had hitherto been predominantly auto-erotic," in maturity, it "is now subordinated to the reproductive function; it becomes, so to say, altruistic" (1905/1962, p. 73).

And where does this reproductive—and heterosexual—definition of mature sexuality leave the gay men and the lesbians? As Freud put it on many occasions, the reproductive definition of mature sexuality makes homosexuality not an illness but "a variant of the sexual function produced by a certain arrest of sexual development" (letter to an American mother, quoted in Bayer, 1981, p. 27). Over the course of his long career, Freud proposed many different childhood scenarios that could lead to arrested development, all of them in one way or another involving either an unconscious and unresolved fixation on the mother (for males) or a masculinity complex (for females).[10]

Although later psychoanalytic writing about homosexuality eventually transformed Freud's theory of arrested development into a theory of psychopathology, Freud himself made clear in at least three separate statements that homosexuality was not an illness or a pathology. The first statement was a response to a question about homosexuality posed to him by a Viennese newspaper in 1903. He replied in that same newspaper,

> I am . . . of the firm conviction that homosexuals must not be treated as sick people, for a perverse orientation is far from being a sickness. Would that not oblige us to characterize as sick many great thinkers and scholars of all times, whose perverse orientation we know for a fact and whom we admire precisely because of their mental health? Homosexual persons are not sick. (Quoted in Lewes, 1988, p. 32)

Then, in 1921, Freud actually overruled the British psychoanalyst Ernest Jones's decision to exclude an openly homosexual psychoanalyst from membership in the psychoanalytic society simply because of his homosexuality. Jones reasoned that if the candidate could not be psychoanalyzed out of his pathological condition, then he could not reasonably be considered competent to handle the psychoanalysis of others. Freud's response to Jones, which was cosigned by the analyst Otto Rank, denies any necessary connection between being homosexual and being limited in mental or psychological functioning.

> Your query, dear Ernest, concerning prospective membership of homosexuals has been considered by us and we disagree with you. In effect we cannot exclude such persons without other sufficient reasons, as we cannot agree with their legal prosecution. We feel that a decision in such cases should depend upon a thorough examination of the other qualities of the candidate. (P. 33)

Finally, in 1935, Freud wrote his now-famous letter to the American mother who had apparently asked whether psychoanalysis could cure her son's sexual orientation. His response, which was made public in 1951, contains Freud's clearest statement that homosexuality was not the illness or the pathology that later psychoanalysts would try to make it.

> I gather from your letter that your son is a homosexual. I am most impressed by the fact that you do not mention this term yourself in your information about him. May I question you, why you avoid it? Homosexuality is assuredly no advantage, but it is nothing to be ashamed of, no vice, no degradation, it cannot be classified as an illness; we consider it to be a variation of the sexual function produced by a certain arrest of sexual development. Many highly respectable individuals of ancient and modern times have been homosexuals, several of the greatest men among them (Plato, Michelangelo, Leonardo da Vinci, etc.). It is a great injustice to persecute homosexuality as a crime, and cruelty too. If you do not believe me, read the books of Havelock Ellis.
>
> By asking me if I can help, you mean, I suppose, if I can abolish homosexuality and make normal heterosexuality take its place. The answer is, in a general way, we cannot promise to achieve it. In a certain number of cases we succeed in developing the blighted germs of heterosexual tendencies which are present in every homosexual; in the majority of cases it is no more possible. It is a question of the quality and the age of the individual. The result of treatment cannot be predicted.

What analysis can do for your son runs in a different line. If he is unhappy, neurotic, torn by conflicts, inhibited in his social life, analysis may bring him harmony, peace of mind, full efficiency whether he remains a homosexual or gets changed. (Quoted in Jones, 1957, pp. 195–196)

Freud could de-privilege heterosexuality to the extent that he did because of his theoretical premise that the individual's sexual object choice is made during childhood from a sexually undifferentiated starting point, rather than being determined biologically. As we saw in Chapter 3, Freud had similarly argued that masculinity and femininity are made, not born; and in that context, too, he was prevented from following his premise to its most radical conclusion by cultural lenses that he never shed completely. Specifically, just as the androcentrism acquired from his culture prevented him from arguing that the female psyche is not intrinsically inferior to the male psyche, so too his gender-polarizing and biologically essentialist assumption that heterosexuality is the only legitimate context for adult sexual relationships prevented him from arguing that homosexuality is as normal as heterosexuality.

Freud's Psychoanalytic Successors

After 1930 or so, Freud's successors made at least three fundamental changes to the substance of his psychoanalytic theory.[11] Although not all of these changes dealt directly with sexual object choice, their cumulative effect was to destroy not only the radicalism that was inherent in Freud's analysis of heterosexuality but even the social tolerance that was inherent in Freud's analysis of homosexuality.

First, Freud's successors rejected his assumption that both heterosexuality and homosexuality were specialized derivatives of an earlier bisexuality. Specifically, they challenged his assertion that—even in the context of heterosexuality—the sexual instinct and the sexual object are merely soldered together, and they substituted in its place the assertion that a heterosexual object choice naturally develops in everyone unless blocked by some kind of psychological trauma or neurotic conflict. The key figure in this particular revision of psychoanalytic theory was Sandor Rado (1940), who vehemently insisted that although there was a latent heterosexual impulse in every homosexual, there was no complementary homosexual impulse in any heterosexual.

Second, they rejected Freud's assertion that a homosexual object choice represents an arrest of psychosexual development at the oedipal stage, substituting in its place the assertion that a homosexual object choice represents an arrest of development at the preoedipal—or oral—stage. Because the child is said to develop his or her most basic sense of self during the preoedipal period, this shift backward in time represents the homosexual as someone whose "ego" is so undeveloped and so unstable that he or she has what is essentially "a borderline personality structure with . . . primitive object relations" (Lewes, 1988, p. 76); the shift backward also represents the homosexual as someone whose sexual object choice constitutes evidence of an almost psychotic psychic structure. The key figure in the shift to the preoedipal period was Melanie Klein, whose 1932 book, *The Psycho-Analysis of Children,* founded the "object relations" school of psychoanalysis. Edmund Bergler and Charles Socarides, in particular, helped shape the preoedipal analysis of homosexuality.

Finally, where Freud had privileged the sexual instinct as the primary basis for both human motivation in general and human neurosis in particular, his successors substituted in its place an emphasis on various social and interpersonal issues, such as power and dependency. From the perspective of these "interpersonal" or "adaptational" theorists, homosexuality was thus not so much a specialization of the sexual instinct as a symptom, or a sexualizing, of a nonsexual neurotic conflict—hence the use of the term *pseudohomosexuality* in the 1950s. The key figures in the movement away from sexuality were Karen Horney and Harry Stack Sullivan. The key figures in this revisionist view of homosexuality were Clara Thompson, Abram Kardiner, and Lionel Ovesey.[12]

Although not all psychoanalysts agreed with all three revisions, the cumulative effect was to pathologize homosexuality as a mental illness and make it theoretically amenable to psychiatric treatment.[13] That virtually all American psychiatrists agreed with at least the move toward pathologizing homosexuality can be seen in the unquestioned inclusion of homosexuality in the first official listing of mental disorders published by the American Psychiatric Association in 1952; nor was there any question about its continued inclusion when the *Diagnostic and Statistical Manual* (*DSM-I*) was updated and republished in 1968 as *DSM-II*.[14]

This American unanimity on the issue of pathology was underscored by Karl Menninger's introduction to the American edition of the Wolfenden Report, which he wrote in 1963. While applauding the primary conclusion of the British report—that homosexual acts between consenting adults ought to be decriminalized—Menninger completely ignored another important conclusion, which was that homosexuality could be viewed as a mental illness or a disease only if the criteria were "expanded beyond what could be thought of as legitimate" (quoted in Bayer, 1981, p. 222). Without commenting explicitly on this implied critique of the American psychiatric establishment, Menninger wrote that from the standpoint of the psychiatrist, homosexuality "constitutes evidence of immature sexuality and either arrested psychological development or regression. Whatever it be called by the public, there is no question in the minds of psychiatrists regarding the abnormality of such behavior" (p. 39).

American psychiatrists officially pathologized homosexuality until 1973, when homosexuality was finally deleted from *DSM-III* after a bitter and lengthy political battle.[15] They held on to that distortion of classical psychoanalytic theory for so long, in part, because of a ten-year study by Irving Bieber and others on the etiology of male homosexuality, which supposedly found the homosexual male to be the victim of a pathogenic family (Bieber et al., 1962). In spite of many methodological flaws, the most serious of which was the failure to include any homosexuals who were not in therapy, the results of the study were widely seen as vindicating not only the classification of homosexuality as a mental disorder but also the rejection of Freud's belief that homosexuality and heterosexuality were specialized derivatives of a universal bisexuality. As Bieber himself saw it, the investigation of male homosexuality "has documented the severely pathologic parent-child relationship" of the homosexual. "The parental constellation" most likely to produce a homosexual son "is a detached, hostile father and a close-binding, intimate, seductive mother who is a dominating, minimizing wife." These and other findings are "contrary to classical psychoanalytic theory" in indicating "that most men are not latent homosexuals; rather, all homosexuals are latent heterosexuals." He generalized:

> In no other species in which reproduction depends on male-female sexual coupling have deviant types appeared that fear or abhor heterosexual matings and engage in homosexual be-

havior consistently, exclusively, and in highly organized patterns. Fear of and aversion to female genitalia, in themselves, demonstrate the pathology of the homosexual adaptation and the error of assuming that the homosexual deviation occurs within a biologically normal range. (1965, pp. 249–254)

In a recent critique of the evolving perspective on male homosexuality in psychoanalytic theory, Kenneth Lewes (1988) speculates that in the post-Freud years, the psychoanalytic theory of sexual object choice became increasingly negative in its stance toward homosexuals while its theory of femininity became increasingly positive in its stance toward women, in part because although lots and lots of women analysts participated in the revision of the latter, no openly homosexual analysts participated in the revision of the former. On a related note, Lewes also speculates that in the post-Freud years, the psychoanalytic establishment became viciously abusive toward homosexuals in part because it displaced all of its antifemale sentiments—which could no longer be expressed explicitly in its theory of femininity—onto its theory of male homosexuality. In Lewes's words: "The essentially gynephobic stance of early psychoanalysis, having been purged from the theory of femininity, found refuge in the theory of homosexuality, which, unlike the former discourse, did not permit its objects to participate in its formulation" (1988, p. 238). When combined with the unacknowledged need of many analysts to repudiate their own "homosexual strivings," this gynephobic stance produced "an attack on homosexuals conducted with an intemperance, ferocity, and lack of empathy" that is not only "appalling in a discipline devoted to understanding and healing" (p. 239) but is also "a stain on the history of psychoanalysis" (p. 121).

Lewes may or may not be correct about the reason for the psychoanalysts' abusive stance toward homosexuals, but the abusiveness itself is undeniable. The worst offender, according to Lewes, was Edmund Bergler, a preoedipal theorist who published prodigiously in respectable psychoanalytic journals and lay publications over a thirty-year period, especially from the end of World War II to the mid-1950s. According to Bergler, who claimed that he had absolutely "no bias against homosexuals," they are "essentially disagreeable people, regardless of their pleasant or unpleasant outward manner," which is "a mixture of superciliousness, fake aggression, and whimpering." They are "subservient when confronted with a stronger person, merciless when in power, unscrupulous about trampling on a weaker person" (1956, pp. 28–29). They apparently also have a propensity toward criminality, hence "the great percentage of homosexuals among swindlers, pseudologues, forgers, lawbreakers of all sorts, drug purveyors, gamblers, pimps, spies, brothel-owners, etc." And as for bisexuals? Well, said Bergler, "nobody can dance at two weddings at the same time, not even the wizard of a homosexual" (1947, pp. 403, 405).

Abram Kardiner, writing around the same time as Bergler, went so far as to compare what he saw as the male homosexual's "notorious" hatred of women with the Nazis' hatred of Jews (1954, p. 189). Finally, in the midst of the relatively recent battle over whether to delete homosexuality from *DSM-III*, Charles Socarides described male homosexuals as engaged in a compulsive search for "a 'shot' of masculinity." The homosexual, "like the addict, . . . must have his 'fix'" (1970, p. 1201). The pathological nature of homosexuality dooms the homosexual from the start, however. Not only are homosexuals themselves "filled with aggression, destruction, and self-deceit," but whereas heterosexual relationships can frequently provide "cooperation, solace, stimulation, enrichment, healthy challenge and fulfillment," homosexual "masquerades" provide only "destruction, mutual defeat, exploitation of the partner and the self, oral-sadistic incorporation, aggressive onslaughts, attempts to alleviate anxiety and a pseudo solution to the aggressive and libidinal urges which dominate and torment the individual" (Socarides, 1968, quoted in Bayer, 1981, p. 36).

Lest it be thought that Bergler, Kardiner, and Socarides were the only psychoanalysts to invest their writing and presumably their therapy with such condescension and hostility, it should be noted that although the writings of a great many psychoanalysts remained respectful during this era, the writings of a great many others contained hints of Bergler's vituperativeness. But regardless of the actual numbers involved, what is important, as Lewes points out, is that Bergler and the other worst offenders were not rebuked by the psychoanalytic profession. Nor was there self-criticism or self-reflection about the tone of the psychoanalytic discourse until 1980, when an article published in the *American Journal of Pscyhoanalytic Therapy* (Kwawer, 1980) finally suggested that the discourse on homosexuality may have been distorted over the years by the psychoanalysts' unconscious anxieties over homosexuality. I agree with Lewes that for a profession that even has a term for an analyst's distortion of clinical material due to his or her own unconscious anxieties (the term is *countertransference*), it is indeed "extraordinary that it took fully three quarters of a century for psychoanalysis finally to recognize this issue" in the context of homosexuality (Lewes, 1988, p. 228).

This failure by psychoanalysts to keep their own house in order had dire consequences in the post–World War II years, when homosexuality became incorporated into the "demonology" of the McCarthy era (D'Emilio, 1983b, p. 48).[16] At a time when Americans were fearful that subversives might sap their ability to win the Cold War against the Soviet Union, the nation mobilized its resources to root out all persons who were suspected of being either communists or communist sympathizers. As the anticommunist wave grew, gay men and lesbians were likewise labeled a threat to the national security, and they, too, suddenly found themselves the target of a national witch-hunt.

That witch-hunt began in February 1950, the same month when Senator Joseph McCarthy initially charged that the State Department was "riddled with communists" (D'Emilio & Freedman, 1988, p. 292). After a chance revelation by a State Department official testifying in Congress about some several dozen employees having been dismissed for homosexual activity, the "homosexual menace" (D'Emilio, 1983b, p. 43) quickly became a central theme of Senator McCarthy's rhetoric. In June of that same year, the full Senate bowed to McCarthy's pressure and authorized a full-scale investigation into the alleged employment of homosexuals "and other moral perverts" in the federal government (*New York Times,* quoted in D'Emilio, 1983b, p. 42).

That Senate report, which was published in December 1950, stated that a great many homosexuals were indeed employed in government and went on to recommend that homosexuals should henceforth be excluded from all government service. The report justified this extraordinary recommendation on two grounds: the homosexual was a national security risk because of his or her vulnerability to blackmail, and the homosexual had an unreliable "character." Here, the report pulled no punches: "Those who engage in overt acts of perversion lack the emotional stability of normal persons"; "indulgence in acts of sex perversion weakens the moral fiber of the individual"; even "one homosexual can pollute a Government office" (quoted in D'Emilio, 1983b, p. 42).

The response to the report was immediate. Not only did dismissals from civilian posts in the executive branch of government increase twelvefold in the next six months, but in April 1953, President Eisenhower issued an executive order barring gay men and lesbians from all federal jobs throughout the country. Even worse in some ways, as early as 1950, the Federal Bureau of Investigation began to build a national system of surveillance in concert with local vice squads in order to prevent homosexuals from concealing their sexual orientation to gain government employment. Not surprisingly, the federal witch-hunt had serious repercussions at the local level, with police forces around the country now feeling free to harass homosexuals in unpredictable and often brutal ways.

Although the responsibility for this homophobic frenzy cannot be placed entirely in the hands of the psychiatric or even the psychoanalytic establishment, it is reasonable to suppose that if these two august groups had not themselves produced a discourse with such a rigid commitment to pathologizing homosexuality, the federal government might not have so easily justified a policy of systematically denying gay men and lesbians their political and civil rights.

Depathologizing Homosexuality:
The Social Construction of Sexuality

Ironically, the scientific challenge to the psychiatric pathologizing of homosexuality began about the same time as the McCarthy-era witch-hunt against homosexuals. In its earliest form, the challenge was based on two empirical claims: first, that homosexuality was much too statistically common a phenomenon for it to be a pathology of sexuality rather than a normal variant, and, second, that there were many too many homosexuals outside therapy who were mentally healthy for homosexuality to have any intrinsic connection to mental illness.

The first challenge came from landmark studies by Alfred Kinsey and his colleagues (1948, 1953) and by Cleland Ford and Frank Beach (1951). The Kinsey studies, which were based on detailed sexual histories taken from literally thousands of American men and women, found, among other things, that fully 37 percent of American men and 20 percent of American women had had at least one homosexual experience by age forty-five. In much the same spirit, the Ford and Beach study, which was based on a careful review of the available evidence from a wide variety of human societies and animal species, found not only that homosexual behavior existed virtually everywhere they looked but, even more important, that in a full forty-nine of the seventy-six societies they studied, homosexual behavior of some kind was culturally valued.

The second challenge came from a landmark study by Evelyn Hooker (1957) on the relation between sexual orientation and mental health. This study, which was the first in the history of social science to compare homosexuals and heterosexuals who were not in therapy, found that homosexuals were not especially likely to have a disturbed family background. Of even greater consequence was the finding that homosexuals were indistinguishable from heterosexuals on every single measure of psychopathology included in the research.[17]

Although the Kinsey data in particular were misused during the McCarthy era to exaggerate the scope of the "homosexual menace," the writings of all these pioneers were soon put to their rightful purposes by the newly emerging homosexual rights movement (D'Emilio, 1983b); they also served as the springboard for an even deeper challenge to the pathologizing of homosexuality—a challenge that would ultimately call into question not only the naturalness of heterosexuality but the very function of psychiatry. This deeper challenge can be seen as early as the 1950s and 1960s in the writings of at least a half-dozen sociologists and one lone psychiatrist—Thomas Szasz, who was extraordinarily ahead of his time. However, it was not until Michel Foucault (1978) theorized the social and historical construction of what Adrienne Rich (1980) later called compulsory heterosexuality that historians and sociologists finally articulated this social-constructionist challenge in full.[18]

The prevailing belief in Western culture has long been that sexual desire is an ahistorical phenomenon whose "primordially 'natural'" form is heterosexuality (Weeks, 1986, p. 15). The essence of the social-constructionist challenge is that sexual desire is a biohistorical phenomenon whose form can be as differently shaped from one historical and cultural context to another as the form of eating. So yes, humans everywhere engage in sex, just as humans everywhere eat, but what rules they establish about how and with whom they are sexual, what institutions they set up to enforce those "how" and "who" rules, and even what they define as sexual or sexually desirable in the first place have no universal—or ahistorical—form. From this perspective, nothing is sacred or even biologically special about the requirement of exclusive heterosexuality in the mutually exclusive scripts for males and females in contemporary America; that exclusiveness is simply a historical fact about how sexuality happens to be organized in this particular time and place.

To document this biohistorical view of sexuality, scholars from a wide variety of disciplines are undertaking two complementary kinds of studies. They are examining the social organization of sexuality in other times and places, and they are examining the discourses and social institutions in their own societies that have created the particular emphasis on exclusive heterosexuality.

From the research on the social organization of sexuality in other times and places, two conclusions currently stand above all the others. The first conclusion is that even in American society, passionately romantic friendships between individuals of the same sex were not even defined as sexual until the end of the nineteenth century, when the concepts of the invert and then the homosexual were finally invented. Until that time, sexuality was defined in purely behavioral terms—it was not considered an aspect of a person's character or personality—and the rules of sexual behavior concerned, not whether a person's sexual partner was male or female, but whether a person's sexual activity was procreative or non-procreative. The second conclusion was implicit in the discussion of Ford and Beach's early cross-cultural work. That is, in a variety of societies other than the United States, not only is exclusive heterosexuality not included in the mutually exclusive scripts for males and females, but some kind of homosexual activity is included. The best example comes from Sambia, New Guinea, where the culture dictates that the masculinity of a "real" man can be acquired only through the oral-genital transfer of semen from an older man to a younger one.[19]

From the research on the social construction of exclusive heterosexuality in contemporary American society, only one conclusion stands out. That conclusion, which was implicit in the discussion of the McCarthy era, is that two different kinds of social institutions are involved in the construction of exclusive heterosexuality, one kind operating coercively to punish those who transgress and the other kind operating noncoercively to impose what Jeffrey Weeks—paraphrasing Foucault—has called "a grid of definition" on "the possibilities of the [human] body" (1981, p. 100).

In Sambia, that grid of definition leads people to see both heterosexual and homosexual behavior as a natural and expected part of male sexuality, albeit a part that might be considered unnatural if done in a way that violates whatever who and how rules the Sambians have established. In modern-day America, in contrast, that grid of definition—which psychiatry has been instrumental in building—leads people to see *homosexual* and *heterosexual* as describing mutually exclusive types of persons rather than mutually compatible forms of sexual behavior; it also leads people to see homosexuality itself as a pathological aspect of gender deviation. What Weeks called a grid of definition, I myself would call a cultural lens.

In 1973, which happened to be the year that the American Psychiatric Association finally removed homosexuality from its official listing of mental disorders, George Weinberg turned the prevailing notions of health and pathology inside out by introducing the concept of homophobia to explain homosexual oppression. As useful as this concept has been for putting the oppressors of homosexuals on the defensive, the problem with the concept is that it treats homosexual oppression as a pathology or neurosis of the individual oppressor, when, in fact, it is an integral part of the cultural discourses and social institutions of many societies. Put somewhat differently, it depoliticizes the problem of homosexual oppression by obscuring its cultural origin: as much as the fear or abhorrence of homosexuality may be a psychological problem for many individuals, that fear or abhorrence is created by an institutional and ideological emphasis on gender polarization and compulsory heterosexuality.[20]

MASCULINITY-FEMININITY

As noted earlier, the scientific discourse on the inversion of gender and sexuality split into two independent branches, the first concerning homosexuality as a sexual orientation and the second concerning the masculinity or femininity of the individual psyche. Although the second branch was not nearly so unified by psychoanalysis—or, indeed, by any theory—as the first branch, it was just as effective at stigmatizing any nonsexual deviations from the male and female scripts as its more theoretical counterpart was at stigmatizing any sexual deviations from those scripts.

During the course of the twentieth century, at least three separate traditions within psychology and psychiatry have specifically theorized a gender-polarizing link between the sex of the body and the gender of the psyche. These three traditions have been concerned, respectively, with the assessment of masculinity-femininity, the treatment and prevention of masculinity-femininity disorders, especially "transsexualism," and the development of masculinity-femininity in "normal" children.

M-F Assessment

It will be recalled from the chapter on biological essentialism that the late nineteenth century was a time of intense biological theorizing about the origins of female inferiority—which was itself regarded by scientists and laypersons alike as an established fact. In response to all of this biological—and misogynist—theorizing, two of the very first women with doctorates in the new field of experimental psychology, Helen Thompson Woolley and Leta Stetter Hollingworth, at long last harnessed the power of empirical science to look at the question of male-female difference in an open-minded and objective way.[21]

In 1903, these two women published the initial results of their carefully controlled laboratory studies of male-female difference in a variety of intellectual, sensory, motor, and affective abilities; they also published the first of a slew of review articles in which they compiled and evaluated the results of all the research on male-female difference in the field of psychology.[22] These publications were so carefully reasoned and so meticulously documented that by 1936, even the psychologist who had constructed the Stanford-Binet IQ Test, Lewis Terman, had no choice but to concede that "the essential equality of the sexes" has been demonstrated "with respect to general intelligence and the majority of special talents," including "musical ability, artistic ability, mathematical ability, and even mechanical ability" (Terman & Miles, 1936, pp. 1–2).

In conceding the essential equality of the sexes, however, Terman did not mean to imply that the sexes were fundamentally alike in "personality type" (p. 2) or "temperament" (p. vi). Quite the contrary. Even after reading all of the published work by Woolley and Hollingworth, Terman still believed so strongly that "the sexes differ fundamentally in their instinctive and emotional equipment and in the sentiments, interests, attitudes, and modes of behavior which are the derivatives of such equipment" (p. 2) that he took it upon himself to document this difference once and for all by constructing the very first test of "mental masculinity and femininity" (p. 3).[23]

By his own admission, Terman had a second reason for constructing this test. He thought it would enable him to locate the population of inverts from which "homosexuals are chiefly recruited." Terman's interest in quantifying "the degree of inversion of the sex temperament" (p. 467) was obviously related to the tradition of research on the nature of gender deviation that I have been describing.

To construct this first "M-F test," Terman and his coauthor, Catharine Cox Miles (1936), pretested hundreds and hundreds of items that seemed likely to distinguish between males and females, retaining on the test itself only those 455 items that the pretest males and females did, in fact, answer differently. The overall flavor of the test can readily be sampled.

On the Interests subtest, individuals got femininity points for liking—and masculinity points for disliking—nursing, *Rebecca of Sunnybrook Farm,* babies, and charades; they got masculinity points for liking—and femininity points for disliking—soldiering, *Robinson Crusoe,* people with loud voices, and hunting. On the Introversion-Extroversion subtest, individuals got femininity points for agreeing—and masculinity points for denying—that they "nearly always prefer for someone else to take the lead," that they are "extremely careful about" their manner of dress, and that they are "often afraid of the dark"; they got masculinity points for agreeing—and femininity points for denying—that they "rather dislike" to take a bath, that as children, they were "extremely disobedient," that they "can stand as much pain as others can," and that they have "found school a hard place to get along in."

Because of the way the items were selected, the multiple-choice alternatives for every item on every subtest could easily be characterized ahead of time as either significantly more typical of males or significantly more typical of females. This distinction between male-typical and female-typical responses served as the basis for the scoring of the Terman-Miles M-F test. On the test, individuals received a femininity point for every item they answered in female-typical fashion and a masculinity point for every item they answered in male-typical fashion. Their femininity points were then subtracted from their masculinity points to obtain their total M-F score. This method of scoring forces masculinity and femininity to be bipolar ends of a single dimension. That is, on every single item and on the test as a whole, people must be *either* masculine *or* feminine (or, more accurately, they must be male-typical or female-typical); they cannot be *both* masculine *and* feminine.

Terman and Miles's circular method of pretesting numerous items and then including on the test itself only those items that had already distinguished empirically between males and females enabled them to document—with new samples of males and females—that the two sexes differed in "mental masculinity and femininity" (p. 3). They differed so much, moreover, that only about ten out of a thousand males and females had scores that even reached the mean of the other sex.

In designing their new test of mental masculinity and femininity, Terman and Miles saw themselves as bringing the same kind of quantification, clarity, and exactness (p. vi) to the concepts of masculinity and femininity that IQ tests had earlier brought to the concept of intelligence. In fact, they did much more. Whether they realized it or not, they also gave scientific legitimacy to three problematic assumptions about the nature of maleness and femaleness.[24]

First, Terman and Miles reified mental masculinity-femininity as a deep-seated and enduring aspect of the human personality. Although the idea of such a dimension had existed in Western culture for hundreds of years, now, for the first time in history, there was a scientific test specifically designed to measure it and a single score specifically designed to represent it. In other words, masculinity-femininity became a "real" entity legitimized by science as existing within the personality of every individual.

In recent years, critics of the Terman-Miles M-F test have argued that it does not measure any deep-seated or enduring aspect of the human personality; it measures instead the individual's adherence to the cultural norms of masculinity and femininity that were operative in early twentieth-century America. The very close match between the content of the test and the cultural norms of the times was of so little significance to Terman and Miles themselves, however, that it didn't even temper their assertions about the fundamental reality of masculinity and femininity. As they saw it:

> Masculinity and femininity are important aspects of human personality. They are not to be thought of as lending to it merely a superficial coloring and flavor; rather they are one of a small number of cores around which the structure of personality gradually takes shape. The masculine-feminine contrast is probably as deeply grounded, whether by nature or by nur-

ture, as any other which human temperament presents.
(p. 451)

In addition to reifying the concepts of masculinity and femininity, Terman and Miles polarized these concepts as mutually exclusive—or bipolar—ends of a single dimension. Polarization affected the scoring of the test and, even more important, gave scientific and psychological legitimacy to the tradition of having two, and only two, mutually exclusive scripts for males and females. That is, it gave scientific and psychological legitimacy to the longstanding cultural belief that a person could be either masculine or feminine, but not both.

Finally, Terman and Miles theorized a direct link between masculinity-femininity, homosexuality, and psychological normality. Given the way this link was conceptualized—with M-F inverts as the pool of defective personalities from which homosexuals were chiefly recruited—it gave further scientific legitimacy not only to the cultural stigmatizing of homosexuality but also to the more general cultural belief that to be anything other than conventionally masculine or feminine was evidence of psychopathology. Terman and Miles described this link as follows:

Estimates by the best informed students of the subject [of homosexuality] place the proportion of males so afflicted between 3 and 5 percent. . . . The M-F test does not measure homosexuality, as that term is commonly used, . . . [but] it does measure, roughly, degree of inversion of the sex temperament, and it is probably from inverts in this sense that homosexuals are chiefly recruited. . . . The use of the test will [thus] help to center attention on the developmental aspects of the abnormality, just as intelligence tests have done in the case of mental deficiency. It is well known that the milder grades of mental deficiency can now be detected years earlier than was possible a generation ago. The same will in time be true of the potential homosexual. Early identification of the latter deviant is particularly to be desired, because we have so much reason to believe that defects of personality can be compensated for and to some extent corrected. . . . At present no one knows whether the M-F deviant is primarily a problem for the neurologist, biochemist, and endocrinologist or for the parent and educator. (P. 460)

In the thirty-five years immediately following the publication of the Terman-Miles M-F test, empirical research on the so-called personality trait of masculinity-femininity flourished within the field of psychology. At least five or six new measures were developed to assess the trait, the best known of which was probably the masculinity-femininity scale of the Minnesota Multiphasic Personality Inventory. In addition, a series of empirical studies was done on the antecedents and correlates of masculinity-femininity in children and adults.[25]

Embedded in most of this masculinity-femininity research were the three assumptions that Terman and Miles had insinuated into their M-F test: the reifying assumption that masculinity-femininity is a core dimension of the human personality, the bipolarity assumption that masculinity and femininity are opposite ends of a single dimension and hence that a person must be either masculine or feminine but not both, and the mental health assumption that anything other than conventional masculinity or femininity is evidence of pathology.

Treatment and Prevention of Gender Identity Disorders

With psychiatry in the Freudian age tending to define homosexuality and even transvestism as pathologies related to sexuality, not to gender, there was little discussion of gender inversion—or what Terman and Miles had called "the inversion of the sex temperament"—until 1952, when Christine Jorgensen created an international sensation by going to Denmark as a man and returning to America as a woman. Although the explosion of interest in people wanting, and getting, sex-change operations would not reach its peak until the late 1960s and early 1970s, as early as 1953 an endocrinologist by the name of Harry Benjamin began crusading to have what he called the gender identity disturbance of transsexualism recognized as a discrete psychopathology. According to Benjamin, many desperate people suffered from this unrecognized disease, and he himself had been treating a number of them with hormones since the 1920s.

The recognition that Benjamin had been crusading for finally came in 1980, when the American Psychiatric Association's *DSM-III* created a new category of "gender identity disorders" and named transsexualism as a disorder within that category. Ironically, this first official pathologizing of gender identity disorders appeared in the same *DSM* in which, for the first time in psychiatric history, there was no official pathologizing of homosexuality. Perhaps this was no coincidence. Perhaps the psychiatric establishment still believed so completely in the pathology of gender nonconformity that if the politics of the times would not allow it to express that belief through homosexuality, then it would instead express it where and how it could.[26]

According to *DSM-III*, the three diagnostic criteria for transsexualism are having a "persistent discomfort and sense of inappropriateness about one's assigned sex," having a "persistent preoccupation for at least two years with getting rid of one's primary and secondary sex characteristics and acquiring the sex characteristics of the other sex," and having reached puberty. Although not essential to the diagnosis, *DSM-III* further describes most transsexuals as "almost invariably having had a gender identity problem in childhood," often finding their genitalia "repugnant," often complaining "that they are uncomfortable wearing the clothes of the assigned sex and therefore dress[ing] in clothes of the other sex," often engaging "in activities that in our culture tend to be associated with the other sex," and to varying degrees adopting "the behavior, dress, and mannerisms" of the other sex. With respect to their history of sexual orientation, transsexuals are said to be totally variable, with some being asexual, some homosexual, some heterosexual, and some "unspecified." The estimated prevalence of transsexualism is said to be one per 30,000 for males and one per 100,000 for females; the male-to-female ratio among those seeking help at clinics specializing in transsexualism is said to vary from a high of 8:1 to a low of 1:1 (pp. 74–76).

There was always a great deal of controversy, even among psychiatrists, about the appropriate treatment for transsexualism. Many psychiatrists rejected sex-reassignment surgery from the beginning because, they said, it treated only the most obvious symptom of the transsexual's disease rather than its underlying cause. Still, by the late 1960s, when doctors at prestigious American institutions like Johns Hopkins University and the University of Minnesota began performing such operations in their newly established gender-identity clinics, sex-reassignment surgery was well on its way to becoming the treatment of choice among psychiatrists, as well as among transsexuals.

Regarded for a while as a virtual panacea, sex-reassignment surgery lost credibility in the late 1970s, when a follow-up study of fifty transsexuals who had applied for a sex change found so little difference between those who had the surgery and those who didn't have it (Meyer & Reter, 1979) that the Johns Hopkins clinic—the first in the

United States to perform the surgery—stopped doing it altogether.[27] Meanwhile, both transsexualism and sex-reassignment surgery had become household words, thanks largely to the publicity given a few very visible transsexuals, including Jan Morris, who wrote her personal account of becoming a woman in a book entitled *Conundrum* (1974), and Renée Richards, who created a sports controversy when she tried, after surgery, to compete on the women's tennis circuit.

Given how profoundly disturbed and how resistant to psychotherapy the transsexual's gender identity appeared to be, a number of psychiatrists soon considered that it might be far more effective therapeutically to identify children "at risk" for transsexualism, and then to intervene in their development, than to wait for these children to develop full-blown cases of adult transsexualism and then subject them to the mutilating—and not necessarily all that helpful—surgery. In that spirit, some psychiatrists around the country designed programs combining research and therapy to identify, study, and treat boys and girls—but especially boys—who seemed to show an unusual amount of cross-gender behavior, such as wanting to dress in the other sex's clothing, having a preference for the other sex's activities, and making statements about wanting to be the other sex. The first study, which was somewhat preliminary, was published by Richard Green of the University of California, Los Angeles, in 1974. An exhaustive review of all the studies completed in the next ten years was published by Kenneth Zucker in 1985. The final results of Richard Green's own fifteen-year longitudinal study of feminine boys was published in 1987.

The treatment in these programs was varied. In the more coercive programs, like George Rekers's, parents and teachers used behavior-modification techniques to eliminate virtually all behaviors considered gender inappropriate, including not only cross-dressing, playing with cross-gender toys, and playing with cross-sex children but also speaking with a cross-gender voice inflection and moving one's body with cross-gender mannerisms (for example, "limping" one's wrist).[28] In less coercive programs, like Richard Green's, the emphasis was less on ridding the child of every single gender-inappropriate behavior and more on helping the child develop gender-appropriate activities and gender-appropriate relationships that he (or she) could experience in a personally satisfying way.

On the basis of all this research and therapy with "cross-gender-identified" children (Zucker, 1985), a second gender identity disorder was named in the *DSM-III* along with transsexualism: "Gender Identity Disorder of Childhood." The essential features of this disorder, which can be diagnosed only in prepubertal children, are "persistent and intense distress in a child about his or her assigned sex," and "the desire to be, or insistence that he or she is, of the other sex." In addition, a *girl* must demonstrate "either persistent marked aversion to normative feminine clothing and insistence on wearing stereotypic masculine clothing, or persistent repudiation of her female anatomic characteristics," and a *boy,* "either preoccupation with female stereotypic activities, or persistent repudiation of his male anatomic characteristics" (p. 71).

To distinguish the child who is truly gender-disordered from the child who merely fails to conform to gender stereotypes, *DSM-III* explicitly states: "This disorder is not merely a child's nonconformity to sex-role behavior as, for example, in 'tomboyishness' in girls or 'sissyish' behavior in boys, but rather a profound disturbance of the normal sense of maleness or femaleness" (p. 71). Consistent with the view that this distinction might not be nearly so clear as the psychiatrists would have us believe, however, the *DSM* reports, without comment, that "in clinic samples there are many more boys with this disorder than girls" (p. 72). We shall see in Chapter 5 that gender-nonconforming boys are much more stigmatized and ostracized than gender-nonconforming girls. Perhaps perceiving more boys than girls as gender disordered is one way that the culture expresses that social intolerance.

Although the rationale for intervening in the development of gender-disordered children was that they are at risk for transsexualism, the emphasis soon shifted to their being at risk for homosexuality. The evidence responsible for this shift is summarized in *DSM-III*: "Very few" gender-disordered children "develop Transsexualism in adolescence or adulthood," but "from one-third to two-thirds or more of boys with the disorder develop a homosexual orientation during adolescence," as do "some" of the minority of girls who "retain a masculine identification" (p. 72). This link between a gender-disordered childhood and homosexuality is supported by Zucker's analysis of all the studies published by the mid-1980s that traced the development of gender-disordered children into adolescence or adulthood, as well as by Green's more recent study—hence its title, *The "Sissy Boy Syndrome" and the Development of Homosexuality.*

Two explanations are offered for the "low yield rate for a transsexual outcome" (Zucker, 1985) among gender-disordered children. First, therapeutic intervention may itself alter the developmental course of the disorder. Second, transsexual adults are so much rarer in the general population than gender-disordered children that from a purely statistical viewpoint, demonstrating much of a relation between the two would not be possible unless working with a very large sample of gender-disordered children, which these intervention studies have not been able to do. Homosexuality, on the other hand, is not a rare phenomenon; hence it is much easier to demonstrate any childhood correlates that exist. That studies tracing the development of gender-disordered children ended up demonstrating a link, especially in boys, between adult homosexuality and what has in other contexts been called "gender nonconformity" in childhood is not surprising, for at least one major retrospective study of adult homosexuals (Bell, Weinberg & Hammersmith, 1981) has already demonstrated the same link in U.S. society.

Given the low yield of transsexuals and the high yield of homosexuals among the children in these intervention studies, one pair of critics has charged that the intervention itself is an "insidious attempt to stamp out the development of gay identity in young children" (Morin & Schultz, 1978, p. 142). This charge might be even more applicable to someone like George Rekers—who would be happy to stamp out homosexuality, which he sees as a sexual perversion that has been "sold to the unwary public as a right between consenting adults" (1982b, p. 88)—than for someone like Richard Green, who not only played a key role in getting homosexuality removed from the *DSM* but who also sees himself as merely trying to help children who are the unhappy victims of intense social ostracism and intense dissatisfaction with the sex that they really are. Still, in neither case is the child being helped to cope *in a self-affirming way* with social ostracism. Rather, the child is being pathologized and asked to alter a part of the self that may deserve just as much cultural respect as religion or race. As the critics might put it, a democratic and pluralistic society like the United States doesn't deal with discrimination against religious or racial minorities by asking people to convert or bleach themselves. By the same token, it shouldn't deal with discrimination against gender minorities by asking them to "straighten out" or have a sex-change operation.

It is bad enough that psychiatry may have pathologized and treated children who did not have a mental disorder after all. But even worse, as Janice Raymond (1979) and Thomas Szasz (1979) have pointed out, psychiatrists have once again used their almost priestly power to define mental health and mental illness in order to reinforce the highly polarized scripts for males and females in this society. They have once again naturalized the gender conformist and pathologized the gender deviant by creating a new category of mental illness, just as they did in an earlier era with sexual inversion and homosexuality.[29]

People who are desperately unhappy with their biological sex do need some kind of help. But even from a mental health perspective, transsexualism would be much better conceptualized as a *social* pathology than as an *individual* pathology. To put it somewhat differently, transsexualism would be much better conceptualized as the underside of the same process of gender polarization that also produces highly conventional males and females. In a less gender-polarizing culture, after all, it would matter much less if the individual's personality and behavior did not cohere into a tightly gender-polarized package that matched her or his biological sex. In addition, so much less would be defined as masculine or feminine in the first place that sex would not so drastically limit the kind of a person that one could be, and hence people would have much less reason to be desperately unhappy with the particular sex they happened to be born with.

The Development of Masculinity-Femininity in "Normal" Children

Although the existence of a *DSM* category called Gender Identity Disorder of Childhood demonstrates irrefutably that at least a small percentage of children in America do not conform to the gender scripts of the culture, almost every parent, teacher, and developmental psychologist already knows that the large majority of American children—especially those of preschool age and early elementary-school age—are rigidly gender conforming. Children regard a broad range of artifacts and activities as exclusively appropriate for only one sex or the other, and even more important, they strongly prefer same-sex playmates and gender-appropriate toys, clothes, and activities for both themselves and their peers.[30]

Until twenty-five years ago, most developmental psychologists assumed that this pattern of early gender traditionalism was learned in some fashion from the gender-polarizing practices of the social community. In the past twenty-five years, however, at least one prominent branch of developmental psychology has implied something very different: namely, that this early gender traditionalism is a natural—and almost inevitable—by-product of the young child's own cognitive processing.[31]

This naturalizing of the young child's conformity to gender scripts began in 1966, when Lawrence Kohlberg adapted Jean Piaget's theory of cognitive development to the domain of gender. Although Piaget's vision of the child as an active cognitive-processor had profound, and positive, effects on the field of psychology, Kohlberg's adaptation of Piagetian theory to the domain of gender so completely ignored the gender-polarizing practices of the child's social community that it portrayed early gender traditionalism as almost completely emergent from the mind of the child.

What Kohlberg basically argued, following Piaget, is that young children are not passive or mindless pawns of the socializing community but are, instead, active cognitive-processors trying to understand the nature of the physical and social world and the place of the self within that world. In other words, they are pattern seekers struggling to discover whatever categories or regularities exist in the world around them; and once they discover those categories or regularities, they spontaneously construct a self and a set of social rules consistent with them.

For Kohlberg and those working in the Kohlbergian tradition, what follows from this argument in the domain of gender is that "since sex is a stable and easily discriminable *natural* category" (Martin & Halverson, 1981, p. 1129, emphasis added), children are almost inevitably led by their own cognitive processing to choose gender as the organizing principle for the social rules that govern their own and their peers' behavior. Quite independent of anything that the society or the socializing community might do to foster or temper its own gender polarization, the young child spontaneously discovers the male-female dichotomy in nature and then categorizes—and evaluates—both the self and others in terms of that dichotomy. As Kohlberg himself put it: "Basic self-categorizations determine basic valuings. Once the boy has stably identified himself as male, he then values positively those objects and acts consistent with his gender identity" (1966, p. 89).[32]

When combined with what is alleged to be the natural perceptual salience of the male-female dichotomy, the child's natural predilection for pattern seeking could theoretically explain why preschool children organize their social world on the basis of gender. But, continues the Kohlbergian argument, something else about young children also leads them to apply the male-female dichotomy rigidly rather than flexibly—and thereby to become the rigid gender traditionalists that they usually are. That something else is the child's preoperational stage of cognitive development, which lasts—according to Piaget—from approximately eighteen months to seven years of age. This stage has a number of intrinsic cognitive limitations associated with it, only two of which are relevant to this discussion.[33]

First, the preoperational child is an egocentric "moral realist" (Piaget, 1932), predisposed to treat all rules and regularities as absolute and universal. No distinction is made between the physical, the social-conventional, and the moral. Every rule is a moral obligation; every regularity, an immutable moral law. Kohlberg describes the connection between egocentric moral realism and rigid gender traditionalism by noting that the "physical constancies" underlying gender "tend to be identified with divine or moral law, and the need to adapt to the physical regularities of one's identity is defined as a moral obligation." Children think same-sex behavior is "morally required," and they "express punitive sentiments to children who deviate from sex-typed behavior" (1966, p. 122).

Second, the preoperational child cannot yet mentally "reverse" a perceptual transformation that has been performed on some object in the real world; hence, he or she is unable to "conserve invariance"—to understand that the basic identity of an object remains the same—even across perceptual transformations. The preoperational child is thereby perception-bound, that is, focused on the surface properties of objects and predisposed to treat them as defining even when they are not. This second limitation of preoperational thought should make it difficult for the child to understand that even when a person's outward appearance changes dramatically, his or her sex remains the same. It should also make the child even more rigidly gender conforming than he or she would otherwise be, because from the child's perception-bound perspective, an individual has to both look and act male or female to actually be male or female.

Kohlberg's deepest characterization of the child seems fundamentally right: children do seem to be active participants in the process of gender acquisition, who not only find the male-female dichotomy perceptually and emotionally compelling but who also spontaneously translate that perceptual and emotional compellingness into a rigid set of gender rules for both the self and others. But Kohlberg's implication that rigid gender traditionalism is therefore a natural—and almost inevitable—feature of early childhood seems fundamentally wrong. For one thing, the male-female dichotomy may be perceptually and emotionally compelling to children in the first place not because of its having any kind of *natural* perceptual primacy over other dimensions or categories but because the gender-polarizing practices of the child's social community have made it perceptually and emotionally compelling. For another thing, even preschool children may think about gender in a rigidly gender-polarizing way not because of any preoperational stage of cognitive development but because they have not yet learned what makes a person a biological male or female.

Consistent with the possibility that young children may find the male-female dichotomy perceptually and emotionally compelling because of the gender-polarizing practices of the socializing community are the following two empirical findings, both of them replicated on numerous occasions. First, although fully 80 percent of American two-year-olds can readily distinguish males from females on the basis of purely cultural cues like hairstyle and clothing, as many as 50 percent of American three- and four-year-olds still fail to distinguish males from females if all they have to go on are biologically natural cues like genitalia and body physique. In other words, it is not biologically natural sex differences that young American children find so perceptually and emotionally compelling but culturally constructed gender differences. Second, by twenty to twenty-four months of age, preschool children generate much more restrictive gender rules for their male peers than for their female peers, an asymmetry for which there is no obvious source in either cognitive development or biology but for which there is an obvious source in the culture, which prescribes much harsher treatment for male gender deviance ("sissies") than for female gender deviance ("tomboys").[34]

Consistent with the possibility that young children may think about gender in a rigid way not because they are in a preoperational stage of cognitive development but because they lack sufficient biological knowledge is a panoply of empirical findings that derive from a recent challenge in developmental psychology to the very existence of fixed, universal, and chronological Piagetian-like stages in human development. According to these antistage theorists, one main reason young children fail to perform competently on a variety of Piagetian reasoning tasks—including those tasks that have anything to do with gender—is that they do not yet have enough knowledge about the subject matter being tested. Test the reasoning of very young children in a domain where they have sufficient knowledge—ask even the youngest dinosaur experts to reason about dinosaurs, for example—and their reasoning will not look preoperational but as mature as an adult's.[35]

The implication of this antistage argument for the domain of sex and gender should be clear. If even the youngest children demand the most rigid gender conformity from themselves and their peers, they do so, in part, not because they are in a preoperational stage of cognitive development but because they have not yet learned—or, more to the point, they have not yet been taught—that the genitalia constitute the defining attributes of male and female. Consistent with this antistage perspective is the finding from a recent study of my own. Only about half of the three-year-olds, four-year-olds, and early five-year-olds that I tested had the genital knowledge necessary to correctly identify, in color photographs, the sex of four toddlers who were nude from at least the waist down. But of those who did have that knowledge, fully 74 percent could conserve the sex of two other toddlers across the dramatic changes in physical appearance that are pictured on the following two pages (Bem, 1989).

Recent empirical evidence does call Kohlberg's theory of gender acquisition into question, then, but for purposes of this particular discussion, the important point is that Kohlberg naturalized gender polarization, situating the source of the motivation for a gender-polarizing match between sex and behavior within the mind of the preoperational child—just as Freud naturalized androcentrism by situating the source of the androcentric valuing of the penis within the mind of the oedipal child.

Deconstructing Masculinity-Femininity

In their own different ways, the psychological and psychiatric discourses on masculinity and femininity that we have been discussing all privilege gender traditionalism and pathologize gender deviance by naturalizing what is essentially just conformity to the cultural requirement that the sex of the body match the gender of the psyche. The discourse on masculinity-femininity assessment does this not only by conceptualizing gender as a bipolar dimension around which the

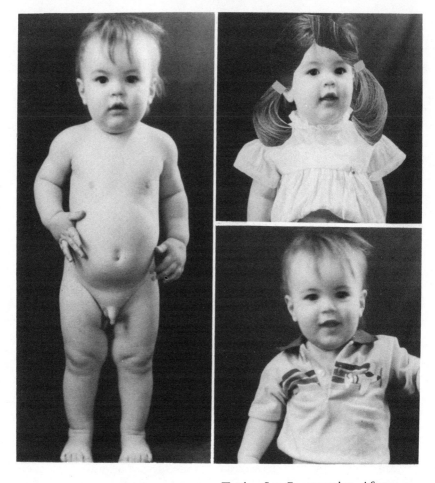

Testing Sex Conservation. After briefly seeing the photograph of a nude toddler, children are asked to identify the sex of that toddler from other pictures in which the toddler's genitalia are not visible—pictures in which the toddler is clothed and/or coiffed in, first, a sex-inconsistent way and, second, a sex-consistent way. Children who correctly identify the toddler's sex in all six pictures have passed the test. Such children clearly understand that sex remains invariant even across changes in cultural gender markers.

GENDER POLARIZATION

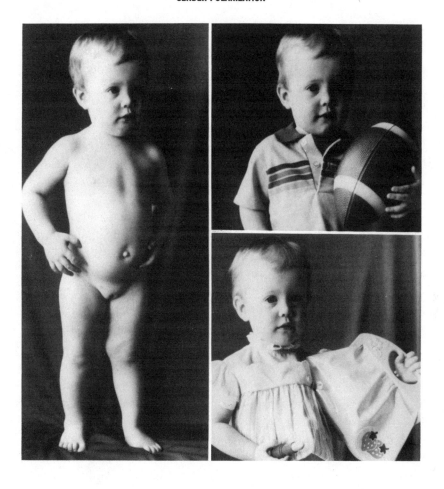

human personality inevitably takes shape but also by stigmatizing masculine and feminine inverts as the pool from which homosexuals are chiefly recruited; the discourse on gender identity disorders does this by explicitly pathologizing children and adults who fail to achieve the culturally required match between body and psyche; and finally, the discourse on gender development in "normal" children does this by treating the phenomenon of early gender traditionalism as an all-but-inevitable by-product of the interaction between the natural perceptual salience of the male-female dichotomy and the natural cognitive processing of the preoperational child.

This legacy of naturalizing gender conformity and pathologizing gender nonconformity held sway within the field of psychology until the early 1970s, when feminism finally took hold in both psychology and the culture at large. In this new feminist zeitgeist, a number of feminist psychologists—myself included—independently began to question the problematic assumptions about masculinity and femininity at approximately the same time. Several early contributions stand out as landmarks in this growing critique of the field.

In 1970, Inge Broverman and her colleagues not only documented empirically but also criticized the double standard of mental health applied by clinical psychologists, psychiatrists, and social workers, which bore a striking resemblance to the gender stereotypes then prevalent in American culture. My own theoretical and empirical research on the concept of androgyny began in 1971, with the development of the Bem Sex Role Inventory. Two years later, in 1973, Ann Constantinople published a critique of all the masculinity-femininity scales that psychologists had produced before 1970, and Jeanne Block published an article about androgyny based on her own longitudinal research. Finally, in 1974, Janet Taylor Spence, Robert Helmreich, and Joy Stapp published their instrument for assessing androgyny, the Personal Attributes Questionnaire.[36]

Although the concept of androgyny was not unproblematic, the early theoretical and empirical work on androgyny did challenge the longstanding psychological assumptions about masculinity-femininity in a new way. Because this early work on androgyny was so central to the early feminist critique of the gender polarization within psychology itself, I shall discuss it here in some detail, then go on to the work that was designed to overcome the conceptual limitations of androgyny.[37]

The Bem Sex Role Inventory, or BSRI, is a paper-and-pencil self-report instrument that asks the respondent to indicate on a seven-point scale how well each of sixty different attributes describes him or her. Twenty of the attributes reflect the definition of masculinity in this culture (for example, assertive, independent), twenty reflect the definition of femininity (for example, tender, understanding), and twenty are fillers. The respondent is unaware of these categories. Although the BSRI appears to be a standard measure of masculinity-femininity, a number of its features directly challenge the three problematic assumptions that we earlier traced all the way back to Terman and Miles (1936).[38]

First, and perhaps most important, the masculine and feminine items on the BSRI were selected, not on the basis of how males and females describe themselves, but on the basis of what was culturally defined as gender appropriate in the United States in the early 1970s. Judges who screened the pool of items for the test were thus treated as "native informants" about the culture—to use the anthropological term—rating each item not by how well it described themselves personally but by how desirable they thought it to be "in American society generally" for either a man or a woman. This procedure was designed to locate masculinity and femininity in the discourse of the culture rather than in the personality of the individual and itself constituted a challenge to Terman and Miles's reification of masculinity-femininity as a core dimension of the human personality. The procedure was also designed to accord with a concept of the conventionally gendered—or "sex-typed"—individual as someone whose self-definition and behavior are thoroughly intertwined with the stereotyped definitions of gender appropriateness in his or her culture.

Second, the scoring of the BSRI did not treat the selected masculine and feminine items as clustering at the two opposite ends of a single masculinity-femininity scale; instead, the items were assumed to represent two fully independent scales of culturally defined masculinity and culturally defined femininity, respectively. This novel scoring procedure enabled individuals who took the BSRI to describe themselves as high in both, low in both, or high in one and low in the other; in so doing, it reversed Terman and Miles's bipolarity assumption that an individual must be either masculine or feminine, but not both.

Finally, the BSRI contrasted conventionally sex-typed people not with people who were "cross-sex-typed" (or "inverted"), as had almost always been the case before, but with people who were "androgynous."

Both conceptually and methodologically, these androgynous people have been variously defined as (1) having self-concepts that simultaneously incorporate the cultural definitions of both masculinity and femininity or (2) having self-concepts that are not at all intertwined with cultural definitions of gender appropriateness. In either case, the positive value that feminists attached to this contrast group suggested that rather than being the most mentally healthy of all individuals, conventionally sex-typed people might actually be "prison[ers] of gender" (Heilbrun, 1973, p. ix). This revaluation challenged Terman and Miles's mental health assumption that anything other than conventional sex-typing was evidence of pathology.

Each respondent to the BSRI receives a Femininity Score equal to the total number of femininity points in his or her self-concept, a Masculinity Score equal to the total number of masculinity points in his or her self-concept, and a Femininity-Minus-Masculinity Difference Score equal to the difference between the individual's total number of femininity and masculinity points. When the BSRI was designed, respondents were defined as sex-typed, cross-sex-typed, or androgynous on the basis of their Femininity-Minus-Masculinity Difference Score, with small difference scores indicating androgyny and large difference scores indicating either sex-typing or cross-sex-typing.

Somewhat later, the decision was made to reserve the term *androgynous* for those individuals who earned their small difference scores by scoring high in both masculinity and femininity and to label as *undifferentiated* those who earned their small difference scores by scoring low in both masculinity and femininity. Although this decision made sense for certain empirical reasons, it did tend to obscure that the BSRI had been designed to distinguish conceptually and empirically between two particular groups of individuals: those who are highly motivated to keep both their self-concept and their behavior consistent with the cultural standards of gender appropriateness (the conventionally sex-typed group) and those for whom the cultural standards of gender appropriateness are not particularly important to either their self-concept or their behavior (the androgynous group).

As I saw it at the time, and as I still see it today, the concept of androgyny challenged gender polarization in psychology and in the American culture as almost nothing up to that time had done. Whereas it had earlier been assumed that masculinity and femininity were core dimensions of the human personality, now it was being suggested that masculinity and femininity were merely cultural stereotypes to which people conformed at their peril. Whereas it had earlier been assumed that mental health required men to be masculine and women to be feminine, now it was being suggested not only that everyone could be both masculine and feminine but, even more important, that standards of mental health should be genderless. Finally, whereas it had earlier been assumed that sex should determine the kind of self-concept an individual should develop and the kind of behavior she or he should engage in, now it was being suggested not only that an individual should be free to have her or his own unique blending of temperament and behavior but, even more important, that the very division of attributes and behaviors into the two categories of masculine and feminine was somewhere between problematic and immoral.

The revolutionary nature of the concept of androgyny so perfectly matched the feminist spirit of the early 1970s that it achieved instant celebrity within the field of psychology and was also independently discovered and idealized by at least two feminists working within the humanities, the literary scholar Carolyn Heilbrun and the poet Adrienne Rich. Carolyn Heilbrun introduced her work on androgyny, which was a major book tracing "the hidden river of androgyny" (1973, p. xx) from its source in pre-Hellenic myth through the literature of the twentieth century, with the following words:

> "When a subject is highly controversial," Virginia Woolf observed to an audience forty-five years ago, "and any question about sex is that, one cannot hope to tell the truth. One can only show how one came to hold whatever opinion one does hold." My opinion is easily enough expressed: I believe that our future salvation lies in a movement away from sexual polarization and the prison of gender toward a world in which individual roles and the modes of personal behavior can be freely chosen. The ideal toward which I believe we should move is best described by the term "androgyny." This ancient Greek word—from *andro* (male) and *gyn* (female) . . . seeks to liberate the individual from the confines of the appropriate. . . . It suggests a spectrum upon which human beings choose their places without regard to propriety or custom. (Pp. ix–xi)

Adrienne Rich provided no such introduction, but her poem, "The Stranger," spoke for itself:

Looking as I've looked before, straight down the heart
of the street to the river
walking the rivers of the avenues
feeling the shudder of the caves beneath the asphalt
watching the lights turn on in the towers
walking as I've walked before
like a man, like a woman, in the city
my visionary anger cleansing my sight
and the detailed perceptions of mercy
flowering from that anger

if I come into a room out of the sharp misty light
and hear them talking a dead language
if they ask me my identity
what can I say but
I am the androgyne
I am the living mind
you fail to describe
in your dead language
the lost noun, the verb surviving
only in the infinitive
the letters of my name are written under the lids
of the newborn child
(1973, p. 19)

As anyone who has followed the history of contemporary feminist thought knows, the concept of androgyny came under severe criticism almost as quickly as it had become idealized. By 1974, Adrienne Rich had thus already expunged her androgyny poem from her volume of collected poems; by 1976, she had written a brief critique of the whole concept in *Of Woman Born*; and by 1978, in *The Dream of a Common Language,* she had written a new poem entitled "Natural Resources" in which she dropped the word itself from her lexicon. A portion of that poem reads as follows:

There are words I cannot choose again:
humanism   androgyny

Such words have no shame in them, no diffidence
before the raging stoic grandmothers:

their glint is too shallow, like a dye
that does not permeate

the fibres of actual life
as we live it, now
(P. 66)

Although the many critiques of androgyny that have appeared
during the last fifteen years have varied enormously with the political
and the disciplinary backgrounds of the critics, three criticisms seem to
me to be responsible for the swiftness with which androgyny became a
dirty word among so many feminist theorists.[39]

First, the history of the concept has been neither so glorious nor so
gender neutral as Heilbrun suggested in her original tracing of the
concept. Quite the contrary. According to Barbara Gelpi, androgyny
has been used throughout the history of Western culture as a vision of
how the "perfect *man*" (1974, p. 153) could be created, as a vision, in
other words, of how the "masculine vessel" could be "filled and fulfilled
by feminine emotion and physicality" (p. 152). In the "brave new world
of male androgynes" (p. 157), men could thus be androgynous while
women would still be androcentrically defined in relation to men.
Many say this androcentric history and emphasis are represented in
the term itself—which places *andro* before *gyne*.

Second, and even more important, the concept of androgyny is
simultaneously so gender neutral, so utopian, and so devoid of any real
connection to historical reality that it doesn't even acknowledge the
existence of gender inequality, let alone provide a conceptual or historical analysis of that inequality. This failure shows up most clearly in the
evenhanded treatment of masculinity and femininity. Although both
men and men's activities have been the locus of cultural value in almost
all times and places, the concept of androgyny by itself does nothing to
point this inequality out. Nor does it make women and women's activities *more* valued or men and men's activities *less* valued.

Apart from the too evenhanded treatment of what males and females have represented historically, the concept of androgyny is theorized at too private and too personal a level to be of any value politically. The elimination of gender inequality will require institutional
change, not just personal change. By focusing on the person rather
than the patriarchy, androgyny provides no conceptual or political

analysis of gender inequality; in fact, it diverts attention away from such analysis.

Finally, the concept of androgyny reproduces—and thereby reifies—the very gender polarization that it seeks to undercut. It does this by assuming masculinity and femininity to be conceptual givens, if not set personality structures; by emphasizing the complementarity of masculinity and femininity, which, in turn, implies the naturalness of heterosexuality; and by focusing attention on the male-female distinction itself rather than on, say, the class or power distinction.

Although I think there is some truth in all of these critiques—and although my own sense of the limitations of the concept had taken me beyond androgyny as early as 1977, when I began to do work on gender schematicity—still, I do not find any of the critiques so devastating as to justify the exclusion of *androgyny* from the feminist lexicon.[40] Yes, androgyny has apparently had an androcentric history, but it need not be used androcentrically—and has not been used androcentrically— by modern feminists. And yes, androgyny is devoid of any analysis of gender inequality, which is why I have so much enjoyed being able, in this book, to finally discuss the concept after a full discussion of androcentrism. But even if androgyny does fail to theorize gender inequality, it is not without political consequence. At a certain historical moment for feminist theorists, and even today for many people confused about how to behave as a man or a woman, androgyny provides both a vision of utopia and a model of mental health that does not require the individual to banish from the self whatever attributes and behaviors the culture may have stereotypically defined as inappropriate for his or her sex. To my mind, that revolution in the discourse of the culture was— and is—a worthy political accomplishment.

This reference to masculinity and femininity brings me at last to the third critique of androgyny: it reifies the gender polarization that it seeks to undercut. Here I think a distinction has to be made not only between different users of the androgyny concept but also between its different meanings. For early androgyny theorists like Carl Jung (1953), masculinity and femininity were conceptually defined as deeply embedded personality structures whose complementarity suggested the naturalness of heterosexuality; and androgyny was itself defined as the bringing together of those two complementary structures within either a single person or a heterosexual marriage.

For later writers like Carolyn Heilbrun and myself, however, masculinity and femininity were conceptualized as stereotyped definitions embedded within the cultural discourse, rather than as personality structures embedded within the individual, and androgyny was usually defined as the absence of any concern with those cultural definitions of masculinity and femininity, rather than as the integration of masculinity and femininity. Put somewhat differently, the "moral" of androgyny was that "*behavior* should have no gender," where behavior includes one's choice of sexual partners (Bem, 1978, p. 19).

I do not think, however, that the concept of androgyny adequately conveys that masculinity and femininity have no independent or palpable reality. Androgyny inevitably focuses more on the individual's being both masculine and feminine than on the culture's having created the concepts of masculinity and femininity in the first place. Hence, androgyny can legitimately be said to reproduce precisely the gender polarization that it seeks to undercut, and to do so even in the most feminist of treatments.

In 1977, to convey more forcefully that masculinity and femininity are cultural lenses that polarize reality, I shifted the focus of my own research from the concept of androgyny to the concept of gender-schematic information processing, or gender schematicity. Simply put, gender schematicity is the internalizing of the gender polarization in the culture, the learned readiness to see reality as carved naturally into polarized sex and gender categories, not carved—whether naturally or unnaturally—into some other set of categories. It is the imposition of a gender-based classification on social reality, the sorting of persons, attributes, behaviors, and other things on the basis of the polarized definitions of masculinity and femininity that prevail in the culture, rather than on the basis of other dimensions that could serve equally well.

This focus on gender-schematic information processing emerged, in part, from my more general theory of how male and female newborns become conventionally masculine and feminine adults, a theory known as gender schema theory (Bem, 1981b). Gender schema theory applies to the domain of gender the same ideas about the internalization of cultural lenses that I will develop more generally in Chapter 5. Specifically, gender schema theory argues that because American culture is so gender polarizing in its discourse and its social institutions, children come to be gender schematic (or gender polarizing) themselves without even realizing it. Gender schematicity, in turn, helps lead children to become conventionally sex-typed. That is, in imposing a gender-based classification on reality, children evaluate different ways of behaving in terms of the cultural definitions of gender appropriateness and reject any way of behaving that does not match their sex. In contrast to Kohlberg's cognitive-developmental account of why children become sex-typed, this alternative account situates the source of the child's motivation for a match between sex and behavior, not in the mind of the child, but in the gender polarization of the culture.

As a real-life example of what it might mean to be gender schematic, consider how a college student at Cornell might go about deciding which new hobby to try out from among the many possibilities that are available. He or she could assess how expensive each possibility is, whether it can be done in cold weather, whether it can be done between and among classes, exams, and term papers, and so forth. In Ithaca, New York—where the seasons are described only semifacetiously as "winter and July"—the answers to all of these questions would make knitting an obvious choice. Being gender schematic, however, means being ready to look at this decision through a gender-polarizing lens. The student would ask early on, What "sex" is the hobby? What sex am I? Do they match? If sex and hobby match, then the hobby would be considered further. If not, then it would be rejected forthwith.

By shifting the focus of my research from androgyny to gender schematicity, I wanted to establish that masculinity and femininity were, in my view, cultural constructions; I also wanted to do with research on individual differences *within* a culture what anthropologists frequently try to do with the differences *between* cultures. Just as they use the differences between cultures to illuminate, or expose, a particular culture's way of organizing reality, so my theoretical and empirical work on gender schematicity was an attempt to use the differences between gender-schematic and gender-aschematic people within American culture to illuminate, or expose, not just the gender schematicity of sex-typed people in particular but the gender polarization of American culture in general. I was thus conceptualizing the sex-typed people in my research not just as gender-schematic individuals but as highly enculturated natives whose mode of processing information could serve as a window into the consciousness of the culture as a whole.[41]

This novel use of individual differences made good sense methodologically because, as noted earlier, people are defined as conventionally sex-typed on the BSRI if and only if their self-descriptions conform to the highly polarized definitions of gender appropriateness that prevail in the culture. Put somewhat differently, people defined as sex-typed on the BSRI could just as well have been defined as highly enculturated with respect to gender. When successful, both strategies—looking at cultural differences or at individual differences—manage to expose previously invisible cultural lenses. That is, they enable us to look *at* the lenses of a culture rather than *through* them by showing us previously unimagined alternatives and thereby teaching us that a culture's nonconscious—and dominant—way of organizing reality is not the only way of organizing reality.

If there is a feminist moral to the concept of gender schematicity, it is thus not that each of us should be free to explore both the masculine and the feminine within ourselves. It is rather that, in our current historical context, the culturally constructed dichotomy between masculine and feminine need not—and should not—be reproduced in either the instruments of culture or the identities of individuals. This is precisely the same feminist moral that is implicit in at least certain interpretations of androgyny.

BEYOND SCIENCE: THE CELEBRATION OF FEMALE DIFFERENCE

In the history of feminist thought, there has been a longstanding split between the minimizers of male-female difference, like Carolyn Heilbrun and myself, who seek to undermine whatever gender polarization exists in cultural discourses and social institutions, and the maximizers of male-female difference, who seek to reclaim, and thereby revalue, those aspects of female experience that have been denigrated or rendered invisible by an androcentric history. This split can be seen in the first wave of feminist advocacy, when the minimizers like Elizabeth Cady Stanton and Susan B. Anthony argued that women should be granted the right to vote on account of their being more like than unlike men, and the maximizers like Lucy Stone argued that women should be granted the right to vote on account of their unique attributes—including their nurturance and their better developed sense of morality. This split can also be seen in the many varieties of feminist theory that have been battling each other since the emergence of the second wave of feminist advocacy in the 1960s.[42]

Although the minimizers had a heyday during the androgyny era of the late 1960s and early 1970s, much of the feminist discourse of the

1980s has been organized around the celebration of female difference and the development of a critique of masculinity. The major contributors to this maximizing discourse have not always agreed on the source of the male-female difference they postulate, but they have been very much in agreement about the value and the content of the prototypically male and female "standpoints" (Harding, 1986), or "voices" (Gilligan, 1982).

What virtually all of the woman-centered theorists have seen as a woman's special virtue is her ability to easily transcend the many isolated little units and artificial polarities that men are said to almost compulsively invent. For Jean Baker Miller (1976), it is thus a woman's capacity to develop and grow *through* relationships, rather than to artificially dichotomize independence and dependence, that is central; for Carol Gilligan, it is "seeing a world comprised of relationships rather than of people standing alone, a world that coheres through human connection rather than through systems of rules" (1982, p. 29); for Hilary Rose, it is the unifying of "hand, brain, and heart" (1983, p. 73), rather than the separation of the manual from the mental from the emotional.

This tendency to see everyone and everything as interconnected and hence needing to be in balance has implications not only for a woman's psyche and her interpersonal relationships but also for the kinds of values that she would be inclined to espouse and the kinds of institutions that she would be inclined to build. Had women been the ones with the power to construct the dominant cultural institutions, it thus follows from the woman-centered perspective that we human beings would now be in much less danger of destroying both ourselves and our planet than we are; we would also have a radically different conception not only of science and morality but of just about every other domain of human life as well. Implicit in this vision of a brave new world constructed by women is a devastating critique of the current world, which was built by men. According to these woman-centered theorists, the problem with men and the institutions they build is that they are altogether too concerned with separation, dominance, and hierarchy and not concerned nearly enough with connectedness, mutual empowerment, and harmony.

Because the woman-centered theorists are much less in agreement about the source of the postulated male-female difference than about its content and value, they make a range of assumptions about origins, from the biologically essentialist through the child-developmental to the social-psychological.

At the more biologically essentialist end of the spectrum are people like Adrienne Rich (1976) and Mary Daly (1978), who both seem to emphasize the metaphysical nature of the female body. Adrienne Rich, to quote her once again, says that "as the inhabitant of a female body," she finds "the boundaries of the ego . . . much less crudely definable than the words 'inner' and 'outer' suggest."

> In love-making . . . there is, often, a strong sense of *inter*penetration, of feeling the melting of the walls of flesh, as physical and emotional longing deliver the one person into the other, blurring the boundary between body and body. The identification with another woman's orgasm as if it were one's own is one of the most intense interpersonal experiences: nothing is either "inside" me or "outside" at such moments. . . . In pregnancy . . . I experience the embryo . . . as something inside and of me, yet becoming hourly and daily more separate, on its way to becoming separate from me and of-itself. . . . Far from existing in the mode of "inner space," women are powerfully and vulnerably attuned both to "inner" and "outer" because for us the two are continuous, not polar. (Pp. 47–48)

> I am really asking whether women cannot begin, at last, to *think through the body*, to connect what has been so cruelly disorganized—our great mental capacities, hardly used; our highly developed tactile sense; our genius for close observation; our complicated, pain-enduring, multipleasured physicality. . . . In such a world women will truly create new life, bringing forth not only children (if and as we choose) but the visions, and the thinking, necessary to sustain, console, and alter human existence—a new relationship to the universe. (Pp. 290–292)

Taking a more developmental perspective, in contrast, are people like Evelyn Fox Keller (1985) and Carol Gilligan (1982), who argue, following Nancy Chodorow (1978), that in different ways, both Western science (Keller) and Western morality (Gilligan) have become as committed to objectivity as they have been—that is, as committed to the separation of self from other and of subject from object—in part, because the psyches of the Western males who constructed those domains were shaped by a mother-infant relationship that simultaneously made separation essential and connectedness problematic.

Finally, taking a more social-psychological perspective on male-female difference are a whole variety of woman-centered theorists who argue, in one way or another, that what shapes women's and men's differing constructions of reality are their differing positions in society. For most of these more situationally minded people, including Jean Baker Miller (1976), Sarah Ruddick (1989), Dorothy Smith (1987), Hilary Rose (1983), and Bettina Aptheker (1989), what seems to loom largest in the "dailiness" (Aptheker, 1989) of a woman's position in society is her caregiving role in the division of labor, including her experience of mothering. For others, including Nancy Hartsock (1983) and Sandra Harding (1986), what seems to loom largest is her daily experience of being subordinated—or what bell hooks calls "on the margin." Marginality is, in turn, presumed to produce an "oppositional consciousness" (hooks, 1984).[43] Ironically, these last three theorists could almost be considered minimizers, for they focus not so much on the difference of being a woman but on the difference of being marginalized.[44]

The woman-centered, or difference-centered, discourse of the 1980s emerged as a corrective not only to the long history of androcentrism in Western culture but also to certain unfortunate aspects of feminist theorizing in the late 1960s and early 1970s. The targets included the emphasis on female oppression, or patriarchy—which treated women as victims—and the emphasis on gender neutrality and androgyny, both of which treated women as all but invisible. Given the celebration of women in the feminist discourse of the 1980s, women are certainly not invisible any longer, nor are they any longer represented merely as victims. The question must be asked, however: Has this maximizing discourse managed to expose and thereby dislocate any of the three lenses that have differentially shaped the lives of males and females since the beginning of Western culture, or has it merely reproduced those lenses in yet another context? In my own view, the woman-centered discourse of the 1980s has vigorously, and unfortunately, reproduced both gender polarization and biological essentialism; at the same time, however, it has been truly provocative—if somewhat problematically so—with respect to androcentrism.

With respect to gender polarization, the case is clear. For all of its emphasis on a woman's unique ability to transcend the artificial polarities that men are said to invent, the woman-centered perspective has so completely polarized women and men, along with what it defines as the male and female modes of relating to reality, that for all practical purposes, both men and women are as limited by homogenized visions of themselves as ever before. Granted that it is now men rather than women who are being denigrated, and granted also that the words *masculinity* and *femininity* are not being used explicitly, still, these are not real women being celebrated and real men being pilloried. These homogenized visions are but the flip side of the polarized, gender caricatures of androcentrism.

With respect to biological essentialism, the verdict is a little muddier because of the diversity among the theorists on the question of origins. This diversity notwithstanding, the woman-centered theorists concentrate so much more on the psychological differences between males and females than on their differing social contexts, they spend so little time debating the all-important question of where those psychological differences come from, and they make those psychological differences seem so intimately connected to the essence of what it means to be either male or female that, in the end, the impact of the discourse is to make those psychological differences between males and females seem natural, not socially constructed.

This brings us, finally, to the issue of androcentrism. If we read the woman-centered discourse as it often seems to invite being read—that is, as a description of empirical difference between real males and real females—then what we get, unfortunately, is a problematic—if mildly delicious—disruption of the androcentric lens. The disruption is mildly delicious because it reverses the androcentric value system, making women and women's modes of functioning the locus of cultural value, rather than men and men's modes of functioning. At the same time, however, the disruption is problematic, because it is just as one-sided and distorted as the lens it is intended to disrupt. Put somewhat differently, flesh-and-blood women and men aren't all as good and evil, respectively, nor as homogeneous, as the woman-centered discourse seems to imply.

On the other hand, if we read the woman-centered discourse in a way that is more analogous to how I read my own research on gender schematicity—that is, not primarily as an empirical study of human differences but as a strategy for exposing an invisible cultural lens—then the two concepts that were problematically represented in the woman-centered discourse as the prototypically male mode of functioning and the female difference become, respectively, the androcentric lens and the *idealized* female voice, which can also be thought of as a gynecentric, or woman-centered, lens. Even more important, the woman-centered discourse itself becomes not just a problematic discussion of individual male and female psychology but a truly provocative discussion of the androcentrism that lies hidden in even the most gender-neutral-seeming social institutions.

In Chapter 3, I argued that men used their positions of power to construct a social world that defined women and women's roles in relation to men and men's roles. What the woman-centered discourse of the 1980s has made clear, however, is that men in power androcentrically defined more than that; they androcentrically defined science, morality, mental health, work, politics, law, and every other institution of society as well.

To say that men in power constructed these institutions androcentrically is not simply to say that they excluded women from them, although they did that, too. It is to say that they unconsciously built into those institutions whatever fundamental assumptions about reality they came to have by virtue of their particular position in the social structure. Because they were privileged in the social hierarchy and emotionally and physically distanced from the activity of intimate caregiving, the institutions they built were predisposed to take on precisely the characteristics that the woman-centered theorists have so eloquently—and so poisonously—described in the language of sexual difference.

As guilty as the woman-centered discourse may thus have been of reproducing biological essentialism and especially gender polarization, its indirect critique of cultural androcentrism has been wonderfully illuminating.

5

THE CONSTRUCTION
OF GENDER IDENTITY

The theoretical perspectives on the social construction of gender that have dominated the social science literature for the past fifty years have emphasized socialization, situational constraint by the social structure, psychodynamic conflict, or identity construction by the individual. The first and second emphasize something that the culture does to the individual, whereas the third and fourth emphasize something that goes on within the individual's psyche.[1] In examining these perspectives and then moving beyond them, we move from a cultural analysis of the gender lenses in society, which occupied us in the previous chapters, to a social-psychological analysis of the processes by which the individual acquires those gender lenses and thereby constructs a conventionally gendered self, or resists acquiring those gender lenses and thereby becomes a gender subversive.

Although all socialization theories emphasize the molding of the child into some preestablished cultural pattern, or template, the theories deriving from sociology and anthropology emphasize a different facet of this process than do the theories deriving from psychology. Sociologists and anthropologists begin their analyses of socialization, not with the individual child or the individual socializer, but with the overarching need of society to prepare each succeeding generation of young people to take their required places in the social structure. Because that social structure is everywhere based on a gendered division of labor, this preparation must include the gender-differentiated molding of not only skills but psyches as well; male and female children must be shaped to fit their very different adult roles.

Three analyses of gender socialization reflect this more societal (or functional) tradition: those by Talcott Parsons and Robert Bales (1955), Herbert Barry, Margaret Bacon, and Irvin Child (1957), and Beatrice Whiting and Carolyn Edwards (1988). The analysis by Whiting and Edwards is of special interest because it suggests that in anticipation of their adult roles, boys and girls are almost everywhere put into different "learning environments" (p. 2) with different categories of "social partners" (p. 6). It also demonstrates empirically—and in places as varied as Africa, India, the Philippines, Okinawa, Mexico, and the United States—that nurturance is elicited in interaction with children under one year of age, who are much more likely cross-culturally to be found in the learning environments of girls than in the learning environments of boys. This finding harks back to the argument I made at the end of Chapter 2 about women and girls being everywhere more motivated to take care of infants and children than men and boys are, not because of any "maternal instinct," but because the sexual division of labor forever and always places women and girls in the "contact" condition, and men and boys in the "no-contact" condition.

In contrast to the sociologists and the anthropologists, who begin their analyses of gender socialization with social structure, the psychologists begin their analyses with the gender-stereotyped expectations of the individual adults who populate that social structure. The basic psychological model here is that of the self-fulfilling prophecy. In the simplest possible case, the adults in the child's social community treat girls and boys differently because of their gender-stereotyped preconceptions of what girls and boys are supposed to be like. That differential treatment then causes girls and boys to become different from one another in the way that the adults' preconceptions determined.[2]

Perhaps the most elegant empirical demonstration of this kind of gender socialization was orchestrated by Beverly Fagot, who carefully recorded the behavior of both teachers and children in a toddler playgroup at two different points in time (Fagot et al., 1985). During the first series of observations, the twelve-month-old boys and girls communicated to their teachers and to one another in very similar ways; but the teachers, because of their gender stereotypes, unwittingly reinforced the girls for communicating more gently and reinforced the boys for communicating more assertively. As a result of this different treatment, those same boys and girls displayed dramatically different styles of communicating when they were again observed some twelve months later, thereby demonstrating that the gender preconceptions of adults do indeed become the gender-differentiated reality of children's social behavior.

Like socialization theories, social-structural, or situational, theories also emphasize what the culture does to the individual. Unlike socialization theorists, however, social-structural theorists do not see the culture as having a deep-seated and enduring impact on the psyche of the developing child. Rather, they see both the child and the adult as being constrained by their situations. What is responsible for the construction of conventionally gendered women and men is not childhood socialization, then, but the assignment of women and men to different and unequal positions in the social structure. That different and unequal assignment constrains both children and adults psychologically, by channeling their motivations and their abilities into either a stereotypically male or a stereotypically female direction. It also constrains them more coercively, by restricting their ability to step outside their assigned positions should they be motivated to do so.

The social-structural perspective on gender has been cogently argued in recent years by Alice Eagly (1987) and Cynthia Epstein (1988). Two of the best known empirical studies in this tradition were done ten years earlier, however. Rosabeth Moss Kanter, in *Men and Women of the Corporation* (1977), argued that women are less motivated than men to get ahead in the world of paid employment not because of any intrinsic differences in their personalities but because their mostly low-level clerical and service jobs provide them with precious little opportunity for advancement. Nancy Henley, in *Body Politics* (1977), argued that men's and women's differing styles of verbal and nonverbal communication are similarly derived from their differing status in the social structure.

The psychological implication of the social-structural perspective should be clear: change a woman's position in the social structure, and her motivation and ability will quickly change as well. The political implication should also be clear: if women are ever to have political and economic equality, what needs to change is not the psyche—or even the socialization—of the individual; what needs to change is the androcentric social structure that operates systemically and in the here and now to preserve male power.

In contrast to both socialization and social-structural theories,

which focus in one way or another on what the culture does to transform male and female into masculine and feminine, psychoanalytic
theories focus on how the child's psychic conflicts accomplish this
transformation. These psychic conflicts are presumed to develop
whenever the child's own impulses and desires are made emotionally
problematic.

As we saw in Chapter 3, Freud proposed that the child's desire for
the mother is itself made emotionally problematic by the castration
anxiety and the penis envy that develop in boys and girls, respectively,
when they discover the existence of the infamous genital difference. In
boys, this internal psychic conflict leads to masculinity through identification with the father; in girls, it leads to femininity through an accep-
tance of female inferiority and a shift from mother love to father love.

In more recent psychoanalytic formulations, Freud's presupposition of female inferiority and even his interpretation of the Oedipal
conflict have been questioned. In the highly influential account by
Jacques Lacan, for example, it is not the discovery of simple anatomical
difference but the realization of what the phallus signifies in a patriarchal society that causes males to identify with privilege and power
and females to identify with inferiority and subordination.[3]

In the account by Nancy Chodorow (1978, 1989), in contrast, the
critical event occurs earlier, in the preoedipal period, and involves a
conflict in boy-children over dependency and symbiosis. Building on
ideas from object relations theory and on the fact that childcare is
universally assigned to mothers, rather than fathers, Chodorow argues
that because mothers are much more likely to relate to their boy-
children as different and separate from themselves—and to their girl-
children as close to and like themselves—boys develop "a self that denies relatedness" while girls develop "a self-in-relation" (1989, p. 15); in
addition, boys grow up with such a strong need to deny their relatedness to women in general that, as men, they use whatever forms of
power are available to them in order to cast women as the other (p. 14).

In a modern democratic society, where individuals choose adult
roles for themselves instead of having those roles assigned to them on
the basis of some ascribed characteristic, psychological identities are,
perhaps inevitably, seen as all-important. They are also seen as something people construct for themselves instead of something people
acquire through their cultural socialization, their status in the social
structure, or even their psychic conflicts. Although the earliest theories

of identity either ignored the issue of gender altogether or considered a woman's identity to be held in abeyance until it could be organized around the identity of the man who would be her husband, identity-oriented psychologists and sociologists have recently begun to see masculinity and femininity, and even sexual orientation, as resulting in part from an individual's personal and conscious commitment to a particular aspect of the self.[4]

This image of the individual actively constructing an identity around either sex or sexuality appears in three different theoretical and empirical contexts. It appears in Lawrence Kohlberg's Piagetian account of how young children construct their masculinity or femininity, which we discussed in Chapter 4. It appears in the analysis of how transsexuals construct ways of talking about themselves and conducting themselves that enable them to pass as members of the sex they wish to be. At least some sociologists see this construction of a masculine or feminine self by transsexuals as different from non-transsexuals' self-construction in only its level of awareness and desperation.[5] Finally, the image of the individual building a self-identity appears in recent theoretical analyses of how same-sex sexuality was transformed during the twentieth century from sin, vice, or sickness into, first, a homosexual identity and, later, an even more self-affirming gay male or lesbian identity.[6]

An individual can construct more than a personal identity by making a commitment to some aspect of the self. As the identity politics of the movements for gay rights, women's rights, senior citizens' rights, and black rights eloquently testify, an individual can extend a personal sense of identity into the political arena and construct a whole political movement on the basis of that commitment.

Each of these four perspectives has something profound to say about the process whereby male and female infants are transformed into the kinds of masculine and feminine adults who willingly accept the different—and unequal—roles assigned to them in an androcentric and gender-polarizing society. The insight of socialization theories is that the adult woman or man is, in part, the product of the child's encounter with the culture. The insight of psychodynamic theories is that because the process of socialization necessarily regulates the child's natural impulses, the adult psyche inevitably contains repressed desires and psychic conflicts. The insight of identity-construction theories is that even a child is never merely the passive object of cultural forces;

both children and adults are active makers of meaning, including the meaning of their own being. And finally, the insight of social-structural theories is that at least some portion of who people are, even as adults, is not what they have become inside but what their current level of status and power requires or enables them to be.

The enculturated-lens theory of individual gender formation to be presented here seeks to incorporate these critical insights, as well as situate the individual from birth to death in a social and historical context containing the lenses of androcentrism and gender polarization. The challenge for the theory is thus to explain how a society manages to transfer its lenses from the culture to the individual. How, in general, does a society create a cultural native? How, in particular, does it create a *gendered* cultural native, transforming male and female children into masculine and feminine adults?

During the past fifteen years or so, a number of feminist scholars have turned to psychoanalytic theories, especially Nancy Chodorow's theory of mother-infant relations, because other social-constructionist theories appear to locate the psychology of gender at too superficial a level within the individual's psyche. Although the concept of an internalized gender lens may not deal as narrowly or as specifically as Chodorow's theory does with either the mother-infant relationship or the psychological dimension of emotional connectedness versus emotional separation, the concept does offer to both feminists and psychologists as deeply psychological and as profoundly cultural an explanation of individual gender formation as it also offers for the acquisition of a native consciousness.

ENCULTURATION

Gender schema theory, outlined in Chapter 4, maintains that children in gender-polarizing societies internalize the lens of gender polarization and thereby become gender polarizing (or gender schematic) themselves. This internalized lens, in turn, helps lead children to become conventionally gendered. That is, in imposing a gender-polarizing classification on social reality, children evaluate different ways of behaving in terms of the cultural definitions of gender appropriateness and reject any ways of behaving that do not match their sex.

Gender schema theory contains two fundamental presuppositions about the process of individual gender formation: first, that there are gender lenses embedded in cultural discourse and social practice that are internalized by the developing child, and, second, that once these gender lenses have been internalized, they predispose the child, and later the adult, to construct an identity that is consistent with them. The theory to be presented here retains these presuppositions but elaborates and extends the gender schema account in two important ways.

One way it does so is by adding the lens of androcentrism to the earlier account. Because society is not only gender polarizing but androcentric, the males and females living within it become androcentric and gender polarizing themselves. The inclusion of this second lens dramatically alters the consequences of internalizing the gender lenses. Whereas before, the individual had been nothing more than a carrier of the culture's gender polarization, now the individual is a deeply implicated—if unwitting—collaborator in the social reproduction of male power.

Another way the earlier theory is expanded is in spelling out the processes of enculturation that are presumed to transfer the lenses of androcentrism and gender polarization from the culture to the individual. This model of enculturation is sufficiently general to explain how all cultural lenses are transferred to the individual, not just gender lenses. The analysis of how conventionally gendered women and men are made is thus but a special case of how cultural natives are made. Consistent with this premise, I preface my theoretical analysis of individual gender construction with a more general analysis of the two enculturation processes that are critical to the making of a cultural native: the institutional preprogramming of the individual's daily experience into the default options, or the historically precut "grooves," for that particular time and place, and the transmission of implicit lessons—or metamessages—about what lenses the culture uses to organize social reality.[7]

The Making of a Cultural Native

Preprogramming an individual's daily experience into the default options of a particular culture is apparent in the most superficial analysis of how children have been made into unmistakably different kinds of social beings in different cultures and different historical epochs.[8] Consider the institutionally structured experience of children in modern middle-class America, for example, where everyone from six to sixteen spends seven hours a day, five days a week, forty weeks a year, in rigidly age-segregated classrooms being taught material that frequently has no immediate value to either themselves or anyone else in their communities. Now compare that to the institutionally structured experience of children in a more traditional culture, where skills critical to making a living are learned every day by participating with adults in productive labor and where the child's daily labor—like the adult's—is essential to the economic well-being of family and community.

The point should be clear. The kinds of human beings that children and adults become depend on their daily social experiences; and these social experiences are, in turn, preprogrammed by institutionalized social practices—which are themselves but one embodiment of the same cultural lenses that are also embodied in cultural discourse.

As important as this structuring of daily experience is to the making of a cultural native, however, the less visible process of tacitly communicating what lenses the culture uses to organize reality is equally important. This tacit communication of cultural metamessages about what is important, what is of value, which differences between people and other entities are to be emphasized and which are to be overlooked, which dimensions are to be used in judging how similar or dissimilar people and other entities are in the first place, and so on and so forth, helps to make a cultural native because it nonconsciously transfers the lenses of the culture to the consciousness or the psyche of the individual.

According to the anthropologist Clifford Geertz, the hallmark of a native consciousness is not being able to distinguish between reality and the way one's culture construes reality; in other words, the reality one perceives and the cultural lenses through which one perceives it are "indissoluble" (1983, p. 58). Although this kind of consciousness can sometimes be retained by adults who live in a sufficiently homogeneous society, it can be acquired only by children, who learn about their culture's way of construing reality without yet being aware that alternative construals are possible. In contrast to the adult visiting from another culture, the child growing up within a culture is thus like the proverbial fish who is unaware that its environment is wet. After all, what else could it be?

There are at least two different ways to talk about this nonconscious transfer of lenses from the culture to the child, both of which presuppose that the information to be transferred is embedded within the social practices of the culture. Insofar as social practices communicate metamessages to the child, the acquisition of cultural knowledge can be considered a kind of subliminal pedagogy. Insofar as the child gradually deciphers the meaning embedded in social practices, the acquisition of cultural knowledge can be considered more a matter of picking up information than transmitting it; in this case, the culture itself is more a text to be read—and read by an active, meaning-constructing reader—than a lesson to be taught.

This simultaneous transmission and pickup of information is initiated every time the active, pattern-seeking child is exposed to a culturally significant social practice. Take, for example, the practice of wearing a wristwatch that tells the time to the nearest minute. Simultaneously communicated by this practice and picked up by the child is that time must be quantified precisely and that human behavior must be scheduled precisely. Cultures that tell time by the sun and the seasons communicate a very different conception of social reality.

In real life, social practices cannot be neatly divided into those that prestructure daily experience and those that communicate cultural metamessages. All institutionalized social practices simultaneously do both, as can be seen in the following analysis of how the American middle-class family creates the kinds of radically individualistic people that anthropologists regard as distinctively Western, if not distinctively American.[9]

The process of molding American infants into individualistic American adults begins almost immediately after birth. Although children in many other cultures spend years in close physical contact with their mother—feeding from her breast, being carried on her back, and even sleeping in her bed—American children in families that can afford it are typically put out of their parents' beds and even out of their parents' bedrooms from the start. They are also typically weaned by the time they are one year old. The distinction between self and other is tacitly but forcefully imposed.

Americans structure into their children's daily lives the further notion that this separate self is a privileged entity, with boundaries that should not be violated and with needs, wants, and preferences that should be satisfied if at all possible. Parents communicate that the self has inviolable boundaries by giving children their own bedrooms and knocking on the door before entering, and by giving them diaries—complete with keys—in which to write their private thoughts. They communicate that children's needs, wants, and preferences should be satisfied—and that they *have* needs, wants, and preferences—by asking even toddlers what they want to eat and by responding even to infants as if their every vocalization were the expression of a desire that the parents should try to satisfy. Other, more sociocentric cultures give such rights and privileges to neither children nor adults.

By structuring their social interactions with children in these highly individualistic ways, American parents are doing two things simultaneously. First, they are situating the children in social contexts that will shape them into persons who have strong internal desires and who expect those desires to be satisfied. Second, they are communicating the shared cultural conception of a person.

Not only the American child lives in a social world that treats the individual as if he or she were the fundamental unit of all social life. The American adult lives in a social world that does exactly the same thing.

Consider first, for example, the American institution of "going away to college." Although possible, in principle, for almost any young adult to get an outstanding college education while still living at or near the family home, going to college, for those who can afford it, means going *away* to college. That is, it means being separated geographically, culturally, and psychologically from those with whom the young adult has always shared the bonds of love. The separation of the individual from the family is thus treated as a natural and desirable developmental stage; and connection, as a mark of immaturity and an encumbrance to social mobility.

Consider the American institution of getting married—and then divorced. Although marriage was once seen as a lifetime commitment to be dissolved only in the most extreme circumstances, if ever, it is increasingly seen as a limited partnership to be sustained if and only if it contributes substantially to the growth and development of both partners. Getting a divorce has become easier, not only legally but socially and psychologically as well. Again, separation is the norm, and connection an encumbrance to self-development.

Consider the American institution of going into therapy. So many people who can afford it now seek counseling whenever they experience any sense of dissatisfaction with their lives that some sociologists (like Robert Bellah et al., 1985) see the therapist as a significant cultural figure in late twentieth-century America. From their perspective, the growing prevalence of therapy is significant, in part, because the therapeutic dyad may constitute the kind of self-serving interpersonal relationship that Americans now seek in their personal lives—that is, a relationship that not only makes no demands or moral judgments but that also gives priority to individual self-enhancement rather than to the common good of any larger social unit. Again, connection is desirable if and only if it is not an encumbrance to the individual.

Finally, consider that most fundamental of capitalist institutions—private ownership. Private ownership is so ubiquitous in the daily lives of Americans that even the communal ownership of a neighborhood lawn mower is almost unthinkable. Nor are material things all that Americans have difficulty sharing; even the personal space around the body is treated as if it were private property. This peculiarly American pattern of laying claim to a relatively large amount of personal space is exhibited in face-to-face interactions at international gatherings, where the Americans inch backward to preserve the space around them and their conversational partners from many other cultures inch forward.[10]

Given the highly individualistic social world in which Americans live from the time they are born until the time they die, no wonder that in Tibetan, Americans are known as *nga dangpo,* which roughly means "me-firsters."[11]

The Making of a Gendered Native

Just as American society constructs me-firsters by situating people in a culture whose discourses and social practices are organized around the lens of radical individualism, so, too, does it construct conventionally gendered women and men by situating people in a culture whose discourses and social practices are organized around the lenses of androcentrism and gender polarization. In Chapters 3 and 4, I exposed the androcentrism and the gender polarization in some important discourses of Western culture. My purpose here is to expose the androcentrism and the gender polarization in some social practices. These social practices program different and unequal social experiences for males and females; they also transfer the androcentric and gender-polarizing lenses of the culture to the psyche of the individual.

The androcentrism of American social practices can be seen most easily in the world of paid employment, where most women are still segregated into occupations which themselves embody the same three androcentric definitions of a woman discussed in Chapter 3.[12] The androcentric definition of a woman in terms of her domestic and re-productive functions is embodied in those many women's jobs that provide administrative and logistical support to some higher-status male, including secretary, administrative aide, research assistant, para-legal, dental hygienist, and nurse. The androcentric definition of a woman in terms of her power to stimulate or satisfy the male sexual appetite is embodied in jobs that cater to male sexuality directly—prostitute, stripper, and go-go dancer come to mind—as well as in jobs that cater to male sexuality indirectly by emphasizing a woman's sexual attractiveness, including flight attendant, receptionist, and even televi-sion news anchorwoman. And the androcentric definition of a woman as an inferior departure from the male standard is embodied in the very definition of what constitutes a normal work life in America: con-tinuous full-time work (with time off only for illness) throughout early and middle adulthood. The definition of full-time work is itself a his-torical construction, varying—even for men—from something like forty hours or fewer per week for those in "working-class" jobs to a great deal more than forty hours per week for fast-track young profes-sionals in legal practices and financial firms. But whatever the social class of the job, neither the biological fact of female pregnancy nor the cultural and historical fact of female childcare is factored into the defi-nition of a normal work life, which means that women in the world of paid employment are still being forced to cope with social practices (for example, the lack of pregnancy leave and childcare) that were institu-tionalized at a time when women themselves were still excluded from that world by law.

It should be clear from the discussion of how cultural natives are made that all of these androcentric social practices do two things simul-taneously. First, they situate men and women in markedly unequal positions in the social structure, positions where men have much more opportunity than women to earn money, acquire marketable skills, advance in their careers, and wield power. This unequal positioning provides men and women with daily social experiences that, in turn, give rise to drastically different ways of construing reality.

Second, these androcentric social practices communicate to all the participants in the social world, both male and female, as well as to any spectators—children, say, watching representations of that social world in movies or on the television news—that males are the priv-ileged sex and the male perspective is the privileged perspective. That is, these practices communicate that males are the central characters in the drama of human life around whom all action revolves and through whose eyes all reality is to be interpreted. Females, in contrast, are the peripheral, or marginal, characters, defined in terms of their relationship to the central characters. In the words of Simone de Beauvoir, females are the second sex, or the other.

This androcentric message is communicated by many institutionalized social practices. An example is the much-criticized practice of generically using *he, him,* and *man* to include *she, her,* and *woman.* Contrary to what at least some antifeminist pundits (playing on Freud) have condescendingly claimed, the feminist objection to this linguistic convention is not a case of "pronoun envy"; it is a sophisticated critique of a social practice that makes women invisible and treats men as the standard-bearers for the whole species.[13] Another linguistic example is the practice of having a woman take her husband's name and the title Mrs. (Mrs. John Smith) upon marriage. Apart from how androcentric this practice is in form, it gives the father's name to any children that the couple may have and makes it much more important to the couple to have at least one male child—because only a male child can carry on what is euphemistically known as the family name.

Like the androcentrism of the world beyond the family, the androcentrism within the family extends well beyond linguistic convention. In keeping with the androcentric definition of a woman in terms of her domestic and reproductive functions, even the employed wife is thus expected to provide whatever support services her husband requires to earn his living. In keeping with the androcentric definition of a woman in terms of her ability to stimulate and satisfy the male sexual appetite, the wife is also expected to provide her husband with sexual intercourse on demand, which is why the concept of marital rape is so often treated as an oxymoron.

This refusal to acknowledge the reality of marital rape is but one example of how the androcentric privileging of the male has left women with no legal recourse when their husbands abuse them. Still another example is the longstanding policy of the criminal justice system to look the other way when husbands beat their wives.

In some cultures, androcentrism organizes the social practices that impinge on children just as much as it organizes the social practices that impinge on adults, with many more newborn baby girls being killed because of limited resources than newborn baby boys, for example, and with many more school-age girls being denied the kind of an education that would make them literate. In late twentieth-century America, in contrast, where compulsory education and antidiscrimination laws now mandate that girls and boys receive virtually identical formal educations, androcentrism impinges on most children in more subtle ways: school systems treat boys' reading problems more seriously than girls' problems with math and computers, for example, and the culture as a whole treats sissies much more harshly than tomboys. This differential treatment of sissies and tomboys highlights a critically important interaction between androcentrism and gender polarization; we shall return to it below.

Even in late twentieth-century America, however, gender polarization organizes the daily lives of children from the moment a pink or blue nametag is taped to the bassinet to signal the newborn's sex, as it is in almost every American hospital. (In my daughter's case, a pink bow was also taped to her bald head.) Gender polarization continues at home, where parents dress their children in pink or blue, coif them (as soon as possible) with long hair or short, put them into bedrooms decorated with ballet dancers or football players, and tell them in no uncertain terms that they can't wear or play with either this item of clothing or that toy because it's "just for boys" or "just for girls."

Toys and clothes are not the only things defined as inappropriate for one sex or the other; so are a great many natural human impulses. Defined as gender inappropriate for females, for instance, is the desire for autonomy and power; defined as gender inappropriate for males are feelings of vulnerability, dependency, and affection for same-sex others.

Again, all of these gender-polarizing social practices do two things simultaneously. They program different social experiences for males and females, respectively, and they communicate to both males and females that the male-female distinction is extraordinarily important, that it has—and ought to have—intensive and extensive relevance to virtually every aspect of human experience.

Children pick up this gender-polarizing message both from practices that divide reality into masculine and feminine and from certain more subtle aspects of the language. Consider what is being communicated, for example, when a three-year-old is corrected for saying about Grandpa that "she" is eating an apple, or when a four-year-old is taught a song in which "the fingers are ladies and the thumbs are men," or when a five-year-old is taught to keep track of the date by pinning boy paper dolls on the odd-numbered days and girl paper dolls on the even-numbered days. On the surface, these language lessons may be about grammar and body parts and calendars. At the meta level, however, they teach children to look at social reality through a lens that is gender polarizing.

Gender polarization does not end with childhood. During adulthood there is at least as much emphasis on the gender polarization of the body, as well as a strong emphasis on the gender polarization of erotic desire and sexual expression. Males and females alike are all but required to conform to the cultural mandate for exclusive heterosexuality.

This heterosexual mandate is institutionalized in a great number of social practices privileging heterosexuality and marginalizing homosexuality. Examples are (1) the criminalization of same-sex sexual activity, which has been upheld by the Supreme Court as recently as 1986 in *Bowers v. Hardwick*; (2) the denial of the right to marry to gay male and lesbian couples, which also denies them the spousal benefits that accrue to married heterosexual couples, including employment-based fringe benefits, survivorship rights, and legal authority over medical decisions for the partner should he or she become incapacitated by illness or accident; (3) the barring of gay males and lesbians from military service; (4) the refusal of many churches to accept openly gay males and lesbians into their congregations; (5) the organization of almost all postpubescent social life around the heterosexual couple, with dates and dances at the high school and dinner parties in suburbia all but denying the existence of gay male and lesbian relationships; and (6) the similar denial of gay male and lesbian existence by the programming and advertising of the mass media. Although this virtual censorship of same-sex sexuality in the mass media has had to be modified somewhat in the context of the recent AIDS epidemic, news reports and even occasional episodes on sitcoms that are designed to provide information on how the HIV virus is transmitted do not begin to challenge the privileging of heterosexuality as much as a single ad for toothpaste featuring a same-sex romantic couple undoubtedly would.

Besides communicating that the male-female distinction requires attention in all domains of human social life, gender-polarizing social practices also communicate a corollary of that metamessage: that another important distinction is to be made between a *real* male or female and a *biological* male or female. This corollary is first communicated when parents teach children their earliest definitions of male and female.

In my critique of Kohlberg's cognitive-developmental theory in Chapter 4, I pointed out that although children as young as three years of age have the capacity to understand that it is biological attributes like the genitalia that define a person as male or female, fully 50 percent of American three-, four-, and five-year-olds are able to distinguish male from female only when those males and females are clothed and coiffed in a fully gender-polarizing way.

From an enculturation perspective, the reason so many young American children pay more attention to hairstyle and clothing than to genitalia is that they have picked up an implicit—if somewhat erroneous—cultural metamessage about what sex is. Americans tend to dress prepubertal males and females differently and to give them different hairstyles—that is, to polarize their physical appearances—precisely so that their sex will be apparent even when their genitalia are hidden from view. Moreover, in supermarkets, on playgrounds, and in every other social context, parents readily identify people as male or female for their children even when they have no specific information about those people's genitalia. In doing these things, adults not only rely on visually salient cultural cues themselves but they also unwittingly teach children a social or cultural definition of sex rather than a biological one.

As I see it, the legacy of learning a social definition of sex lasts long after a child has learned about the special significance of the genitalia as the defining attributes of male and female. Not only does the social definition set up a pattern of behavior that is culturally consistent with whatever sex the child is told he or she is; it also instills in the child the never-to-be-fully-forgotten feeling that being male or female is something to work at, to accomplish, and to be sure not to lose, rather than something one *is* biologically.

If the lifelong pressures and demands of the mutually exclusive cultural scripts did not nourish that germ of an idea, perhaps it would wither and die once the child learned about the genitalia. But because the scripts do nourish it, it grows to become a deeply rooted insecurity, which, in turn, motivates many adults to try to enhance their sense of being either a "real" man or a "real" woman through the kinds of behavioral choices they make in their everyday lives.

This insecurity is profoundly exacerbated by the requirement in a gender-polarizing society that people repress at least some of their most natural human impulses. Polarization of the human impulses exacerbates gender insecurity—as Freud himself would have understood—because no matter how well people manage to keep them under control, those gender-inappropriate impulses not only produce a certain level of conflict and contradiction within the individual psyche; they also constitute an eternal internal threat to the male or female selves that people work so hard to construct and maintain.

In principle, parents could communicate a very different metamessage not only about what sex is but also about when sex matters. They could communicate that sex is a narrowly construed biological concept that does not need to matter outside the domain of reproduction, which is the antithesis of the traditional cultural metamessage that sex matters very much indeed in virtually all domains of human activity. In my own family, I tried to teach my children at the earliest possible age that "being a boy means having a penis and testicles; being a girl means having a vagina, a clitoris, and a uterus; and whether you're a boy or a girl, a man or a woman, doesn't need to matter unless and until you want to make a baby."

Both the liberation that can come from having a narrow biological definition of sex and the imprisonment that can come from not having such a definition are strikingly illustrated by an encounter my son, Jeremy, had when he naively decided to wear barrettes to nursery school. Several times that day, another little boy insisted that Jeremy must be a girl because "only girls wear barrettes." After repeatedly insisting that "wearing barrettes doesn't matter; being a boy means having a penis and testicles," Jeremy finally pulled down his pants to make his point more convincingly. The other boy was not impressed. He simply said, "Everybody has a penis; only girls wear barrettes."[14]

Although the gender-polarizing concepts of a real man and a real woman give both men and women the feeling that their maleness or femaleness is something they must continually construct and reconstruct, rather than something they can simply take for granted, in the context of an androcentric culture it is the males in particular who are made to feel the most insecure about the adequacy of their gender. Androcentrism exacerbates the male's insecurity about his status as a real man in at least two different ways. It so thoroughly devalues whatever thoughts, feelings, and behaviors are culturally defined as feminine that crossing the gender boundary has a more negative cultural meaning for men that it has for women—which means, in turn, that male gender-boundary-crossers are much more culturally stigmatized than female gender-boundary-crossers. At the same time, androcentrism provides such an unreachable definition of what a real man is supposed to be that only a few men can even begin to meet it.

During childhood, the cultural asymmetry between male gender-boundary-crossers and female gender-boundary-crossers can be seen in the merciless teasing of sissies, as opposed to the benign neglect or even open admiration of tomboys. Asymmetry can also be seen in dress and play codes for children: although a girl can now wear almost any item of clothing and play with almost any toy without so much as an eyebrow being raised by her social community, let a boy even once have the urge to try on a princess costume in the dress-up corner of his nursery school, and his parents and teachers will instantly schedule a conference to discuss the adequacy of his gender identity. Although the terms *sissy* and *tomboy* do not apply to adults who have crossed the gender boundary, the asymmetry between male boundary-crossers and female boundary-crossers is as strong as ever for those who have left childhood behind. This is why a woman can wear almost any item of male clothing—including jockey underwear—and be accepted socially, but a man still cannot wear most items of female clothing without being stigmatized.[15]

This heavy-handed suppression of impulses in males that are culturally defined as even slightly feminine—including what I see as the natural impulse to adorn oneself in vibrant colors and silky textures—makes it extraordinarily difficult for many men to acknowledge the existence within themselves of desires that have even the slightest hint of femininity; the layers of their psyches are thus filled with the kinds of repressed impulses that cannot help but constitute a continuous internal threat to the security of their gender identities. Although theoretically, women are also subject to this kind of internal threat, the androcentrism in American culture now allows females to so freely express many impulses that are culturally defined as masculine (including, for example, the impulses to political leadership and athletic mastery) that there are probably not nearly so many repressed masculine impulses in the psyches of women as there are repressed feminine impulses in the psyches of men.

But apart from making gender boundary crossing asymmetrical, androcentrism provides a definition of a real man that is so thoroughly intertwined with being powerful and privileged that it inevitably puts all those millions of men without power and privilege at risk for feeling not just insufficiently powerful and privileged but insufficiently masculine as well. The risk of feeling emasculated—or neutered—is especially intense when a man has to acknowledge a woman who is more powerful or privileged (or even competent) than himself.

This widespread risk to the common man's sense of masculinity might threaten the foundation of an androcentric society if not for two countervailing social practices that enable even those millions of men without power and privilege to feel at least marginally like real men: (1) the historical exclusion of women from positions of public power and the development of a religion and a science presupposing men's natural right, as men, to dominate women, which together enable even those men without power and privilege to confirm at least their male *right* to that power and privilege, and (2) the cultural marginalizing of homosexuals, which enables men without power and privilege to confirm their status as real men by defining themselves not only in terms of their natural difference from all women but also in terms of their natural difference from men who are obviously not real men.

None of this is to say that androcentrism provides a definition of a real woman that is easy for all women to attain. In a culture that androcentrically defines women in terms of their domestic and reproductive functions, women who are unable to have children almost inevitably experience a sense that they are not real women. Moreover, the extraordinary cultural emphasis on a real woman's being sexually attractive to men makes a great many women over forty (or maybe even thirty) worry that their status as real women may be gone forever; it also makes women of every age spend an inordinate amount of time, energy, and money in pursuit of beauty.

SELF-CONSTRUCTION

Where androcentric and gender-polarizing social practices so narrowly constrain the roles of women and men that there are few choices, if any, about how to be a woman or a man, the internalized lenses of androcentrism and gender polarization serve exactly the same function in individual gender formation that all internalized cultural lenses serve in creating a cultural native. That is, they make the preprogrammed societal ways of being and behaving seem so normal and natural that alternative ways of being and behaving rarely even come to mind.

A transitional society like the United States, however, makes an almost infinite variety of options available to the individual but then not so subtly communicates that the individual's adequacy as a man or a woman depends on the selection of a limited subset of those options. Here, the internalized lenses of androcentrism and gender polarization so rigorously guide the individual's selection of alternatives that the construction of the self seems to lie as much with the individual as with the culture. This constructed self comprises a gendered personality, a gendered body, an androcentric heterosexuality, and the abhorrence of homosexuality.

The Gendered Personality

I have repeatedly suggested that the social reproduction of male power is aided and abetted by the cultural transformation of male and female into masculine and feminine. In other words, I have argued that the institution of male power depends for its survival on the construction of males and females whose gendered personalities mirror the different and unequal roles assigned to them in the social structure. The assumption here may seem to be that a gendered personality is a static collection of masculine or feminine traits that has already been shaped by enculturation—that it is a finished *product*, so to speak, rather than a psychological *process*. But a gendered personality is both a product and a process. It is both a particular collection of masculine or feminine traits and a way of construing reality that itself constructs those traits.

The collection of masculine or feminine traits that constitute the gendered personality have long been seen as representing two important, if complementary, modes of human functioning. Different theorists have different labels for these modes. According to Talcott Parsons (Parsons & Bales, 1955), masculinity is associated with an "instrumental" orientation, a cognitive focus on getting the job done or the problem solved, whereas femininity is associated with an "expressive" orientation, an affective concern for the welfare of others and the harmony of the group. Similarly, David Bakan (1966) has suggested that masculinity is associated with an "agentic" orientation, a concern for oneself as an individual, whereas femininity is associated with a "communal" orientation, a concern for the relationship between oneself and others. Finally, Erik Erikson's distinction between "inner and outer space" represents an anatomical analogue to a similar psychological distinction between a masculine "fondness for 'what works' and for what man can make, whether it helps to build or to destroy" and a more ethical feminine commitment to "resourcefulness in peacekeeping . . . and devotion to healing" (1968, p. 262).

In the late 1960s and early 1970s, what the many feminist proponents of androgyny were basically arguing was that although instrumental and agentic traits were traditionally reserved for men and expressive and communal traits were traditionally reserved for women, this gender polarization was tragically and unnecessarily limiting human potential, allowing each person only that half of the total personality potential that matched the cultural definitions of gender appropriateness. This limitation might not matter, the argument continued, if all that was at stake was a set of trivial possibilities—like wearing pants or using lipstick—but because everyone was forfeiting a profoundly important way of relating to the world, the limitation was tragic and unnecessary for everyone personally and was, furthermore, worth placing near the center of a feminist revolution.

By the time people reach adulthood, however, it is not just the culture that is limiting them to half their potential. It is also their own readiness to look at themselves through the androcentric and gender-polarizing lenses that they have internalized from the culture and thereby to see every possibility that is consistent with those lenses as normal and natural for the self and every possibility that is inconsistent with those lenses as alien and problematic for the self. In other words, they are limited by their enculturated readiness to constantly ask, "Does this possible way of being or behaving adequately match my culture's conception of a real man or a real woman?" and to answer the question with, "If not, I'll reject it out of hand. If so, I'll consider exploring it further."

To say that the enculturated individual asks this question is not to say, however, that he or she is always—or ever—consciously aware of doing so. More often than not, the culture seems to have tuned the individual's antennae to an androcentric and gender-polarizing station, so they automatically pick up whatever signals that station is sending. Once this tuning is completed, the internalized lenses of androcentrism and gender polarization not only shape how individuals think about the self but also how they feel. Put somewhat differently, the individual's deepest thoughts and feelings about what is alien to the self and what is not alien are shaped by internalized cultural definitions of what a man and a woman ought to be.

The gendered personality, like the gendered culture, thus has a readiness to superimpose a gender-based classification on every hetero-geneous collection of human possibilities that presents itself. The gen-dered personality is more than a particular collection of masculine or feminine traits, then; it is also a way of looking at reality that produces and reproduces those traits during a lifetime of self-construction. This conceptualization of the gendered personality as both process and product is consistent with a longstanding tradition in personality psy-chology that sees each individual as constructing his or her own unique reality by bringing, say, a particular style of social interaction into all situations. It is also consistent with a longstanding tradition in cognitive psychology that sees human perception itself as a constructive process that always involves some degree of selection, organization, and inter-pretation on the part of the perceiver.[16]

In Chapter 4, I introduced my empirical research on gender lenses as part of a conceptual challenge to the theoretical tradition of gender polarization in psychology. But the research also comprises an empiri-cal test of the psychological claim being made here that the gendered personality is both process and product. More specifically, the research tests the theory that conventionally gendered women and men *limit themselves* to only half their potential by nonconsciously imposing a gender-based classification on social reality.

The overall strategy of the research was first to identify people who are conventionally gendered—whose self-described traits on the mas-culinity and femininity scales of the Bem Sex Role Inventory mirror the highly polarized definitions of gender appropriateness in Ameri-can culture—and then to ask whether these prototypes of masculinity and femininity are significantly more likely than anyone else to orga-nize information on the basis of gender. If so, there is reason to believe that the gendered personality is both process and product, as well as reason to believe that the process itself may be partially responsible for the product. (Because these studies predate my theorizing about an-drocentrism, they address only the lens of gender polarization.)

In one of these studies, subjects were shown a list of sixty-one words and then asked to recall as many of those words as they could in whatever order the words happened to come to mind. The list included animals, verbs, articles of clothing, and people's first names in random order. Half of the people's names were male and half were female; one-third of the words within each of the other categories had masculine connotations (*gorilla, hurling, trousers*), one-third had feminine connotations (*butterfly, blushing, bikini*), and one-third had no gender connotations (*ant, stepping, sweater*). Research in cognitive psychology has shown that if an individual has stored a number of words in memory in terms of an underlying schema or network of associations, then thinking of one schema-related word enhances the probability of thinking of another. Accordingly, an individual's sequence of recall will reveal runs or clusters of words that are linked in memory by the schema; after thinking of one animal word, for example, he or she is likely to think next of another animal word. Subjects in this study could cluster words either according to semantic category (animals, verbs, clothing, names) or according to gender.

The results showed that conventionally gendered subjects clustered significantly more words by gender than did other subjects. For example, if a conventionally gendered subject happened to recall a feminine animal like a butterfly, he or she was more likely to follow that with another feminine word, such as *bikini*, whereas subjects who were not conventionally gendered were more likely to follow *butterfly* with the name of another animal. (Conventionally gendered subjects were not more likely than others, however, to cluster according to the semantic categories; everyone did that.) As the theory predicted, then, conventionally gendered individuals were more likely than others to organize information in terms of gender—to view reality through the lens of gender polarization (Bem, 1981b).

In a study by Deborrah Frable and myself (1985), subjects listened to a group discussion and were then asked to recall who said what. Of interest here was how frequently subjects erroneously attributed statements made by male discussants to other males, rather than to females, and statements made by female discussants to other females, rather than to males. Such within-sex errors indicate that the subject is confusing the members of a given sex with one another, that is, that he or she is noting, sorting, and remembering people on the basis of their sex. The results showed that conventionally gendered subjects were especially likely to do this, revealing once again that their perceptual and conceptual worlds are organized around gender. (A control condition showed that conventionally gendered subjects were not more likely than other subjects to make within-*race* errors; in other words, the effect was specific to gender.)

In a third study (Bem, 1981b), the sixty masculine, feminine, and neutral attributes from the BSRI were all projected onto a screen one at a time, and the subject was asked to push one of two buttons, ME or NOT ME, to indicate whether the attribute was or was not self-descriptive. It was found that conventionally gendered subjects responded more *quickly* than others when endorsing gender-appropriate attributes or rejecting gender-inappropriate attributes and more *slowly* than others when endorsing gender-inappropriate attributes or rejecting gender-appropriate attributes. This implies that conventionally gendered individuals have a readiness to decide on the basis of gender which attributes to associate and dissociate with their self-concept. It also suggests that when filling out the BSRI, conventionally gendered individuals sort the attributes into equivalence classes on the basis of gender in order to describe themselves.

The next important question is whether the spontaneous use of this classification limits conventionally gendered women and men to that half of their human potential that matches the definitions of gender appropriateness in the culture. To test this hypothesis, a second series of laboratory studies was conducted in which it was asked whether people who describe themselves as conventionally gendered on the BSRI are also significantly more likely than others to restrict their behavior in accordance with cultural definitions of gender appropriateness.

The first study in this series (Bem & Lenney, 1976) demonstrated that conventionally gendered people are more likely than other people to avoid even trivial everyday activities like oiling a squeaky hinge or ironing a cloth napkin if those activities are culturally defined as not appropriate for their sex; furthermore, if conventionally gendered people find themselves in a situation where they must perform such activities, they are more likely than others to report having negative feelings about themselves.

The other studies in the series (Bem, 1975; Bem, Martyna & Watson, 1976) confirmed that this pattern of cross-gender avoidance extends beyond the trivial activities of everyday life to the more profound activities included within the instrumental (or agentic) domain and within the expressive (or communal) domain. Thus, only androgynous women and men managed *both* to stand firm in their opinions when faced with a group unanimously giving an opposing opinion *and* to behave nurturantly toward a baby and a lonely peer. In contrast, conventionally gendered women and men managed to do well only at whichever of these behaviors the culture defines as appropriate for their sex. In other words, conventionally masculine men were independent but not nurturant, and conventionally feminine women were nurturant but not independent.[17]

The conventionally gendered women and men in this program of research represent in purer form all who are enculturated in American society. As such, they serve as a window into the consciousness of the culture as a whole. That cultural consciousness, in turn, includes not just gender polarization but also androcentrism. In real life, it is thus the lenses of androcentrism and gender polarization that together shape perceptions of what feels natural for the self, for other people, and for the social arrangements within the culture.

As an example of how an individual's androcentric and gender-polarizing lenses can shape the perception of other people, consider one of my favorite studies in social psychology. Subjects looking at a photograph of male and female graduate students seated around the two sides and head of a rectangular table rated the group members on leadership and dominance. Consistent with the basic premise that androcentric and gender-polarizing lenses make it seem more normal and natural for a male, not a female, to be in a position of power, it was found that subjects seeing a male seated at the head of the table considered him the leader of the group, but the same benefit of position was not extended to a female seated at the head of the table—she was not perceived as a leader.[18]

As an example of how androcentric and gender-polarizing lenses can together shape the perception of the social arrangements in the culture as a whole, consider the prototypical American view of whether there are now far too many men or just about the right percentage of men in positions of power and influence in American society. Although the gender lenses were able at one time in U.S. history to make even the total legal exclusion of women from such positions hardly worthy of comment, today the lenses not only make the presence of but one woman out of nine on the Supreme Court and one woman out of fifteen in the House and one out of fifty in the Senate seem like a reasonable ratio; they also make the prototypical American blind to the fact that the culture is miscontruing the continued male domination of its social institutions as at least a first approximation of sexual equality. The androcentric and gender-polarizing lenses would not allow the analogous mistake if females dominated those institutions instead of males.

Finally, as an example of how androcentric and gender-polarizing lenses can together shape the perception of what feels natural for the self, consider the observation made plausible by many studies that males and females alike see other males and females, as well as themselves, as subject to one standard of judgment if female and another standard of judgment if male. More specifically, whereas males see themselves and other males as both competent and deserving until proven otherwise (at least if they are white), the burden of proof is on each individual female to demonstrate to herself and to others why she in particular should be seen as either competent or deserving. This burden-of-proof difference is precisely what that social-psychological study showed when it found males—but not females—more likely to be selected as the group leader when they just happened to be seated at the head of the table. This burden-of-proof difference is also what many other empirical studies showed when they found that women underestimate, and men overestimate, the quality of their own performance and, furthermore, that women underreward themselves, and men overreward themselves, for whatever their level of performance actually is.[19]

This androcentric and gender-polarizing way of looking at the self predisposes females to reject any way of being or behaving that treats females as people whose needs, desires, abilities, and interests are to be taken seriously. This includes such things as requesting a merit raise from an employer, submitting an article for publication, competing head on head, or, for that matter, taking one's talents and interests seriously enough in the first place to embark on an important personal project. It also predisposes females to elaborate ways of being and behaving that subordinate their own needs, desires, abilities, and interests to those of the men and the children in their lives.

In addition to putting females at risk for giving themselves too little priority in relationships with others, this androcentric and gender-polarizing way of looking at the self also puts males at risk for giving themselves too much priority in relationships with others. Specifically, it predisposes males to reject any ways of being and behaving that put them in a subordinate position—a predisposition that is exaggerated whenever the more dominant position is to be held by a woman. It also predisposes males to elaborate any ways of being or behaving that put them in a more dominant or powerful position.

With this whole discussion of androcentric and gender-polarizing lenses as a conceptual backdrop, it is clear that women are culturally predisposed to give themselves much less priority than they rightfully deserve while men are culturally predisposed to give themselves much more priority than they rightfully deserve. It is also clear that on psychological grounds alone, the heterosexual marriage is a perfect breeding ground for inequality because it brings a male assumer of privilege together with a female denier of privilege.

But as powerful as the internalized gender lenses are, and as critical as they are to the self-construction of gendered personalities, it would be wrong to suppose that men's and women's different and un-equal ways of being and behaving are created only by acts of self-perception and self-construction. Their ways of being and behaving are simultaneously constructed by the androcentric and gender-polarizing social practices of the culture, which continue to situate males and females in different and unequal positions in the social structure throughout their life cycle. There is thus never just a psycho-logical force responsible for the construction of real men and real women; there is always a structural or situational force operating in the same direction.

The Gendered Body

The gendered personality does not exist as pure or disembodied spirit. It is physically embedded in a biological structure, the human body, which is as subject to the processes of androcentric and gender-polariz-ing self-perception and self-construction as the human personality it-self. The construction of the gendered body demonstrates nearly as well as the construction of the gendered personality just how deeply the androcentric and gender-polarizing lenses can shape people's feel-ings about what is alien to the self and what is not. By the body itself, I mean not just how people look, with and without their clothes on, but also how they function physiologically, how they move around in space, and even how they experience and express their sexual desires.

Consider first people's feelings about how their bodies are sup-posed to look, even when naked and standing still. Looking through the lens of gender polarization makes people uncomfortable about virtually every feature of their bodies that spontaneously appears more frequently in the other sex. Women with visible hair on their legs and faces and short men with little upper-body muscle development find these features so alien to their sense of self—that is, they feel so much as if these features don't rightfully belong on their particular bodies— that the women use razors, depilatories, and bleaches, and the men use body-building equipment, shoe lifts, and hormone injections to try to manipulate their bodies into conformity with their gender-polarizing vision of who they really are.

This widespread desire to improve on the biological sexual differ- ence by making bodies even more male or female in appearance than nature did attests to just how much of an impact the gender-polarizing lenses can have on the way people perceive and construct their selves; it also suggests that what "normal" gender-polarizers feel about their bodies may be different only in degree (and direction) from what trans- sexuals feel about their bodies.

People's feelings about their bodies are never shaped solely by the lens of gender polarization, however. The lenses of androcentrism and gender polarization are always inextricably linked together, which is why males in American society are predisposed to value and affirm the body, whereas females are predisposed to feel ambivalent about—and hence to deny—the body. This asymmetry between the sexes derives from androcentric beliefs: although these beliefs perfectly comple- ment gender polarization in the context of males, they so conflict with gender polarization *and* biology in the context of females that virtually no realizable female embodiment is fully able to satisfy the require- ments of both lenses.

With males, the androcentric predisposition to privilege whatever is male and to otherize whatever is female so beautifully harmonizes with the gender-polarizing predisposition to accentuate the natural sexual difference that the male's motivation to affirm and enhance the maleness of his body can only be increased. With females, the interac- tion of the two lenses has a more paralyzing effect. On the one hand, the lens of gender polarization impels females to accentuate their natu- ral sexual difference so they won't look at all like men. On the other hand, the lens of androcentrism impels them to minimize their natural sexual difference so they won't look very much like women, either.

This androcentric minimizing of the female body has been a part of American culture since at least the 1920s, when women seeking to broaden the boundaries of the female world strapped down their breasts and wore long-waisted dresses to reduce the visibility of their body contours. Although this minimizing of the female body was briefly put aside during the post–World War II era of Marilyn Monroe, motherhood, and the feminine mystique, it returned in full force in the 1970s and 1980s, when the ideal dressed-for-success woman not only wore a man-tailored business suit to work but, underneath that business suit, had so little body fat that few female contours needed to be hidden.

In 1899, Thorstein Veblen speculated in *The Theory of the Leisure Class* that among wealthy people, female beauty is equated with "delicate and diminutive hands and feet and a slender waist" (p. 148) because such features conspicuously display a husband's ability to support a wife who is completely unfit for productive labor. In other words, both "the constricted waist" of Western culture and "the deformed foot" of the Chinese are "mutilations" of the female body that have come to be seen as physically attractive because they visibly demonstrate a husband's "pecuniary reputability" (p. 149).

One aspect of Veblen's analysis is particularly relevant to the question of why female beauty in middle-class America today is so strongly associated with thinness. Just as the corseted waist and the bound foot squeezed women's bodies down to a biologically pathological size, the current ideal of female thinness violates the female body's natural biological tendency to put on adipose tissue—or fat—at every single developmental milestone from puberty to pregnancy to menopause. Besides being inconsistent with the gender-polarizing message that women should not look at all like men, the androcentric equating of female beauty with female thinness is thus also inconsistent with female biology.[20]

Between 1966 and 1970, over 7,500 male and female adolescents were asked in a national survey whether they would rather be heavier, thinner, or about the same (Dornbusch et al., 1984). Consistent with my claim that the lenses of androcentrism and gender polarization predispose males to affirm their bodies and, at the same time, leave females with no biologically realizable embodiment that can satisfy their conflicted vision of what a woman ought to look like, the adolescent boys in this study either became increasingly satisfied with their bodies during the course of their normal sexual development or they stayed the same, whereas the adolescent girls became increasingly dissatisfied with their bodies. Among adolescents at the highest level of sexual maturity, there was thus a vast gender difference, with over 80 percent of the males expressing happiness with their bodies and over 60 percent of the females expressing unhappiness.

The androcentric lens not only makes women ambivalent about the femaleness of their bodies; by thoroughly associating an autonomous self with males, it also creates ambivalence in women about having an autonomous body at all. Even a female body takes up a certain amount of space in the physical world, space that might be seen as rightfully belonging to males and males alone, and it also has the kinds of autonomously motivated needs and urges that only the males in an androcentric world are supposed to have. Accordingly, females are predisposed to position their bodies in ways that take minimal space and to move their bodies in ways that are unintimidating, vulnerable, and accommodating to men rather than in ways that are strong, confident, and interpersonally dominating.[21] Females are also predisposed to feel uncomfortable with almost any overt expression of a physiological need or function. To a woman who is androcentric and gender polarizing, everything from having sexual urges to burping and farting to eating a lot can thus feel as ego-alien as having visible body hair.

This female denial of bodily appetites has taken different forms in different historical periods. In the nineteenth century, for example, it appeared primarily as the suppression of female sexual desire. Today, in contrast, it appears primarily as the suppression of the desire for food—which, in extreme form, becomes anorexia nervosa.[22]

This shift in the form of female self-denial from sex to food should not be seen as implying, however, that sexuality is no longer a critically important context for the self-perception and self-construction of maleness and femaleness. Human sexuality continues to have the particular form that it has in U.S. culture in part because the lenses of androcentrism and gender polarization continue to make whatever is consistent with them seem normal and natural and whatever is inconsistent with them seem alien and problematic. Although this power to shape what feels alien to the self and what feels natural has many consequences in the domain of sexuality, I want to discuss two consequences in some detail: the construction of an androcentric heterosexuality, or the eroticizing of female inequality, and the abhorrence of homosexuality.

Androcentric Heterosexuality

In recent years, an increasing number of Americans have finally begun to acknowledge the epidemic of male violence against women, which feminists have been insistently calling to everyone's attention ever since Susan Brownmiller published *Against Our Will* in 1975. Although the conventional wisdom conceptualizes such violence as the pathological product of a criminal or demented mind, what follows logically from both feminist analysis in general and the cultural analysis in this book in particular is that all forms of female brutalization—including rape and wife beating—are but an exaggeration of the male dominance and the female objectification that have come to seem normal and natural in the context of everyday heterosexuality. Put somewhat differently, the everyday way of experiencing heterosexual desire is itself so shaped by the androcentric and gender-polarizing conception of male dominance as normal and natural, and anything other than male dominance as alien and problematic, that the sexual brutalization of a woman by a man is not just an isolated act, a case of an individual man taking out his psychological problems on an individual woman. It is rather the inevitable cultural by-product of an androcentric heterosexuality that eroticizes sexual inequality.

This eroticizing of sexual inequality can be seen in what most Americans think of as perfectly normal and natural heterosexuality. First, although neither women nor men in American society tend to like heterosexual relationships in which the woman is bigger, taller, stronger, older, smarter, higher in status, more experienced, more educated, more talented, more confident, or more highly paid than the man, they do tend to like heterosexual relationships in which the man is bigger, taller, stronger, and so forth, than the woman.

Second, both women and men see it as normal and natural for the male to play a more dominant or assertive role in a heterosexual encounter and for the female to play a more yielding or accommodating role. They also see it as emasculating for the man and defeminizing for the woman if those assertive and yielding roles are reversed on a regular basis. In normal, everyday heterosexual eroticism, the male is thus supposed to be superior in a wide variety of personal characteristics related to status and to play the dominant role in virtually every aspect of the heterosexual encounter from initiating the date to arranging and paying for the entertainment to guiding the sexual activity.

Finally, both women and men see the female in general and the female body in particular as more the object of male sexual desire than as a desiring sexual subject (or agent). This objectification, which manifests itself in the extraordinary emphasis on a woman's physical attractiveness in American culture, as well as in the almost continuous display of the nude or seminude female body in art, advertising, and the mass media, constitutes an eroticizing of sexual inequality—as opposed to merely a celebrating of female sexuality—because it implicitly imposes a male perspective on the definition of female sexuality. It androcentrically defines women—and predisposes women to define themselves—not in terms of their own sexual desires but in terms of their ability to stimulate and satisfy the male's sexual desires.

It is no accident that American culture has no comparable tradition of displaying the nude or seminude male body. The culture has so completely constructed females and nudes as the objects of male sexual desire that when Americans see a display of a nude or a seminude male body, they instantly assume that it is not a heterosexual woman's object of desire but a gay man's object of desire. This perception, in turn, so arouses their abhorrence of homosexuality that they end up judging the display of the nude male body itself as inherently pornographic.

Given how thoroughly embedded male dominance and female objectification are in even these three "normal" and taken-for-granted aspects of heterosexual desire, it follows that date rape would be a frequent occurrence. After all, when looking through androcentric and gender-polarizing lenses, the man finds it normal and natural to keep pushing for sex even when the woman is resisting a bit, and the woman finds it alien and problematic to assert herself so forcefully and unmistakably that the man will have no choice but to stop what he's doing or use force. Now, however, the norm is so much for men to keep making sexual advances and for women to keep resisting those advances without making a scene or even being impolite that many date rapists do not perceive the sexual intercourse they manage to get as an act of rape.[23]

And if the frequency of date rape is not surprising, given the gender lenses that men and women wear, nor should it be surprising that so many men in American society find violence against women to be so sexually arousing, so affirming of their masculinity, or both, that they brutalize women directly or participate in such brutalization vicariously through violent pornography.

The Abhorrence of Homosexuality

Two interconnected phenomena need to be analyzed next: why Americans in general are predisposed to find homosexual impulses abhorrent and why this abhorrence of homosexuality—which is usually called homophobia—seems to involve males even more than females.[24] The pieces of my own analysis of these phenomena are scattered through this chapter and the previous one, on gender polarization, so let me pull together all of the pieces that have to do with an individual's looking through androcentric and gender-polarizing lenses.

For most of the twentieth century, in psychiatry and the culture at large, homosexuality and heterosexuality have been defined as mutually exclusive sexual orientations; heterosexuality has also been defined as the sine qua non of psychological normality, and homosexuality, as proof positive of psychopathology. Prior to the twentieth century, in contrast, homosexuality was conceptualized more as a non-procreative sexual act than as a permanent condition of a person. This didn't mean that the procreation-centered society embraced it as good, but neither was it seen as nearly so central to the self-definition of a male or a female.

Now that homosexuality is considered central to self-identity, however, the gender-polarizing individual is predisposed to see all conformity to the culture's gender scripts as normal and natural and all deviations from the culture's gender scripts as alien and problematic. The gender-polarizing individual is also predisposed to see homosexual deviations as especially problematic, whether in the self or others. This concern about homosexuality is exacerbated by the gender-polarizing concept of a real man or woman, as opposed to a biological man or woman, because that concept makes males and females alike feel tenuous and insecure about their identity as males and females.

These several facets of gender polarization interact in the psyche of the individual to make homosexuality the quintessential threat to one's status as a man or a woman. More specifically, the gender-polarizing concepts of a real man and a real woman interact with the gender-polarizing vision of homosexuality as a permanent pathology to make even a single homosexual impulse an irreversible threat to normality. No wonder that gender-polarizing males and females are predisposed to repress whatever homosexual impulses they feel and to find abhorrently unnatural whatever homosexual impulses they perceive in others.

This abhorrence of homosexuality implicates males even more than females. Female sexuality in an androcentric society is so defined from a male perspective that the lesbian herself is all but rendered invisible. In addition, the cultural definition of a real man makes males feel much more insecure about the adequacy of their gender than females, for the definition unrealistically requires them not only to suppress every human impulse with even the slightest hint of femininity but also to attain the kind of power and privilege in their social community that will produce respectful deference in women and less powerful men.

This higher level of gender insecurity among males makes the affirmation of maleness much more emotionally charged for men than the affirmation of femaleness is for women; it also predisposes men to engage in two destructive forms of masculinity building that are directly related to homosexuality. First, it predisposes them to suppress virtually all cross-gender impulses, including the desire for physical intimacy with their fathers or their sons. The only exception to this taboo occurs in contexts that are clearly defined by the culture, whether appropriately or inappropriately, as unquestionably masculine, the football field being a prime example. Second, gender insecurity predisposes men to define themselves in terms of their "natural" difference from both women and homosexual men. In some cases, this *psychological* otherizing of the feminine is sufficient to assuage the male's insecurity about being adequately masculine; in more extreme cases, however, more destructive forms of defensive masculinity building are required, including, for example, the dominance of women and the bashing of gay men.

For American men in general, the abhorrence of homosexuality in both themselves and other males is thus produced by their gender-polarizing vision of heterosexuality as normal and homosexuality as pathological, as well as by a defensive need to use their own constructed difference from homosexual men to shore up their own very vulnerable sense of being adequately masculine. None of this is to say, however, that the abhorrence of homosexuality is best conceptualized as a psychological problem, rather than as a cultural one. On the contrary. Even the perpetrators of anti-homosexual hate violence take out their aggressions and their frustrations on gay males and lesbians in particular because these groups have been institutionally otherized in U.S. culture in much the same way that Jews were institutionally otherized in Nazi Germany.

THE MAKING OF A GENDER NONCONFORMIST

Let us turn from the identity construction of gender conformists to the identity construction of gender nonconformists. Included in this category are all of the people whose lives seriously violate the androcentric, gender-polarizing, and biologically essentialist definition of a real man or a real woman—all of the people, in other words, who would have been thought of as sexually inverted in the late nineteenth and early twentieth centuries: gay men, lesbians, bisexuals, transsexuals, transvestites, and "gender-disordered" children, who continued to be pathologized even after the concept of sexual inversion had gone out of fashion. Also included in the category are feminists, both male and female, who actively oppose the gender scripts of the culture, and even the relatively traditional women and men who become gender nonconformists merely by reversing some critical aspect of the male or female script—by choosing, if they are women, to sacrifice marriage and children for an ambitious full-time career, and by choosing, if they are men, to do the reverse.

Although these many different kinds of gender nonconformists may not seem to belong in the same overarching category, they share two related attributes that are more important to this discussion than any of the differences among them. By virtue of their existence, all of these gender nonconformists challenge the presumed naturalness of the link between the sex of the body and the gender of the psyche. And because they fail to follow the gender scripts of the culture, they must find a way to construct a viable identity in a society that insistently denies them any legitimacy.

Since the end of the nineteenth century, most discussions about the pathologized group of gender nonconformists have focused on the twin questions of cause and cure. The underlying assumption has always been the same: something has misfired in the biology or the experience of these individuals and needs to be fixed.

In addition to pathologizing the gender nonconformists, the question, What went wrong? contains an even deeper assumption: that homogeneity within each sex is natural and diversity is unnatural. This deeper assumption is apparent even in discussions that do not explicitly pathologize the gender nonconformist but merely assume that the psychic outcome of the nonmasculine male, the nonfeminine female, and the nonheterosexual male or female requires causal explanation. Again it is assumed that something is natural about all of the "matches" between the sex of the body and the gender of the psyche and unnatural about all of the "mismatches."

As I see it, however, there are too many "mismatches" in too many times and places for them to be other than completely natural. What these so-called mismatches show is that the nature of human gender and sexuality is not predetermined in the individual or the culture by either nature or nurture; rather, at both the individual and the cultural levels, they are the outcome of an interaction between biology and history. And because of that interaction, the potential for diversity is enormous, across different cultures and across different males and females within the same culture.[25]

The best analogy here is with food preferences. Human beings are born with a general desire to eat and a general capacity to desire whatever specific foods are defined as edible in a particular time and place. At the cultural level, this openness to experience interacts with differences in the availability of different foods and with a whole variety of other historical factors to produce the enormous diversity of food preferences that exists from culture to culture. At the individual level, this same openness interacts with individual differences in personal experience and with any individual differences that may exist in the biology of taste to produce the enormous diversity of food preferences that also exists from person to person within the same culture.

This biohistorical model of human food preferences has many implications for the domain of gender and sexuality. Most critical here, however, is that it reverses the usual assumption about what kind of relation to expect between the sex of the body and the gender of the psyche. Specifically, it suggests not gender polarization between males and females but richness and diversity across different cultures, as well as among males and females within the same culture.

With this one critical assumption reversed, the psychological question that the gender nonconformists in American society bring to mind is no longer, What went wrong? or even, Why do they exist? Nothing went wrong, and they exist, in one form or another, because gender diversity is natural. Rather, the psychological questions that gender nonconformists bring to mind are these: First, if gender diversity is the human norm, then why are so many people in U.S. society so committed to constructing selves that are not only exclusively heterosexual but also masculine (if they are male) or feminine (if they are female)? And second, how do gender nonconformists manage to construct viable identities in a society that so insistently denies them even the claim to psychological normality?

The first question was addressed earlier in this chapter. To address the second, it will be helpful to consider the historical development of gay male and lesbian identity during the course of the twentieth century. I focus on this group in particular because their more recent experience of living in a homophobic and heterosexist world—like the historical experience of Jews living in an anti-Semitic world—highlights the need of every otherized group to look *at* the lenses of the dominant culture rather than *through* them and thereby to develop an oppositional consciousness. Put somewhat differently, their experience highlights the need of every otherized group to articulate a perspective that challenges the meaning assigned to them by the dominant culture and, further, challenges the very neutrality of the dominant perspective.

In contrast to the Jews, however, who long ago articulated a history of themselves and a set of traditions that they can still use today to buffer their children against the anti-Semitic lenses of the dominant culture, lesbians and gay men have generally been forced to develop their sense of being different with no such psychological protection against the cultural stigmatization of homosexuality. Perhaps nothing can be done about the childhood isolation of lesbians and gay men, who almost inevitably grow up in a family that does not share their status as members of a stigmatized minority group. But something can be done, and is being done, to provide the coming generations of lesbians and gay men with an articulated tradition affirming the value of their difference from the dominant group.[26]

Prior to World War II, even the large urban areas in the United States did not yet have stable and easily accessible homosexual communities; hence most gay men and lesbians discovered their own homosexual desires in isolation from others like themselves. Although their own particular interaction of biology and personal experience had obviously not been sufficient to give them gender-conforming psyches, their internalization of the gender lenses was almost certainly sufficient to make their emerging gender nonconformity seem pathological to themselves.

That self-perception was exacerbated if they went to their local library or their local therapist for further information or help. At the library, they would find novels like *The Well of Loneliness* (1928) by Radclyffe Hall, which represented the lesbian as a poor "freak of a creature . . . hideously maimed and ugly . . . flawed in the making" by "God's cruel[ty]" (quoted in Faderman, 1981, p. 321)—and hence more to be pitied than scorned. At the therapist's, they would find all manner of therapeutic techniques to rid them of their homosexual desires, including psychoanalysis, hypnosis, "adjustment therapy," hormone medication, pharmacologic shock, electroshock, aversion therapy, castration, hysterectomy, and even lobotomy.[27]

In this socially isolating and pathologizing context, virtually every gay man and lesbian in the United States had to cope alone with the formidable problem of constructing a viable identity in a hostile culture; they had to invent themselves from scratch, unaided, and without either social or ideological support for their gender nonconformity. Although some surely managed to build satisfying identities and satisfying lives despite their situation—by putting their homosexuality aside, for example, and organizing their lives around some other aspect of the self—and although a few lesbians in particular may even have managed to find (or construct) supportive communities of unmarried professional women in which to explore their many differences from the dominant culture, for most gay men and lesbians of the time, both their own isolation and the pathologizing of homosexuality by the larger community placed them at serious risk for defining the self, rather than defining the culture, as inherently pathological. In the worst cases, this self-definition led to suicide; in many cases, it led to futile attempts to try and change the self through some kind of medical or psychological therapy.

The risks associated with constructing an identity in the absence of social and ideological support are brought into sharp relief not only by the pre–World War II experiences of lesbians and gay men but also by the experiences of those defined today as transsexuals. Looking through the lenses of the dominant culture, these gender-nonconforming women and men are made so unhappy by the mismatch between the sex of their body and the gender of their psyche that they manage to convince themselves that they are perfectly "normal" males and females who just happen to be trapped in the body of the other sex, and then they seek to change their physical sex through a series of mutilating surgical procedures.

Although this belief may seem incomprehensible in a modern scientific community, my hypothesis is that it is partly an exceedingly rare extension into adulthood of the erroneous—and nonbiological—lesson that almost all American parents teach their young children about what male and female are. The reason transsexuals alone hold on to this nonbiological lesson is that it provides them with a viable way to construct an identity that is consistent with the cultural definition of male and female.

For whatever reason, the transsexual starts life with extremely gender-nonconforming preferences in activities, playmates, clothing, and the like. After learning erroneously—like almost every other child—that the sexes are defined by these cultural gender markers, he or she attaches the "wrong" sex label to the self, then carries that label into adulthood because, ironically, it provides the transsexual with a viable identity as a "real" woman or man.

The social isolation of the gay men and the lesbians in American society came to an end during World War II, when massive numbers of young people left their homes and began to live together in sex-segregated contexts in the armed services or in urban boardinghouses, where they stayed while earning money away from their families. Once in contact with one another, gay men and lesbians began to build the kinds of social institutions for themselves (bars, newspapers, softball teams, churches, fashions) that would create a rich social life separate from the dominant culture. In so doing, they transformed themselves from a collection of separate lesbian and gay male individuals into a dynamic and interconnected lesbian and gay male subculture, or community.

Although this community did not immediately do a great deal to challenge the pathologizing of homosexuality by the dominant culture, and although that pathologizing continued to take its toll on the community as a whole, as well as on the individuals within the community, still, these gender nonconformists no longer had to cope with their difference from the dominant culture in total isolation. They now had a kind of "home" or "family" where they could be with others like themselves and where they could develop a psychological identity as a member of a deviant sexual group, rather than as an isolated—and pathological—individual.

That identification with a deviant sexual group took on a new meaning in the 1970s and 1980s, when the homosexual subculture was catapulted into a gay rights movement, which increasingly provided its constituents not just with social support for their gender nonconformity but with political and ideological support as well. Although a multitude of historical factors were responsible for this transformation—among them, the earlier formation of the black power movement, the women's liberation movement, and the Vietnam War protest movement—the one historical moment most often celebrated as the birth of the gay rights movement occurred on Friday, June 27, 1969, when a police raid on a gay bar in Greenwich Village sparked the several days of rioting that came to represent the beginning of gay political resistance to the heterosexism of the dominant culture.

The name of the gay bar was the Stonewall Inn. And in the post-Stonewall period, lesbians and gay men have increasingly been able to create exactly the kind of oppositional consciousness that an otherized group needs if it is ever to construct a viable identity. Specifically, lesbians and gay men have increasingly constructed *politicized* sexual identities that not only challenge the meaning assigned to lesbians and gay men by the dominant culture but also challenge the very neutrality of the dominant cultural perspective. These two aspects of the gay male and lesbian challenge correspond, as I see it, to two more-or-less chronological developments within the gay rights movement itself, the first emphasizing gay pride and the second emphasizing the gay perspective. (Like the generic use of the word *man* to encompass both women and men, the generic use of the word *gay* to encompass lesbians and bisexuals as well as gay men is androcentric. Hence I avoid it as much as possible and use it only when I can find no satisfactory alternative. The term *queer,* which some activists have recently suggested for this purpose, is not widely accepted, nor would it be appropriate for historical phrases that use the word *gay*—like *gay rights* and *gay pride.*)

Although the gay rights movement has always included strong resistance to institutional policies that discriminate against gay men and lesbians, that resistance was at first most strongly associated with the concept of gay pride. This was a period when, besides fighting for their civil rights as members of an oppressed minority group, gay men and lesbians were also challenging the stigma of pathology that for so long had prevented them from developing a positive sense of self. They thus emphasized coming out of the closet and celebrating their identity as gay men and lesbians. Within the lesbian-feminist community in particular, this celebration of identity was enhanced by the claim that only lesbian feminists were committed enough to the cause of women's liberation to devote 100 percent of their energies to women; heterosexual feminists, in contrast, were said to divide their energies between women and men.

Although significant political conflicts within the gay rights movement sometimes split the interests of gay men from the interests of lesbians and the interests of gay men and lesbians from the interests of bisexuals, those conflicts have so receded in the years since the conservatism of the Reagan administration, AIDS, and the associated upswing in the level of anti-gay violence in the United States that by the early 1990s, the identity and the unity of these several groups were once again being celebrated and affirmed. Several new umbrella groups and organizations were formed, as well as the new academic field of lesbian, gay, and bisexual studies. Scholars in this field seek to uncover the hidden history of those it defines as part of the lesbian, gay male, and bisexual past, to analyze the construction of *all* forms of human sexuality, including the traditionally unanalyzed form of exclusive heterosexuality, and to expose the cultural requirement of exclusive heterosexuality as—not a primordially natural form of human sexuality—but the ideological and institutional construction that it really is. Central to the existence of this new field is the presupposition that by virtue of having been marginalized for so long by the dominant culture, sexual minorities have a special perspective that enables them to look *at* the lenses of the dominant culture rather than *through* them.[28]

The emerging field of lesbian, gay male, and bisexual studies is but one example, however, of a gay-affirmative challenge to the dominant culture that has been growing for the past twenty years and that now encompasses essays, novels, poetry, music, art, and so forth. What the development of this gay-affirmative cultural tradition means for the development of individual identity is that coming generations of lesbian, gay male, and bisexual people no longer need to construct their own identities either from scratch or in the context of a heterosexist conceptual framework. True, most lesbians, gay men, and bisexuals will still grow up in families that communicate homophobic and heterosexist metamessages from the moment of birth, but as soon as the individual becomes motivated to seek out information about alternative genders and sexualities, a rich and self-affirming tradition will be immediately available. Someday it may even rival the tradition available to the Jewish child growing up in an anti-Semitic culture.

In the years since the American Psychiatric Association removed homosexuality from its official listing of mental disorders, many psychologists writing about homosexuality have argued that gay male and lesbian identity formation, or coming out, necessarily takes the individual through a predictable series of successive stages.[29] Although the earlier stages in these theories frequently involve anger at the dominant culture for its oppression of sexual minorities and immersion in the politics and the culture of the gay community, the final stage—and hence a mature sexual identity—has the individual putting this *obsession* with sexual identity aside and coming to see that being heterosexual, homosexual, or bisexual is but one aspect of a person's total identity.

Perhaps that would be a reasonable goal in a social world that did not privilege exclusive heterosexuality—although in such a world, there would be nothing to be angry about even in the earlier stages, so the theory would decompose. In the current social world, however, the dominant culture never stops otherizing—or assaulting—those who are gay with anti-gay social policies and social practices.

In this lifelong context of intolerance by the social institutions of the dominant culture, the individual lesbian, gay male, or bisexual person has just two self-affirming alternatives. And to link either of them with the dimension of psychological maturity is to make the mistake of theorizing in a cultural and political vacuum. A person can make opposition to the dominant culture the center of his or her sexual identity, or, on the other hand, construct a personal world that supports his or her sexual identity. Although the stage theories of identity formation favor the latter over the former, at least some gay men and lesbians had to make opposition to the dominant culture the center of their sexual identities or homosexuality would probably still be included in the American Psychiatric Association's official listing of mental disorders. Not only that, but there would not now be emerging exactly the kind of conceptual challenge to the heterosexist orthodoxy and exactly the kind of explosion in gay-affirmative scholarship and creative expression that will someday make it possible for lesbian, gay male, and bisexual adolescents to build their self-affirming identities on the foundations laid by the giants who preceded them.

In the past several years, the politicizing of identity has been both personally empowering and politically effective not just for lesbians, gay males, and bisexuals but for other subordinated groups as well, including African Americans, Hispanics, women, and even physically disabled people. Yet the politics of identity may contain as much inner tension as the earlier politics of psychological androgyny did.

With androgyny, the inner tension derived from the conflict between the moral of androgyny—which was that behavior should have no gender, that is, that masculinity and femininity are cultural constructions that should be abolished—and the concept of androgyny, which nevertheless treated masculinity and femininity as if they had an independent and palpable reality. By the same token, the inner tension in identity politics derives from the conflict between the moral, which is that the identity categories of the dominant culture are ideological and institutional constructions, and the strategy itself, which nevertheless treats those categories of identity as if they had an essential reality.[30]

The fact is, however, that although the concepts of heterosexuality, homosexuality, and bisexuality may be historically and culturally created *fictions,* like the concepts of masculinity and femininity and the concepts of black, Hispanic, Asian, Native American, and white, they are fictions that come to have psychological reality if they are institutionalized by the dominant culture. Accordingly, they can have extraordinary political power both for cultural oppression and for the resistance to cultural oppression.

6

TRANSFORMING THE DEBATE ON SEXUAL INEQUALITY

Since the second half of the nineteenth century, the question of biological sex difference has been the focal point of virtually all American discussions of sexual inequality. It was at issue when the first American feminists were fighting to get women the most basic rights of citizenship and again when the second major wave of feminists swept onto the scene—and has been part of the discussion ever since. The interest in sexual difference is now so integrated into American culture that it is evident in almost any collection of magazines at the local supermarket. Modern science and modern feminism both feed this popular interest—science because of its emphasis on sociobiology and prenatal hormones, and feminism because of its celebration of the distinctively female vision of an interconnected world.

Implicit in this focus on sexual difference is the assumption that how the sexes *really* differ is a question of scientific and political urgency. At the end of Chapter 2, I argued, in contrast, that the question is scientifically misguided. In this chapter, I carry that argument a step further, suggesting that the focus on sexual difference is politically misguided as well. Specifically, I argue that if people in this androcentric, gender-polarizing, and biologically essentialist culture are ever to understand why sexual equality would necessarily require a radical restructuring of social institutions, the cultural debate about sexual inequality must be reframed so that it addresses not male-female difference but how androcentric social institutions transform male-female difference into female disadvantage.

Three assumptions from the theoretical analysis of this book lead directly to this transformation in the cultural debate. First, the existence of at least a subset of sexual differences, like women's capacity for childbearing, is taken as axiomatic. Second, the question of sexual difference is seen as much less central to the matter of female inequality than the question of how the social context interacts with whatever sexual differences may exist. Finally, the social context is itself seen as having two separable—if related—aspects: androcentrism, which every feminist must be committed to eradicating, and gender polarization, whose eradication is more controversial.

THE CONUNDRUM OF DIFFERENCE

Stated in its most dichotomous form, the question that has plagued the debate on female inequality for 150 years is whether women and men are fundamentally the same or fundamentally different. This recurring question of sexual difference has prevented even feminists from achieving consensus on social policy because besides being inherently irresolvable itself, it has generated yet another set of apparently irresolvable dichotomies. These second-order dichotomies are revealed in answers to the following three questions: (1) What is the cause of female inequality? (2) What is the best strategy for ending female inequality? and (3) What is the meaning, or definition, of female equality?

In the current cultural debate, female inequality is typically attributed to one or the other of two causal factors, which need not be treated as mutually exclusive but usually are. Either women are being denied access to economic and political resources by policies and practices that intentionally discriminate against even those women whose situation is most similar to men's, in which case the consensus is that the government must step in to remedy the situation; or, alternatively, women's biological, psychological, and historical differences from men—especially their psychological conflict between career and family—lead them to make choices that are inconsistent with building the kind of career that would enable them to attain those economic and political resources, in which case there is no one to blame for female inequality and hence no consensus about any need for remediation.[1]

Surprising as it may seem at first glance, recent economic studies have demonstrated that women as a group are as economically disadvantaged in U.S. society today as they were in 1960, with only the subgroup of young, white, unmarried, and well-educated women showing any substantial economic progress and with everyone else so segregated into the lowest-paid occupations and part-time work that overall, women as a group still earn a mere 65 percent or so of what men earn.[2] Although this persistent female inequality after thirty years of antidiscrimination law is frequently taken as evidence that discrimination against women is not nearly so important a cause of female inequality as female choice, I think this persistent female inequality is instead a testimony to the inadequacy of the understanding of how discrimination against women actually works.

Ever since the Supreme Court ruled in *Muller v. Oregon* (1908) that protective legislation could be used to compensate women for their "disadvantage in the struggle for subsistence," two opposing strategies for ending female inequality have been at the center of the debate on gender policy. Gender neutrality, also known as gender blindness, mandates that no distinctions of any sort ever be made on the basis of sex; and special protection for women, also known as sensitivity to sexual difference, mandates that special provision be made in the workplace to compensate women for their biological and historical role as the caregivers for children.

The gender-neutral approach to sexual equality was popular during the 1960s and early 1970s, as indicated not only by the Supreme Court's willingness in *Reed v. Reed* to finally declare explicit discrimination against women to be unconstitutional but also by the willingness of almost all feminists of the day to enthusiastically support the passage of that most gender-blind of all feminist proposals, the equal rights amendment. The gender-neutral approach was so popular because it was consistent with three important facts that feminists were just then managing to bring to the attention of the general public: (1) discrimination on the basis of sex had long denied women the equal protection under the law that should have been guaranteed to all citizens by the Fourteenth Amendment to the U.S. Constitution; (2) protective legislation designed over the years to benefit women in the workplace had done more to hurt them economically than to help them; and (3) women are as inherently intelligent, responsible, and capable of supporting themselves, if given the opportunity to do so, as men—not inherently inferior, as legislators and judges traditionally represented them to be.

By the late 1970s and 1980s, however, champions of equal rights increasingly realized that gender neutrality so deemphasized the differences in the life situations of women and men that as a strategy, it was helping only those few women who were similarly situated to men while doing little, if anything, to help those many women who were locked into low-paying jobs by their gendered life situations as wives and mothers. Not only that, but when applied mindlessly and formulaically in divorce settlements, gender neutrality was actually harming differently situated women by falsely presupposing them to have as much earning potential—and hence as little need for alimony—as their husbands (Weitzman, 1985). Concentrating on this very large group of differently situated women highlighted the shortcomings of gender neutrality and thereby brought special protection back to center stage.

This time around, the advocates of special protection supported, not the kind of special limits for women that were at issue in *Muller v. Oregon,* but, instead, special benefits for women. Specifically, they proposed work-related policies designed to make it possible for women to be both highly paid workers and responsible primary parents, policies such as mandatory insurance coverage for pregnancy leave and a guaranteed return to one's job at the end of such a leave, paid days off for mothers of sick children, and even subsidized childcare. Although demands for these kinds of sex-specific arrangements in the workplace would have been beyond imagining in the difference-blind heyday of the equal rights amendment, they were not all that exceptional in an era when virtually all minority groups were vigorously asserting the values of pluralism and sensitivity to difference—including even physically disabled people, who were at last beginning to get the special access to the mainstream of American life that they need.

In the 1990s, a great deal of support for these kinds of special benefits remains, as does a great deal of resistance to them. The support comes primarily from those feminists who see gender neutrality as having failed and, worse, as having required women to virtually become men to make it in the world of paid employment. The resistance comes from other feminists and from nonfeminists.

The feminist resisters think special protection homogenizes women too much and reinforces the old sexist stereotype that women as a group are inherently incapable of competing successfully with men until and unless special provisions compensate them for their special needs. The nonfeminist resisters, on the other hand, see no justification for making special arrangements to help a group whose economic and political disadvantages derive not from discrimination but from their own decision to invest time and energy in their children, rather than in their careers. As these nonfeminist resisters see it, to prevent employers from doing harm to women through outright discrimination makes sense, but to mandate that employers make special arrangements to help women in a marketplace that is not discriminatory does not.

But as controversial as special protection for a woman's biological and historical role as mother has been since the Supreme Court first upheld it in 1908, yet another form of special protection has become equally controversial since the 1960s. I refer here to the special protection against subtle and indirect discrimination that is embodied in the twin policies of comparable worth and preferential hiring. Comparable worth would move beyond the mandate that women and men doing the same work be paid equal wages to mandate equal wages for women and men doing different work that is of comparable value. Preferential hiring would move beyond simply prohibiting discrimination against women to mandate that an individual woman be hired over an individual man with similar qualifications and that goals and timetables be set for the hiring of a certain percentage of women by a certain time. Setting goals could, in turn, foster the use of quotas to reserve positions exclusively for women.

From the point of view of proponents, comparable worth and preferential hiring are necessary because discrimination against women often targets not women per se but anyone and everyone with the kinds of jobs or job histories that women as a group are much more likely to have than men as a group. From the point of view of opponents of these policies, preferential hiring unfairly deprives innocent males of equal opportunity by violating the almost sacred principle of gender neutrality, and comparable worth violates yet another sacred American principle—the right of employers to set wages in accordance with the free market.[3]

Just as those who emphasize discrimination as the cause of women's inequality, and gender neutrality as the cure, presuppose male-female similarity, then, so those who emphasize female choice as the cause of women's inequality, and special benefits as the cure, presuppose male-female difference. This dichotomy between similarity and difference shows up again in the two opposing definitions of female equality, with one group envisioning that women and men will come to play exactly the same roles both at home and at work and the other group envisioning that women will come to have exactly the same level of economic well-being, or equity, as men, despite continuing to play their traditionally different roles as homemakers and mothers.

Not surprisingly, the sameness conception of female equality was popular during the era when discrimination, gender neutrality, and the equal rights amendment dominated the feminist discourse and the concept of psychological androgyny was being celebrated as well. As feminists then saw it, the only effective way to end the sexist stereotyping of women and the discrimination against women that stereotyping inevitably produces was to abolish gender distinctions once and for all—that is, to move at last toward an androgynous future, where women and men would have not only the same level of economic and political power but the same rights, the same responsibilities, and even the same roles.

Although initially, only antifeminists like Phyllis Schlafly opposed this definition of equality as sameness, on the grounds that it demeaned and destroyed the woman's role within the home, in time a great many feminists came to have that view as well. Defining female equality as sameness to men, they argued, was tantamount to saying that a woman's historical role and the values that it represents are of no intrinsic value.

So yes, the argument continued, women are inherently as competent as men are—there is no disagreement about that—but women are also inherently different from men in a special way having to do with their biological capacity for childbearing; and because of that difference, any worthwhile definition of equality must preserve the woman's biological and historical role as mother and give that role as much cultural value as has traditionally been given to male roles. In other words, the feminist goal should not be to facilitate women's acting exactly like men in order to earn what men earn; rather, women should be able to earn what men earn while still preserving their distinctive concern with the welfare of their own and other children.

After more than a century of dichotomies that relate to the single question of whether women are basically the same as men or basically different from men, feminists have recently begun to concentrate on yet another dichotomy. It is best captured by the following question: Are women of different races, classes, religions, sexual preferences, ethnicities, and perhaps even nationalities sufficiently similar to one another in their needs, goals, and experiences to constitute the kind of a political interest group that could possibly be served by any single program of social change, or are women of different groups so inherently different from one another that there can be little or no common cause among them and hence no possibility of a common feminist solution to their female inequality?[4]

These female-female differences notwithstanding, the historian Estelle Freedman eloquently defends the continuing validity of the feminist struggle: "In a historical moment when the category 'woman' continues to predict limited access to material resources, greater vulnerability to physical and psychological abuse, and underrepresentation in politics, . . . we must avoid the tendency to assume both a false unity across genders and a greater disunity within our gender than in fact exists" (1990, p. 261). Put somewhat differently, if feminists are to keep from getting mired in yet another set of impasse-producing dichotomies, they must not allow their newfound appreciation for the differences among women to undermine the longstanding feminist project of creating a social world in which the category of woman is no longer synonymous with the category of inequality.[5]

With that said, however, the question remains: How can feminists construct the kind of discussion about gender policy that would enable a male-dominated society like the United States to finally create such a social world? How, in other words, can Americans transcend all the irresolvable dichotomies that have plagued even feminist discussions of female inequality for 150 years? My answer is that those dichotomies can be transcended—and a consensus on gender policy can be forged—if a certain level of male-female difference is accepted as axiomatic, and the starting point for the discussion is thereby shifted from difference per se to the society's situating of women in a social structure so androcentric that it not only transforms male-female difference into female disadvantage; it also disguises a male standard as gender neutrality.[6]

TOWARD GENDER NEUTRALITY:
ERADICATING ANDROCENTRISM

In 1984, the feminist legal scholar Catharine MacKinnon exposed the legal myth of gender neutrality as no other writer before her had done. Although she never actually used the term *androcentrism,* her basic argument was all but identical to the one in this book: although males and females differ from one another in many biological and historical characteristics, what is ultimately responsible for every aspect of female inequality, from the wage gap to the rape rate, is not male-female difference but a social world so organized from a male perspective that men's special needs are automatically taken care of while women's special needs are either treated as special cases or left unmet.

Consider, for example, the Supreme Court decisions on disability insurance coverage, discussed in Chapter 3. Although the biological differences here are indisputable, the biological differences themselves were not the reason that pregnancy was excluded from insurance coverage while prostatectomies and circumcisions were included. The reason was a vision of gender neutrality so distorted by androcentrism that the male body was automatically taken as the standard, hence nothing seemed amiss when, in the name of equal protection, total and complete insurance coverage was granted for every one of a man's special needs but not for every one of a woman's.

Consider, for another example, the recent critique of the legal definition of self-defense, which holds that a defendant can be found innocent of homicide only if he or she perceived imminent danger of great bodily harm or death and responded to that danger with only as much force as was necessary to defend against it. That definition always seemed to have nothing whatsoever to do with gender, but it no longer seems quite so gender neutral now that feminist legal scholars like Elizabeth Schneider (1980) and Phyllis Crocker (1985) have pointed out how much better it fits with a scenario involving two men in an isolated episode of sudden violence than with a scenario involving a woman being battered, first in relatively minor ways and then with escalating intensity over the years, by a man who is not only bigger and stronger than she is but from whom she cannot get police protection because he is her husband. The aha experience here comes with the realization that if this woman and this situation had been anywhere near the center of the (male) policymakers' consciousness when they drafted the supposedly neutral definition of self-defense, they might not have placed so much emphasis on the defendant's being in imminent danger at the particular instant when the ultimate act of self-defense is finally made.

Insurance and self-defense do not provide the only contexts in which the male difference from women is "affirmatively compensated" (MacKinnon, 1987, p. 36) by American society while the female difference from men is treated as an intrinsic barrier to sexual equality. To quote MacKinnon:

> Virtually every quality that distinguishes men from women is . . . affirmatively compensated in this society. Men's physiology defines most sports, their needs define auto and health insurance coverage, their socially designed biographies define workplace expectations and successful career patterns, their perspectives and concerns define quality in scholarship, their experiences and obsessions define merit, their objectification of life defines art, their military service defines citizenship, their presence defines family, their inability to get along with each other—their wars and rulerships—defines history, their image defines god, and their genitals define sex. For each of their differences from women, what amounts to an affirmative action plan is in effect, otherwise known as the structure and values of American society. (1987, p. 36)

Of all the androcentric institutions on MacKinnon's list that are typically considered gender neutral, perhaps none is more directly responsible for denying women their rightful share of economic and political resources in the United States than the structure of the work world. Many Americans may think that world of work is as gender neutral as it needs to be now that explicit discrimination against women has been made illegal, but it is, in fact, so thoroughly organized around a male worker with a wife at home to take care of the needs of the household—including childcare—that it transforms what is intrinsically just a male-female difference into a massive female disadvantage.

Imagine how differently the whole social world would be organized if there were no men around (reproduction would be handled somehow), and hence most of the workers in the workforce—including those at the highest levels of government and industry—were either pregnant or responsible for childcare during at least a certain portion of their adult lives. In this context, working would so obviously need to coordinate with birthing and parenting that institutions facilitating that coordination would be taken for granted. There would be paid pregnancy leave, paid days off to tend to sick children, paid childcare, and a match—rather than a mismatch—between the hours of the work day and the hours of the school day. There would probably also be a completely different definition of a prototypical work life, with the norm being, not a continuous forty hours or more per week from adulthood to old age, but a transition from less than forty hours per week when the children were young to forty hours or more per week when the children were older.

The lesson of this alternative reality should be clear. Women's biological and historical role as mothers does not limit their access to economic and political resources. What limits access is an androcentric social world that provides but one institutionalized mechanism for coordinating work in the paid labor force with the responsibilities of being a parent: having a wife at home to take care of the children.

This institutional void affects different groups of women in different ways. Among mothers who work full-time when their children are young, for example, all but the wealthiest must endure the never-ending strain of struggling on their own to find decent and affordable childcare—which in the United States is neither decent nor affordable but all too often passes as such. They must also get up before dawn every weekday morning to take their youngest children to that child-care so that they can get themselves to work on time. All the while, they worry about whether their older children will get into any trouble during their several unsupervised hours before and after school and hope against hope that no school holidays will be declared that week and that none of the children comes down with a fever, because then they will have to leave a child at home alone all day or stay home from work. As if that were not enough to drive them to distraction, they also have to live every single day of their lives with the certain knowledge that— given the sorry state of childcare in the United States—their children are almost certainly not receiving the tender loving care or thoughtful and attentive supervision that they themselves would provide if only they could afford to stay at home while their children are young.

Given these difficulties, it is not surprising that women married to men with high earnings potential frequently make the decision to help maximize their husband's earnings—by, for example, supporting him through medical school before the children are born—so that, instead of having to coordinate paid work and family, they can stay home, at least until the children are in school, and, after that, limit the kinds of jobs they take to those that coordinate well with their children's school schedules. This seemingly rational arrangement may work fine financially for as long as the couple stays married, but if and when they get divorced, as couples often do in the United States, then every bit of the earnings potential that the couple has invested in during the years of their marriage will be embodied in the husband, and the wife will be left with no more ability to support herself on her own than she had when she entered the marriage.

The lives of two remaining groups of women in American society are also affected in dramatically different ways by the absence of institutional supports for coordinating work and family. The first group consists of all those highly career-oriented women who see no way to make it to the top of their fields except by remaining childless. This sacrifice is not ever required of men who make it to the top. In sharp contrast, the second group consists of all those single mothers on welfare, who are culturally stigmatized for their failure to have a male breadwinner in their home when, instead, they should be offered whatever institutional supports would enable them to carry out their dual responsibility as parent and provider.[7]

This emphasis on the need for institutional supports to coordinate paid work and family may seem like just another example of special pleading on behalf of women. Not at all. It is a call for Americans to recognize that their social institutions do not reflect the needs and experiences of both women and men but instead reflect the needs and experiences of men. It is a call for Americans to reconstruct their social institutions to be so inclusive of both male and female experience that neither sex is automatically advantaged or disadvantaged by the social structure.

Pregnancy is the paradigmatic aspect of female experience that must be taken into account institutionally if the concept of gender neutrality as the inclusion of both sexes' experience is to have any real meaning. Pregnancy has this special status for two reasons. First, only women can experience it, and it has sufficient impact on a woman's physical condition that if it is not taken into account institutionally, it automatically advantages men as a group and disadvantages women as a group. Second, although institutionally ignoring pregnancy has often been justified on the grounds that pregnancy disadvantages only those individual women who *elect* to become pregnant, pregnancy is not nearly so elective a condition for the individual woman as this argument implies. Even more important, pregnancy is not an elective condition for the society as a whole; hence the state has a special interest in keeping it an attractive option for even those women who could choose to prevent themselves from ever becoming pregnant.

Almost as paradigmatic of female experience as pregnancy—or childbearing—is the day-to-day responsibility of childcaring. Here, however, the issue is not simply one of providing the institutional supports that would make it as possible for mothers to be paid workers as for fathers to be paid workers. Also at issue is the redefinition of the meaning of work itself so that just as much value is given to the raising of the next generation as to the producing of whatever is currently counted in the gross national product. Such a shift in the androcentric values of the culture would imply that professional childcare should be paid at a much higher rate than it is now and that full-time parenting when children are young should be regarded as much the same kind of personal career sacrifice for the good of the society as serving in the armed forces—in which case the women who do it should be paid for their efforts and should also be helped in their transition into the "civilian" economy with some kind of an analogue to the GI bill.

This inclusive model of gender neutrality has important implications not only for the differences between women and men but also for the differences among women that have recently threatened the idea of a common feminist solution to female inequality. Yes, this model concedes, women of different races, classes, sexual preferences, and so forth, do, to a certain extent, have different needs and different experiences, but those female-female differences should no more be treated as intractable obstacles to a common feminist solution than male-female differences should be treated as intractable obstacles to female equality. The critical issue is not whether female-female differences exist; they clearly do. The critical issue is whether feminist analyses and proposals are framed in sufficiently inclusive a way to deal with the several different ways that androcentric social structures systematically disadvantage different groups of women.

One example of this kind of inclusiveness appears in my own advocacy of subsidized childcare for women (and men) who work outside the home and in the proposed analogue to the GI bill for women (and men) who parent on a full-time basis. Examples of inclusiveness on other important dimensions of female-female difference might be (1) advocating not only that homemakers have a share of their husband's career assets at the time of divorce but also that the fringe benefits available to the spouses of married heterosexuals be available as well to the partners of sexual minorities and (2) advocating that not only abortion rights and birth control but also prenatal and postnatal care be made accessible to women of all social classes.

Implicit in this analysis of how androcentric institutions transform difference into disadvantage are three fundamental lessons from earlier chapters of this book, all having to do with the importance of the environmental context in which the person is situated.

The first lesson, which comes directly from the chapter on biological essentialism, is that as powerful and deterministic as biology may appear, its impact depends in every single instance on the environment with which it interacts. The aspect of this biological contextualism that I wanted to emphasize earlier was the ability of cultural invention to liberate the human organism from what had once seemed its intrinsic biological limitations, hence my interest in such technological innovations as antibiotics, refrigeration, birth control, and baby formula. In this chapter, what I want to emphasize, in contrast, is not the power of cultural invention to liberate, but the power of cultural invention to discriminate—specifically, the power of a male-centered social structure to interact with biology in a way that "naturally" and automatically produces female disadvantage and male advantage.

In my lectures on college campuses, I find that a particular analogy brings this interaction into bold relief. The analogy plays on another one of my nonprivileged attributes, not my femaleness this time, but my shortness. (I happen to be only four feet nine inches tall.) Imagine a community of short people like myself. Given the argument sometimes made in U.S. society that short people cannot be firefighters because they are neither tall enough nor strong enough to do the job, the question arises: Would all the houses in this community of short people eventually burn down? Well, yes, if we short people had to use the heavy ladders and hoses designed by and for tall people. But no, if we (being as smart as short people are) could instead construct lighter ladders and hoses that both tall and short people could use. The moral here should be obvious: shortness isn't the problem; the problem lies in forcing short people to function in a tall-centered social structure.

The second lesson, which comes directly from the chapter on the construction of the individual, is that, as important as it is to eradicate all forms of explicit discrimination against women, a democratic society like the United States constrains its citizens, women in particular, not primarily by coercive confinement but by the provision of social institutions that invisibly and automatically smooth the way toward whatever the historically preprogrammed options—or the conventionally standard behaviors—are for a particular group in a particular time and place. The importance of this institutional smoothing can readily be seen in the changing pattern of behavior that is now occurring in communities like my own Ithaca, New York, where new laws, and new facilitating institutions, have recently been put into place with respect to something as central to daily life as recycling garbage. Before these recycling programs, most community residents never entertained the thought of recycling garbage even for a moment; and the few recycling pioneers could do little with their own recyclable material other than what was then institutionalized as the default behavior—namely, tossing it into the garbage can and having it driven to the local landfill by the weekly garbage collectors.

Now that recycling is mandated by law and facilitated by recycling pickups and ever-increasing varieties of recyclable material, the default behavior of community members alters almost daily. Recycling may not yet be so accepted that a whole new generation never even considers tossing recyclable material away, but neither is recycling any longer so difficult to manage that only a few committed individuals will trouble to do it. Similarly, if women are ever to have their rightful share of the economic and political resources of the United States, social institutions must be built that make it as easy for *any* woman to be a responsible parent and a well-paid worker as it finally is in Ithaca, New York, for anyone and everyone to recycle.

The third lesson in this analysis of how androcentric institutions transform difference into disadvantage comes directly from the chapter on androcentrism. It is that as gender neutral as American institutions may appear now that explicit discrimination against women has been made illegal, in fact, androcentrism so saturates the whole society that even institutions that do not discriminate against women explicitly—like the laws of self-defense—must be treated as inherently suspect.

At the beginning of this chapter, the suggestion was made that the cultural debate about sexual inequality has been bogged down in irresolvable issues that all derive in one way or another from the focus on sexual difference. It should now be clear that by reframing the debate around androcentrism, those issues can be transcended.

Consider, first, the debate over whether women's economic and political disadvantage derives from sex discrimination or from the personal choices that women make themselves. With a shift in focus, these two alternatives no longer seem to be mutually exclusive. Rather, one of the main ways that sex discrimination operates in U.S. society is by forcing women to make their life choices in a social world so androcentric that it provides few institutional mechanisms for coordinating work in the paid labor force with the responsibilities of being a parent. Situating employed mothers in an institutional vacuum has left each woman to piece together her own arrangements for coordinating paid work and family; in addition, it has all but guaranteed that most women's advances in the labor market come at a formidable emotional cost to the individual. The irony here, unfortunately, is that because the culture has so little understanding of how systemic discrimination against women proceeds, it frequently misattributes this cost, not to androcentric institutions, but to the "fallout of feminism" (*Newsweek,* March 31, 1986, p. 58).[8]

Consider, next, the debate over whether the best strategy for ending women's inequality is gender neutrality or special protection. With a shift in focus, these two strategies no longer seem to be in opposition. Instead, current institutions are so thoroughly organized from an androcentric perspective that the only way for them to even begin to approximate gender neutrality is for society to finally begin giving as complete a package of special benefits to women as it has always given to men and men alone. Given how broad and deep these special benefits for men have always been, moreover, it follows that *in the interest of neutrality alone,* the special benefits for women would also have to be broad and deep, including not just insurance coverage for female medical conditions but such things as subsidized childcare, comparable-worth earnings for traditionally female jobs, and even the preferential hiring of those with traditionally female job histories.

To people who don't yet understand that androcentric social institutions constitute an invisible privileging of both males and male experience, these suggestions are bound to seem wrongheaded. They are, after all, based on a concept of group rights, not individual rights. But to define gender justice purely in terms of individual rights only makes sense *after* the playing field that men are always talking about has finally been made so level that both women and men have inclusive group rights. Now, men and men alone have group rights.

As noted in Chapter 1, the androcentric social world was built by rich, white, heterosexual men in particular, not by men in general. Accordingly, most apparently neutral institutions hide discrimination against poor people, people of color, and sexual minorities, as well as discrimination against women. Many examples of hidden discrimination against sexual minorities have been provided in this book, including the extension of an employee's health insurance and other fringe benefits only to those domestic partners who are legally recognized as husbands or wives. Hidden discrimination against the poor disproportionately affects people of color; two examples are the funding of public schools through local property taxes and the providing of health insurance through jobs—and only certain jobs at that. Although none of these policies explicitly mentions race, class, or sexual preference, they fit so much better with the experience of the nonpoor, the white, and the heterosexual that—no matter how neutral they look—they still systematically discriminate against poor people, people of color, and gay men and lesbians; they still systematically give group rights to rich people, white people, and heterosexual people.[9]

Consider, finally, the debate over whether sexual equality should be defined in terms of equality or sameness—in terms of whether women should play exactly the same social roles as men or whether they should have exactly the same level of economic and political power as men while they continue to play their traditionally different roles as wives and mothers. With a shift in focus, whether women and men play the same roles or different roles is not itself the issue. Rather, the issue is whether androcentric institutions turn any role differences between women and men into a package of economic and political disadvantages for women as a group; and *that*, social institutions must be prevented from doing as soon as possible. Whether the role differences between women and men should themselves be abolished is thus an entirely separable issue, and one to be considered below.

TOWARD UTOPIA: ERADICATING
GENDER POLARIZATION

Up to this point, I have tried to lay the groundwork for a feminist consensus on gender policy by reframing the debate around the androcentrism of social institutions. Now, however, I want to move beyond androcentrism to gender polarization and advocate a vision of utopia in which gender polarization, like androcentrism, has been so completely dismantled that—except in narrowly biological contexts like reproduction—the distinction between male and female no longer organizes either the culture or the psyche. This particular utopia is controversial because it challenges the fundamental belief in the differing psychological and sexual nature of males and females, and it is also inconsistent with what is arguably the dominant voice in contemporary American feminist thought—the woman-centered voice, discussed earlier.

Gender polarization is the organizing of social life around the male-female distinction, the forging of a cultural connection between sex and virtually every other aspect of human experience, including modes of dress, social roles, and even ways of expressing emotion and experiencing sexual desire. Accordingly, to dismantle gender polarization requires severing all these culturally constructed connections and cutting back the male-female distinction to a narrow—if critically important—relevance having primarily to do with the biology of reproduction. With complete gender.depolarization, the biology of sex would become "a minimal presence" in human social life (Connell, 1987, p. 289). In other words, the totality of human experience would no longer be divided into cultural categories on the basis of gender, so people of different sexes would no longer be culturally identified with different clothes, different social roles, different personalities, or different sexual and affectional partners any more than people with different-colored eyes or different-sized feet are now.

This absence of gender-based scripts should not be taken to mean that males and females would merely be freer to be masculine, feminine, or androgynous, heterosexual, homosexual, or bisexual, than they are now. Rather, the distinction between male and female would no longer be the dimension around which the culture is organized, which means, in turn, that the very concepts of masculinity, femininity, and androgyny, heterosexuality, homosexuality, and bisexuality, would be as absent from the cultural consciousness as the concepts of a "hetero-eye-colored" eroticism, a "homo-eye-colored" eroticism, and a "bi-eye-colored" eroticism are now.[10]

Although feminists as a whole may not yet have committed themselves to eradicating gender polarization, two separate critiques of gender polarization underlie my own commitment to eradicating it from both the culture and the psyche. The first derives from a broad humanistic concern with the way that gender polarization prevents men and women alike from developing their full potential as human beings, the second from a specifically feminist concern with the foundation that gender polarization provides for androcentrism.

According to the humanistic critique, which was popular among androgyny theorists like myself during the late 1960s and early 1970s, the division of human experience into the masculine and the feminine restricts human potential in at least three related ways.

First, gender polarization homogenizes women and men, rather than allowing either the diversity that naturally exists within each sex or the overlap that naturally exists between the two sexes to flower in social and psychological life. Besides being inconsistent with the diversity of human nature, this homogenization is inconsistent with the American value of freedom to transcend the arbitrary boundaries of ascribed characteristics like sex, race, and caste.

Second, gender polarization dichotomizes not only people but also ways of relating to the world into masculine and feminine types, thereby leaving undefined and unconceptualized not only the androgynous kinds of people who were once the focus of so much feminist attention but also the androgynous ways of relating to the world that so often seem to capture the essence of the human condition. Take, for example, the gender-polarizing dichotomy between male autonomy and female connectedness. Although all human beings everywhere are simultaneously and inextricably separate and autonomous selves, as well as fully interconnected and interdependent members of a human community, no concept in a gender-polarizing culture reflects this two-sided fact about the human condition. Take, for another example, the gender-polarizing dichotomy between male rationality and female emotionality. Although the human psyche is simultaneously and inextricably both rational and emotional, once again, no concept in a gender-polarizing culture reflects this fact.

Finally, gender polarization so dramatically expands the meaning of what it is to be male or female that a paradoxical cultural concept is thereby created: the idea of being a "real" man or woman, as opposed to a merely biological man or woman. This paradoxical concept, in turn, makes both men and women vulnerable to the feeling that their maleness or femaleness cannot be taken for granted but must instead be worked at, accomplished, and protected from loss through misbehavior. The culture has developed no comparable concept of a "real" human being, which is why people have no comparable sense of insecurity about whether they are walking or playing or eating or thinking or having sex in a way that is adequately human; they simply go about the business of doing whatever they have each been biologically enabled to do.

The essence of the humanistic objection to gender polarization is thus that it turns men and women into gender caricatures and thereby denies them the fullest measure of their human possibilities. In contrast, the essence of the specifically feminist objection to gender polarization is that it aids and abets the social reproduction of male power by providing the fundamental division between masculine and feminine upon which androcentrism is built. This antifeminist aspect of gender polarization manifests itself at three levels: the institutional, the psychological, and the ideological.

At the institutional level, gender polarization aids and abets the social reproduction of male power by dichotomizing the social world into the masculine domain of paid employment and the feminine domain of home and childcare, thereby sustaining a gender-based division of labor and obscuring the need for any institutional mechanisms—like paid childcare—that would enable any one individual to easily participate in both domains. Such coordinating mechanisms will continue to be seen as unnecessary as long as gender polarization ensures that different people—that is, men and women—do different things; and the absence of such coordinating mechanisms will continue to promote sexual hierarchy by denying women access to economic and political power.

At the psychological level, gender polarization aids and abets the social reproduction of male power by dichotomizing identity and personality into masculine and feminine categories, thereby providing a concept of *psychological* masculinity and femininity to which the culture can readily assimilate its androcentric conceptions of power and powerlessness. This unholy alliance of androcentrism and gender polarization predisposes men to construct identities around dominance and women to construct identities around deference; it also enables those who deviate from these mutually exclusive identities to be defined, by both the culture and themselves, as pathological.

And finally, at the ideological level, gender polarization aids and abets the social reproduction of male power by prompting the cultural discourse to misrepresent even the most blatant examples of sexual inequality as nothing more or less than sexual difference. Put somewhat differently, gender polarization enables religion, science, law, the media, and so on, to rationalize the sexual status quo in a way that automatically renders the lens of androcentrism invisible. The sexual status quo is not made to seem rational by gender polarization alone, of course; the lens of biological essentialism further rationalizes the sexual status quo by defining difference itself as biologically natural.

In addition to the humanist and feminist arguments against gender polarization, there is an overarching moral argument that fuses the antihumanist and antifeminist aspects of gender polarization. The essence of this moral argument is that by polarizing human values and human experiences into the masculine and the feminine, gender polarization not only helps to keep the culture in the grip of males themselves; it also keeps the culture in the grip of highly polarized masculine values. The moral problem here is that these highly polarized masculine values so emphasize making war over keeping the peace, taking risks over giving care, and even mastering nature over harmonizing with nature that when allowed to dominate societal and even global decision making, they create the danger that humans will destroy not just each other in massive numbers but the planet.

The one good thing about the thoroughness with which gender polarization is embedded in androcentric institutions is that institutional changes designed to eradicate androcentrism will necessarily challenge gender polarization as well. Consider the suggestion made earlier, for example, that society provide institutional ways to coordinate work and family. In addition to challenging androcentrism, this institutional change would begin to break down the boundary between the masculine world of paid employment and the feminine world of home and childcare; it would also begin to challenge the polarization of identity and personality by giving women experience with power and status, and men experience with nurturance and service to others. Although other kinds of institutional changes would deal more directly with gender polarization, my own view is that—apart from the critical issue of ending all forms of discrimination against lesbians, gay men, and bisexuals—the most effective way to begin dismantling gender polarization is to dismantle androcentrism.

Ultimately, gender depolarization would require even more than the *social* revolution involved in rearranging social institutions and re-framing cultural discourses. Gender depolarization would also require a *psychological* revolution in our most personal sense of who and what we are as males and females, a profound alteration in our feelings about the meaning of our biological sex and its relation to our psyche and our sexuality.

Simply put, this psychological revolution would have us all begin to view the biological fact of being male or female in much the same way that we now view the biological fact of being *human*. Rather than seeing our sex as so authentically who we are that it needs to be elaborated, or so tenuous that it needs to be bolstered, or so limiting that it needs to be traded in for another model, we would instead view our sex as so completely given by nature, so capable of exerting its influence automatically, and so limited in its sphere of influence to those domains where it really does matter biologically, that it could be safely tucked away in the backs of our minds and left to its own devices. In other words, biological sex would no longer be at the core of individual identity and sexuality.

NOTES

Chapter 2: Biological Essentialism

1 For this broader feminist critique of science, see Bleier (1988a), Haraway (1989), Harding (1986, 1987), Harding & O'Barr (1987), Keller (1985), Longino (1987, 1990), and Schiebinger (1987, 1989). For more on science as a cultural and historical activity, see Bernstein (1976), Feyerabend (1976), Fiske & Shweder (1986), Kuhn (1962), Polanyi (1967), Rorty (1979), and Toulmin (1972, 1982).

2 Although, to my knowledge, the noted biologist Ernst Mayr has never discussed the biological essentialism in theories of sexual difference and male dominance, he has argued that "the sweeping statements in the racist literature . . . are almost invariably based on essentialistic" thinking (1982, p. 47). For an in-depth analysis of the history of biological essentialism from the perspective of an evolutionary biologist, see Mayr's *Growth of Biological Thought* (1982) and especially his distinction, on pp. 45–47, between essentialist, or typological, thinking (all members of a category are considered to have the same essence) and population thinking (each member of a group is considered biologically unique).

3 This discussion of biological theorizing about class and national origin in the late nineteenth and early twentieth centuries relies heavily on Kamin (1974) and Gould (1981).

4 By the middle of the nineteenth century, this claim about the African's "intrinsic race character" had become completely intertwined with the pseudoscientific theory of "polygenesis," which held that the races had been created as completely separate and distinct species rather than as variations of the same species—a theory that even the noted Harvard biologist Louis Agassiz endorsed. Although the original proponent of polygenesis, Charles

Caldwell, stated explicitly in 1830 that polygenesis should never be used to justify "either enslaving the Africans or destroying the Indians" (quoted in Fredrickson, 1971, p. 73), within a very short span of time, polygenesis was being used as "a scientific apology for Negro slavery and Indian extermination" (Fredrickson, 1971, p. 77). To quote from one of the major books on polygenesis, *Types of Mankind* (1854): "It is manifest that our relation to and management of these people must depend, in great measure, upon their intrinsic race character. While the contact of the white man seems fatal to the Red Indian, whose tribes fall away before the onward march of the frontier-man like snow in the spring (threatening ultimate extinction), the Negro thrives under the shadow of his white master, falls readily into the position assigned him, and exists and multiplies in increased physical well-being" (quoted in Fredrickson, 1971, pp. 77–78). For more on this unholy alliance of science and race in the nineteenth century, see Fitzhugh (1854/1965), Fredrickson (1971), and Jordan (1968).

5 For more on the history of the eugenics movement, see Haller (1963) and Kevles (1985). For two additional documents emphasizing the superiority of "Nordic blood," see Grant (1922) and Stoddard (1920).

6 This discussion of biological theorizing about sex in the late nineteenth and early twentieth centuries relies heavily on Sayers (1982). For more on the biological theorizing of the time and its relation to politics, see Bannister (1979), Gould (1980), Hofstadter (1959), Hubbard (1979), Jordanova (1980, 1989), Merchant (1980), Newman (1985), C. E. Rosenberg (1976), Russett (1989), Shields (1975a, 1982), and Smith-Rosenberg & Rosenberg (1973).

7 Although this critique of sociobiology is very much my own, it has been informed by numerous other critiques, including Bleier (1984), Fausto-Sterling (1985), Flax (1987), Gould (1981), Haraway (1981), Levins & Lewontin (1985), Lewontin (1977), Quadagno (1979), Sahlins (1976), and Sayers (1982). For further discussion of sociobiology, see Caplan (1978).

8 This discussion of the history of, and the evidence for, the prenatal hormone theory relies heavily on Seiwert (1988). For other reviews, see Adkins-Regan (1988), Arnold & Gorski (1984), Beach (1981), Beatty (1979), Feder (1984), Jost (1983), Longino & Doell (1983), Meaney (1988), Meyer-Bahlburg (1984), and Whalen (1968). For other critiques of the prenatal hormone theory, see Fausto-Sterling (1985), Bleier (1984), and especially C. L. Moore (1985), and Birke (1989).

9 For more on how sex differences are mediated by social interaction even among animals, see C. L. Moore (1985), Birke (1989), and Goldfoot & Neff (1987).

10 For a recent review of this whole literature, see Fausto-Sterling (1985). For still other critiques of the Money and Ehrhardt research in particular, see Bleier (1984), Fausto-Sterling (1985), and Quadagno et al. (1977).

11 For an excellent discussion of this debate, see chapter 2 of H. L. Moore (1988).

12 In sharp contrast to the argument being made here, some writers have argued that there is not only a sex difference in the very capacity for this kind of "bonding" but also a limited period of time immediately after birth when bonding can occur. For a thorough critique of this argument in the context of humans, see Myers (1984). For a more recent evaluation of what is known in this whole area, see Fleming (1989). For some fascinating research on how social experiences other than contact can also influence parental motivation, see the work on monkeys described in Goldfoot & Neff (1987); the researchers found that although male and female adults took equally good care of a "stranded" infant with whom they were left alone, those same male adults ignored the infant altogether if a female adult was also available to do the caretaking.

Chapter 3: Androcentrism

1 This brief discussion of the patriarchy concept represents but a tiny fragment of contemporary feminist thought. For more on how contemporary feminist thought has evolved since the 1960s, see Davis (1981), Donavan (1988), Echols (1989), H. Eisenstein (1983), Hull, Scott & Smith (1982), Jaggar (1983), and Nicholson (1986).

2 Even in this brief excerpt, Beauvoir brilliantly foreshadows two related concepts that would later be developed in the fields of linguistics and psychology, respectively. When she notes that man is generally regarded as "both the positive and the neutral," she foreshadows the linguistic distinction between the "marked" and the "unmarked" terms of an opposition. This captures the notion that the typical contrast between opposites like good-bad or long-short or happy-unhappy is not symmetric, with one term representing the positive end of a dimension and the other term representing the negative end; rather, in many, if not most, instances, the contrast is asymmetric. That is, the positive, or unmarked, term can be neutralized in meaning to denote the scale as a whole rather than just the positive end; but the negative, or marked, term can denote just the negative end.

This asymmetry can easily be seen in questions. Questions using unmarked terms, like "How good was the movie?" or "How tall is Chris?" do not imply that the movie was good or that Chris is tall, whereas questions using marked terms, like "How bad was the movie?" or "How short is

Chris?" do imply that the answer is toward the negative end of the scale. The applicability of this distinction to oppositional gender pairs like man-woman, lion-lioness, dog-bitch, and author-authoress should be clear. In each pair, it is the male term that is unmarked and that can therefore be neutralized to include the female.

When Beauvoir writes, however, that "there is an absolute human type, the masculine. . . . Thus humanity is male," the neutralizing of man to include woman is no longer her subject. It is the masculinizing of the whole human species to exclude woman—or at least to otherize her.

Here, Beauvoir foreshadows the psychological concept of prototypicality, which captures the notion that a human category (like bird or even human being) is not a symmetric structure whose members are all defined by a collection of necessary and sufficient features; rather, a human category is an asymmetric structure organized around a prototype and containing both central and noncentral members. All members of a category do not have equal status in the mind of the human perceiver; some members are instead perceived as more equal—or more prototypical—than other members. For example, a robin is a more prototypical bird than a chicken or an ostrich is. The applicability of the prototype concept should be clear. Like the prototypical member of any category, the male is taken to be the cognitive reference point, the standard, for the category of human being; and like the non-prototypical members of any category, the female is taken to be a variation on that prototype, a less representative example of the human species.

For more on the marked-unmarked distinction, see Lyons (1977) and Clark (1969). For more on the concept of prototypicality and its challenge to the "classical" view of concepts and categories, see Rosch (1973), Lakoff (1987), Smith & Medin (1981), and chapter 12 of Gardner (1985).

3 This discussion of the history of the Judeo-Christian heritage relies heavily on Pagels (1976), Phillips (1984), Sanday (1981), and chapters 8 and 9 of Lerner (1986). For more on the ideological struggles within early Christianity, see Pagels (1977, 1988).

4 This discussion of the traditional biblical interpretation of woman relies heavily on Phillips (1984), as well as on Sanday (1981). For feminist rereadings and reconstructions of religious texts and practices, see Plaskow (1990), Reuther (1985), and Sjoo & Mor (1987).

5 This discussion of ancient Greek thought relies heavily on Okin (1979). For more on women in Western political thought, see Saxonhouse (1985) and Bullough, Shelton & Slavin (1988). For a perspective that describes Greek thought as itself derived from an even earlier African civilization, see Bernal (1987).

6 At least one feminist scholar (Saxonhouse, 1985) disagrees with this ranking of Plato and Aristotle. She says Plato denies the female body by artificially making maternity as uncertain as paternity, and Aristotle places a higher value on precisely those virtues that are represented by the woman's role within the family—stability, moderation, and the preservation and education of the young.

7 For an in-depth analysis of natural rights and social contract theory from a feminist perspective, see Pateman (1988).

8 For more on Rousseau's view of women, see Okin (1979). For more on how the sexual temptress theme developed in Judeo-Christian theology from ancient times through the Middle Ages, see Bullough, Shelton & Slavin (1988).

9 For a more detailed introduction to Freud's overall theory, see C. S. Hall (1954).

10 For a more detailed overview of these three feminist reactions, see chapter 8 of Sayres (1982). For more on this early debate between Freud and his contemporaries, see chapter 2 of Gallop (1982) and pp. 121–131 of Mitchell (1974).

11 For more on this third variety of feminist reaction, see part 2 of Eisenstein & Jardine (1980), as well as Mitchell (1974), Gallop (1982, 1985), and Moi (1985).

12 For feminist analyses of this area of American law, see Estrich (1987), Lindgren & Taub (1988), Rhode (1989), and Russell (1982).

13 My discussion of the pre–Civil War era relies heavily on Sachs & Wilson (1978). For more, see Basch (1982), DuBois (1978), Flexner (1959), Gurko (1974), Norton (1980), and Pleck (1987).

14 My discussion of the post–Civil War era relies heavily on Sachs & Wilson (1978), Lindgren & Taub (1988), Taub & Schneider (1982), and Baer (1978).

15 With only a few exceptions, which are clearly noted, the legal opinions quoted in the remainder of this chapter can be found in Lindgren & Taub (1988). The *Slaughter-House* decision quoted here is the first exception; see Sachs & Wilson, 1978, pp. 99–100.

16 Quoted in Sachs & Wilson, 1978, p. 122.

17 Quoted in Baer, 1978, p. 50.

18 My discussion of the modern equality era in this section and the next relies heavily on Baron (1987), Lindgren & Taub (1988), Taub & Schneider (1988), MacKinnon (1987), and Scales (1980–1981).

19 For blacks in particular, there were judicial suggestions of the need for some kind of special scrutiny even before the 1960s. See, e.g., the celebrated footnote in *United States v. Carolene Products* (1938).

20 For more on this strategy and the controversy surrounding it, see Cole (1984).

21 For a fuller discussion of pregnancy and other legal issues related to the female body, see Z. R. Eisenstein (1988).

22 For more on sex segregation in the workplace, see Reskin (1984). For more on comparable worth, see Gold (1983) and Treiman & Hartman (1981).

23 The original study reporting this post-divorce disparity (Weitzman, 1985) claimed the disparity was even greater, with husbands experiencing a full 42 percent rise in their standard of living and wives experiencing a truly extraordinary decline of 73 percent. Those specific figures were later challenged, as reported in Faludi (1991, pp. 19–25).

Chapter 4: Gender Polarization

1 These mutually exclusive scripts are not necessarily identical in every single subculture within the larger society, as the recent work on divergent masculinities across race, class, and ethnicity makes perfectly clear. See, e.g., Segal (1990).

2 In this chapter, the discussion of changing sexual patterns relies heavily on D'Emilio & Freedman (1988). For more on the changing pattern of same-sex relations, see D'Emilio (1983b), Greenberg (1988), Katz (1976), and Duberman, Vicinus & Chauncey (1989). For more on women's same-sex romantic friendships, see Smith-Rosenberg (1975) and Faderman (1978, 1981, 1991).

3 This discussion of nineteenth-century sexology relies heavily on Birken (1988), Chauncey (1982–1983), Faderman (1978), Foucault (1978), Greenberg (1988), Marshall (1981), and Weeks (1981, 1986).

4 For more on sexologists' analyses of feminists and spinsters, see Faderman (1981) and Jeffreys (1985).

5 This description of splitting off the choice of sexual object from sexual inversion has been much informed by Chauncey (1982–1983), Foucault (1978), and D. King (1981). For more on Havelock Ellis, see Robinson (1976) and Weeks (1977).

6 For more on the Victorian view of sexuality and its origins, see Cott (1978) and chapter 3 of D'Emilio & Freedman (1988).

7 This analysis of how sexology evolved is similar to that put forth in Chauncey (1982–1983), D. King (1981), and Marshall (1981). For a somewhat different analysis, see Birken (1988).

8 For more on Freud's Darwinism, see Birken (1988), Marcus (1975), and Sulloway (1979). For a detailed summary of Freud's theory of male homosexuality, see Lewes (1988). For more recent theorizing about lesbians, see Kitzinger (1987).

9 For a thoughtful analysis of this important work, see Stephen Marcus's introduction to the 1975 edition.

10 For a summary of these theories, see Lewes (1988) and C. Thompson (1947).

11 This discussion of Freud's psychoanalytic successors relies heavily on Lewes (1988) and Bayer (1981). For another perspective on the vast post-Freudian psychoanalytic literature, see Friedman (1988).

12 For a critique of the general move away from sexuality, see Marcuse (1955).

13 For a sampling of some of the many treatments that have been tried over the years, see Katz (1976).

14 Note that the *DSM* is listed in the references under the authorship of the American Psychiatric Association.

15 For an excellent analysis of that battle, see Bayer (1981).

16 This brief history of the McCarthy era relies heavily on D'Emilio (1983b) and D'Emilio & Freedman (1988).

17 The work of Kinsey, Ford and Beach, and Hooker is summarized in greater detail in Bayer (1981). For more on Kinsey, see Robinson (1976).

18 Thomas Szasz's (1961) contribution—a challenge to the categories of mental health and mental illness and therefore a challenge to the social power of psychiatry itself—is summarized in Bayer (1981). Some of the first sociologists to theorize the social construction of sexuality were William Simon and John Gagnon (1967), who argued that all sexual conduct is culturally scripted and learned in exactly the same way that other culturally specific kinds of conduct are scripted and learned; Mary McIntosh (1968), who is credited with having first suggested that the homosexual "role" is a recent cultural invention; and Howard Becker (1963), Erving Goffman (1963), Edwin Schur (1965), and Martin Hoffman (1968), who all conceptualized the pathologizing of homosexuality as an exercise in the social control of deviance. For a discussion of these and other sociologists, see Plummer (1981) and pp. 142–144 of D'Emilio (1983b). Because of its historical significance, McIntosh's original article is reprinted in Plummer (1981), along with a more recent interview with her by Jeffrey Weeks and Kenneth Plummer.

19 For a discussion of many cultures where homosexuality is included in the gender scripts, see Greenberg (1988). For an in-depth discussion of the Sambian case, see Herdt (1981).

20 For a more detailed critique of the concept of homophobia, see Plummer (1981a) and Kitzinger (1987).

21 For more on the misogynistic history of psychology and the early feminist counterpoint to that misogyny, see Shields (1975a, 1975b, 1982). For more on early feminist scholarship in the social sciences generally, see R. Rosenberg (1982).

22 In their own reviews of this early sex-differences literature, neither Woolley nor Hollingworth was the least bit shy about criticizing their colleagues for what they saw as truly bad science. As Woolley said in 1910: "There is perhaps no field aspiring to be scientific where flagrant personal bias, logic martyred in the cause of supporting a prejudice, unfounded assertions, and even sentimental rot and drivel, have run riot to such an extent as here" (quoted in Shields, 1975a, p. 739).

The misogynistic rot and drivel to which Woolley referred did not entirely disappear as a result of this first feminist counterpoint. By the time the second wave of feminism emerged in the late 1960s, the social science literature contained a whole new body of research and theory asserting both male-female difference and female inferiority. (For a lengthy literature review in this misogynistic tradition, see Garai & Scheinfield, 1968). In this second feminist moment, yet a second group of women with doctorates in psychology decided to once again harness the power of empirical science to look at the question of sex differences in an open-minded and objective way (e.g., Deaux, 1976; Frodi et al., 1977; Hochschild, 1973; Hyde & Linn, 1986; Sherman, 1971; and especially Maccoby & Jacklin, 1974). For critiques of the tradition in psychology of trying to establish empirically, once and for all, which hypothesized differences between males and females are merely myths and which are reality, see Bleier (1988b), Block (1976), Eagly (1987), Epstein (1988), Hare-Mustin & Maracek (1988, 1990), Sherif (1979), and Unger (1983).

23 I am indebted to Morawski (1985) for pointing out to me this link in the history of psychology between the early findings of no sex differences and the development of the first masculinity-femininity test.

24 This critique of Terman and Miles has been informed by Morawski (1985) and Lewin (1984a). For a critical discussion of IQ tests, see Gould (1981).

25 For reviews of these later tests, see Lewin (1984b) and Constantinople (1973).

26 For a critical history of the concepts of transsexualism and transvestism, see D. King (1981). The works that did the most to establish transsexualism as a discrete psychiatric phenomenon were Benjamin (1966), Stoller (1968), Green & Money (1969), Green (1974), and the American Psychiatric Association's *DSM-III* (1980). The best current social-science sourcebook on the topic of transsexualism is probably Steiner (1985).

27 For a rather negative discussion of sex-reassignment surgery by a psychiatrist who specializes in gender disorders, see chapter 9 of Stoller (1985). For a more positive view of the surgery and its long-term effects on transsexuals, see Blanchard (1985).

28 Rekers's work is described in detail in Zucker (1985). Rekers's work is coercive, and as he has made clear in at least two books written for a lay audience (1982a, 1982b), it is also designed to help stamp out what he sees as sexual perversion.

29 A wonderful new book that does not pathologize transsexuals or transvestites but instead explores the cultural significance of all manner of cross-dressing in history, literature, film, photography, and popular and mass culture is Garber (1992).

30 For the wealth of empirical evidence documenting this assertion, see the review article by Huston (1983).

31 The two specific theories within developmental psychology that best represent these contrasting perspectives are social learning theory (Mischel, 1970) and cognitive-developmental theory (Kohlberg, 1966). For critical discussions of these and other theories of gender acquisition, see Mussen (1969), Maccoby & Jacklin (1974), Huston (1983), and Bem (1985).

32 Those working in the Kohlbergian tradition include Lewis & Brooks-Gunn (1979), Martin & Halverson (1981), and Ullian (1981).

33 For a much more complete introduction to Piagetian theory, see Flavell (1963) and Piaget (1970).

34 Empirical evidence for the claim that young American children can distinguish males from females more readily on the basis of cultural cues than on the basis of biological cues can be found in Bem (1989), Carey (1985), Goldman & Goldman (1982), Katcher (1955), Levin, Balistrieri & Schukit (1972), and Thompson & Bentler (1971). Empirical evidence for the claim that young American children generate more restrictive gender rules for their male peers than for their female peers can be found in Carter & McCloskey (1983–1984), Fagot (1977, 1985), and Stoddart & Turiel (1985).

35 For an exposition of the antistage challenge and empirical evidence supporting that challenge, see Bem (1989), Carey (1985), Chi (1978), Gelman & Baillargeon (1983), Gelman & Gallistel (1978), and Keil (1989).

36 For these early landmarks, see Broverman et al. (1970), Bem (1972, 1974), Block (1973), Constantinople (1973), and Spence, Helmreich & Stapp (1974).

37 Taken together, this section on androgyny and gender schematicity and parts of the next section on the celebration of female difference present two aspects of feminist psychology during the past twenty-five years. For other discussions of feminist psychology during this period, see Crawford & Maracek (1989), Deaux (1984), Fine (1985), Fine & Gordon (1989), Hare-Mustin & Maracek (1988, 1990), Henley (1985), Jacklin (1989), Lykes & Stewart (1986), Parlee (1979), and Wallston (1981).

38 The best current introduction to both the BSRI and other comparable self-report measures related to gender can be found in Lenney (1991). For the original articles describing the BSRI itself, see Bem (1974, 1977, 1981a). Within the field of psychology, there has been a great deal of relatively technical controversy over the scoring and the meaning of the BSRI, as well as over the consistency of the empirical findings based on it. Although this controversy will be of little interest to non-psychologists, the relevant issues are introduced in Bem (1985), Spence (1984), Taylor & Hall (1982), and Frable (1989).

39 This critical discussion of androgyny has been informed by Gelpi (1974), Secor (1974), and Stimpson (1974). For some representative critiques of the androgyny concept from within psychology, see Morawski (1987), Lott (1981), and Sampson (1977).

40 For an update on Carolyn Heilbrun's assessment of androgyny, see Heilbrun (1980).

41 This more anthropological conception of my work on gender schematicity was first made completely explicit in Bem (1987).

42 These theories, and their relation to the minimizing-maximizing split, are discussed by Alcoff (1988), Echols (1983, 1989), Hare-Mustin & Maracek (1988), and especially Snitow (1989). As the Snitow discussion makes clear, the split has had many different labels applied to it. I borrowed the labels *minimizers* and *maximizers* from a 1980 article by Catharine Stimpson.

43 This is a wonderful term. For some interesting history on it, see K. King (1990).

44 For other discussions of these various woman-centered theorists, see H. Eisenstein (1983), Harding (1986), and especially Segal (1987).

Chapter 5: The Construction of Gender Identity

1 For a different analysis of the dominant theoretical perspectives on individual gender formation, see chapter 9 of Connell (1987).

2 Although originally theorized by a sociologist (Merton, 1948), the model of the self-fulfilling prophecy was first tested empirically—and in the context of rat research!—by a psychologist, Robert Rosenthal. After further empirical testing in the context of teachers' expectations for different groups of students (Rosenthal & Jacobson, 1968), the model was applied to gender in the 1970s. For an overview of empirical research on the self-fulfilling nature of gender and other stereotypes, see Snyder (1981).

3 For more on the Lacanian perspective, see the discussion of recent feminist psychoanalysts (including Juliet Mitchell) in Chapter 3.

4 Erik Erikson (1968) is one who thinks women do not acquire a complete identity until they acquire a man in their life. See also Carol Gilligan's critique of Erikson in chapter 1 of *In a Different Voice* (1982).

5 See, e.g., Garfinkel (1967), Raymond (1979), and Kessler & McKenna (1978).

6 See, e.g., the final section of this chapter, as well as D'Emilio (1983b), D'Emilio & Freedman (1988), and Halperin (1990).

7 I am indebted to Berger (1963) for suggesting the first enculturation process and to Shweder (1984) for suggesting the second.

8 This theoretical discussion of enculturation has been greatly influenced by Berger (1963), Shweder & LeVine (1984), Geertz (1973, 1983), and Shweder (1984). For more on the social construction of the child, see Edelstein (1983), Kessen (1979), Kessel & Siegel (1983), Tobin et al. (1989), and especially Wartofsky (1983).

9 This discussion of American individualism has been much informed by Bellah et al. (1985), Geertz (1983), Hsu (1985), Ochs & Schieffelin (1984), and Shweder & Bourne (1984).

10 See chapter 10, entitled "Space Speaks," in E. T. Hall (1973).

11 Anne Z. Parker, University of Oregon Geography Department, personal communication.

12 See Connell (1987) for further discussion of these female job types. For more on sex segregation in the workplace generally, see Reskin (1984), Reskin & Hartmann (1986), and Reskin & Roos (1990).

13 For a sample of this feminist critique, see Martyna (1980); for recommendations on alternative forms, see Frank & Treichler (1989).

14 For more on my own analysis of gender-liberated child-rearing, see the final sections of my 1983, 1984, 1985, and 1989 works.

15 For evidence documenting the greater prohibition of cross-gender activity and clothing choice for boys than for girls, see Carter & McCloskey (1983–1984), Fagot (1977, 1985), Fling & Manosevitz (1972), Langlois & Downs (1980), and Stoddart & Turiel (1985). For a provocative analysis of the cultural significance of cross-dressing in history, literature, film, photography, and popular and mass culture, see Garber (1992).

16 The constructivist tradition in personality psychology is exemplified by Allport (1961), Kelly (1955), Bem & Allen (1974), and Caspi, Bem & Elder (1989). For a discussion of other constructivist personality theories, see Bem (1987). The constructivist tradition in cognitive psychology was solidly established as dominant in the field by Ulrich Neisser's 1967 textbook, *Cognitive Psychology*. For a more accessible introduction to Neisser's views, see Neisser (1976). For an extended introduction to this whole perspective, see Glass & Holyoak (1985) and Gardner (1985).

17 For more detailed summaries of these and other empirical studies on the behavioral limitations of conventionally gendered people, see Bem (1978, 1983, 1985). For a more complete discussion of the unconventionally gendered people, who are interesting in their own right but who are not singled out here because of certain theoretical and empirical complexities unrelated to the current argument, see Bem (1985), Frable & Bem (1985), and Frable (1990).

18 The only exception to this pattern was when the members of the group were all male or all female, in which case the benefit of position was extended to anyone seated at the head of the table (Porter & Geis, 1981; Porter et al., 1983).

19 For a good introduction to this research, see pp. 246–249 of Lott (1987) or pp. 129–137 of Matlin (1987). For another good introduction to the general area of feminist psychology, see Unger & Crawford (1992).

20 For the empirical evidence substantiating this inconsistency with biology, see Rodin et al. (1985) and Dornbusch et al. (1984).

21 For research on sex differences in what psychologists call nonverbal behavior, see Mayo & Henley (1981).

22 For a history of female appetite suppression, see Brumberg (1988).

23 For more on date, or acquaintance, rape, see Parrot & Bechhofer (1991) and Warshaw (1988).

24 Many different kinds of evidence document this connection between homophobia and males, including the greater number of laws in the history of Western culture proscribing male homosexuality and the greater amount of attention given to male homosexuality within psychiatric theory. For empirical evidence documenting that males also have more homophobic attitudes than females, see Herek (1988).

25 For a delightful overview of this cross-cultural diversity, see Newton (1988).

26 The historical analysis that serves as the basis for this discussion of identity comes from D'Emilio (1983a, 1983b).

27 See Katz (1976) for primary source materials for all of these treatments.

28 For writings emphasizing the general concept of a gay perspective, see Brown (1989) and Sedgwick (1990). For one view of the history of the new field of lesbian, gay, and bisexual studies, see Escoffier (1990). As in all developing fields, many important conceptual issues are still a site of struggle. For me, one of the most interesting questions is, Who are to be defined as part of lesbian, gay male, and bisexual history? In other words, what broader category of human beings do today's lesbian, gay, and bisexual people represent, both historically and cross-culturally?

The struggle over this issue to date has most often involved the question of whether some historical figure can be called a lesbian today if she did not define herself that way and if her commitment to women was more emotional or political than erotic or genital (see, e.g., Ferguson, 1990). Still, the question that most interests me is whether the category should be specifically organized around the forming of sexual or affectional bonds with one's own sex or whether it should be reorganized to emphasize having a psyche that *in any way* challenges the gender-polarizing conception of a natural link between the sex of the body and the gender of the psyche. If the latter, then not all women who had intense relationships with other women would necessarily be included in the category represented by today's lesbian, gay male, and bisexual people, but all cross-dressers, all transsexuals, all berdaches, and all boundary-crossing gender pioneers would be included.

Which of these categories one favors depends, in part, on whether one takes the twentieth-century view that sexual desire is the key to the individual's psyche or the nineteenth-century view that sexual desire is related to a larger psychic pattern, or what is today called gender. Living though I do in a twentieth-century world, I myself still retain a bit of the nineteenth-century view.

29 For some examples of these stage theories, see Coleman (1982), Finnegan & McNally (1987), Troiden (1979), and especially Cass (1979, 1983/1984). For an in-depth critique of these theories, see Kitzinger (1987).

30 For more on the inner tensions of identity politics, see Weeks (1987), chapter 7 of Fuss (1989), and Butler (1990). For a thoughtful and provocative discussion of many aspects of gay identity, see pp. 1–90 of Sedgwick (1990).

Chapter 6: Transforming the Debate on Sexual Inequality

1 For a relatively benign example of this "female choice" reasoning, see Kirp et al. (1986).

2 The most concise and convincing presentation of these data is in Fuchs (1988).

3 For other discussions of the overall conflict between gender neutrality and special protection, see Baer (1978), Kaminer (1990), and Kirp et al. (1986). For an excellent introduction to the comparable worth debate, see Gold (1983). For a radical proposal related to the preferential hiring of women, see Hawkesworth (1990).

4 This recent feminist concern with female-female difference grew out of the legitimate accusation made by women of color in the 1970s that feminists, and feminism, were guilty of falsely universalizing what were really just the interests of white, middle-class women; feminists were also accused of denying their own complicity in the racist and classist oppression of people of color, both male and female. For more on the perspectives of feminists from different races and classes, see Davis (1981), hooks (1984), Hull, Scott & Smith (1982), and Joseph & Lewis (1981).

5 Freedman's remarks about the continuing validity of the feminist project were made in 1987 at a Stanford University conference on feminist approaches to sexual difference. Although the conference was much more oriented to theory than to social policy, the collection that grew out of it (Rhode, 1990) nevertheless provides an excellent example of the debate over difference that I have characterized here.

6 This argument that androcentrism turns difference into disadvantage has many features in common with arguments put forth elsewhere by MacKinnon (1987), Okin (1989), and Rhode (1989).

7 For a provocative feminist critique of the current U.S. welfare system, see chapter 7 of Fraser (1989).

8 For more on this antifeminist backlash, see Faludi (1991).

9 For an analysis that considers how apparently neutral institutions systematically discriminate against many nondominant groups—including those who are "different" with respect to race, gender, age, ethnicity, religion, and disability—see Minow (1990).

10 For some thoughts on how sexuality might be organized in the absence of gender polarization, see Newton & Walton (1984) and Rubin (1984).

REFERENCES

Adkins-Regan, E. (1988). Sex hormones and sexual orientation in animals. *Psychobiology, 16*(4), 335–347.

Alcoff, L. (1988). Cultural feminism versus post-structuralism: The identity crisis in feminist theory. *Signs: Journal of Women in Culture and Society, 13,* 405–436.

Alda, A. (1975). What every woman should know about men. *Ms,* October, pp. 15–16.

Allport, G. W. (1961). *Pattern and growth in personality.* New York: Holt, Rinehart & Winston.

American Psychiatric Association. (1980). *Diagnostic and statistical manual of mental disorders* (3rd ed.). Washington, D.C.: American Psychiatric Association.

Aptheker, B. (1989). *Tapestries of life: Women's work, women's consciousness, and the meaning of daily experience.* Amherst: University of Massachusetts Press.

Aristotle (1952a). On the generation of animals. In R. M. Hutchins (Ed.), *Great books of the Western world* (Vol. 9, pp. 225–331). Chicago: Encyclopaedia Britannica.

——— (1952b). Politics. In R. M. Hutchins (Ed.), *Great books of the Western world* (Vol. 9, pp. 445–548). Chicago: Encyclopaedia Britannica.

Arnold, A. P., & Gorski, R. A. (1984). Gonadal steriod induction of structural sex differences in the central nervous system. *Annual Review of Neuroscience, 7,* 413–442.

Baer, J. A. (1978). *The chains of protection: The judicial response to women's labor legislation.* Westport, Conn.: Greenwood Press.

Bakan, D. (1966). *The duality of human existence.* Chicago: Rand McNally.

Bannister, R. C. (1979). *Social Darwinism: Science and myth in Anglo-American thought.* Philadelphia: Temple University Press.

211

REFERENCES

Barash, D. (1979). *The whisperings within.* New York: Harper & Row.

Baron, A. (1987). Feminist legal strategies: The powers of difference. In B. B. Hess & M. M. Ferree (Eds.), *Analyzing gender: A handbook of social science research* (pp. 474–503). Newbury Park, Calif.: Sage.

Barry, H., III, Bacon, M. K., & Child, I. L. (1957). A cross-cultural survey of some sex differences in socialization. *Journal of Abnormal and Social Psychology, 55,* 327–332.

Basch, N. (1982). *In the eyes of the law: Women, marriage, and property in nineteenth-century New York.* Ithaca, N.Y.: Cornell University Press.

Baum, M. J. (1979). Differentiation of coital behavior in mammals: A comparative analysis. *Neuroscience and Biobehavior Review, 3,* 265–284.

Bayer, R. (1981). *Homosexuality and American psychiatry: The politics of diagnosis.* Princeton, N.J.: Princeton University Press.

Beach, F. A. (1981). Historical origins of modern research on hormones and behavior. *Hormones and Behavior, 15,* 325–376.

Beatty, W. W. (1979). Gonadal hormones and sex differences in nonreproductive behaviors in rodents: Organizational and activational influences. *Hormones and Behavior, 12,* 112–163.

Beauvoir, S. de. (1952). The second sex. New York: Knopf.

Becker, H. S. (1963). *Outsiders: Studies in the sociology of deviance.* New York: Free Press.

Bell, N. J., Weinberg, M. S., & Hammersmith, S. K. (1981). *Sexual preference: Its development in men and women.* Bloomington: Indiana University Press.

Bellah, R. N., Madsen, R., Sullivan, W. M., Swidler, A., & Tipton, S. M. (1985). *Habits of the heart: Individualism and commitment in American life.* New York: Harper.

Bem, D. J., & Allen, A. (1974). On predicting some of the people some of the time: The search for cross-situational consistencies in behavior. *Psychological Review, 81,* 506–520.

Bem, S. L. (1972). *Psychology looks at sex roles: Where have all the androgynous people gone?* Los Angeles: UCLA Symposium on Sex Roles.

————— (1974). The measurement of psychological androgyny. *Journal of Clinical and Consulting Psychology, 42,* 155–162.

————— (1975). Sex role adaptability: One consequence of psychological androgyny. *Journal of Personality and Social Psychology, 31,* 634–643.

————— (1977). On the utility of alternative procedures for assessing psychological androgyny. *Journal of Clinical and Consulting Psychology, 45,* 196–205.

—— (1978). Beyond androgyny: Some presumptuous prescriptions for a liberated gender identity. In J. A. Sherman & F. L. Denmark (Eds.), *The psychology of women: Future directions in research* (pp. 1–23). New York: Psychological Dimensions.

—— (1981a). *Bem Sex Role Inventory professional manual.* Palo Alto, Calif.: Consulting Psychologists Press.

—— (1981b). Gender schema theory: A cognitive account of sex typing. *Psychological Review, 88,* 354–364.

—— (1983). Gender schema theory and its implications for child development: Raising gender-aschematic children in a gender-schematic society. *Signs: Journal of Women in Culture and Society, 8,* 598–616.

—— (1984). From biology to feminism: Reply to Morgan and Ayim. *Signs: Journal of Women in Culture and Society, 10,* 197–199.

—— (1985). Androgyny and gender schema theory: A conceptual and empirical integration. In T. B. Sonderegger (Ed.), *Nebraska Symposium on Motivation, 1984: Psychology and gender* (pp. 179–226). Lincoln: University of Nebraska Press.

—— (1987). Gender schema theory and the romantic tradition. In P. Shaver & C. Hendrick (Eds.), *Review of personality and social psychology* (Vol. 7, pp. 251–271). Newbury Park, Calif.: Sage.

—— (1989). Genital knowledge and gender constancy in preschool children. *Child Development, 60,* 649–662.

—— (1992). On the inadequacy of our sexual categories: A personal perspective. *Feminism and psychology, 2,* 435–437.

Bem, S. L., & Lenney, E. (1976). Sex typing and the avoidance of cross-sex behavior. *Journal of Personality and Social Psychology, 33,* 48–54.

Bem, S. L., Martyna, W., & Watson, C. (1976). Sex typing and androgyny: Further explorations of the expressive domain. *Journal of Personality and Social Psychology, 34,* 1016–1023.

Benbow, C. P. (1988). Sex differences in mathematical reasoning ability in intellectually talented preadolescents: Their nature, effects, and possible causes. *Behavioral and Brain Sciences, 11,* 169–232.

Benjamin, H. (1966). *The transsexual phenomenon.* New York: Julian Press.

Berger, P. L. (1963). *Invitation to sociology: A humanistic perspective.* New York: Doubleday.

Bergler, E. (1947). Differential diagnosis between spurious homosexuality and perversion homosexuality. *Psychiatric Quarterly, 21,* 399–409.

REFERENCES

———— (1956). *Homosexuality: Disease or way of life?*. New York: Hill & Wang.

Bernal, M. (1987). *Black Athena: The Afroasiatic roots of classical civilization*. New Brunswick, N.J.: Rutgers University Press.

Bernstein, R. J. (1976). *The restructuring of social and political theory*. New York: Harcourt Brace.

Bieber, I. (1965). Clinical aspects of male homosexuality. In J. Marmor (Ed.), *Sexual inversion: The multiple roots of homosexuality* (pp. 248–267). New York: Basic Books.

Bieber, I., Dain, H., Dince, P., Drellich, M., Grand, H., Gundlach, R., Kremer, M., Rifkin, A., Wilbur, C., & Bieber, T. (1962). *Homosexuality: A psychoanalytic study of male homosexuals*. New York: Basic Books.

Birke, L. I. A. (1989). How do gender differences in behavior develop? A reanalysis of the role of early experience. In P. P. G. Bateson & P. H. Klopfer (Eds.), *Perspectives in ethology: Whither ethology?* (Vol. 8, pp. 215–242). New York: Plenum.

Birken, L. (1988). *Consuming desire: Sexual science and the emergence of a culture of abundance, 1871–1914*. Ithaca, N.Y.: Cornell University Press.

Blackstone, W. (1765–1769/1979). *Commentaries on the laws of England*. Chicago: University of Chicago Press.

Blanchard, R. (1985). Gender dysphoria and gender reorientation. In Steiner, 1985, pp. 365–392.

Bleier, R. (1984). *Science and gender: A critique of biology and its theories on women*. New York: Pergamon.

———— (Ed.). (1988a). *Feminist approaches to science*. New York: Pergamon.

———— (1988b). Sex differences research: Science or belief? In Bleier, 1988a, pp. 147–164.

Block, J. H. (1973). Conceptions of sex role: Some cross-cultural and longitudinal perspectives. *American Psychologist, 28*, 512–526.

———— (1976). Issues, problems, and pitfalls in assessing sex differences: A critical review of "The psychology of sex differences." *Merrill-Palmer Quarterly, 22*, 283–308.

Brigham, C. C. (1923). *A study of American intelligence*. Princeton, N.J.: Princeton University Press.

Broverman, I. K., Broverman, D. M., Clarkson, F. E., Rosenkrantz, P. S., & Vogel, S. R. (1970). Sex-role stereotypes and clinical judgments of mental health. *Journal of Consulting and Clinical Psychology, 34*, 1–7.

Brown, L. S. (1989). New voices, new visions: Toward a lesbian/gay paradigm for psychology. *Psychology of Women Quarterly, 13*, 445–458.

REFERENCES

Brownmiller, S. (1975). *Against our will: Men, women, and rape*. New York: Simon & Schuster.

Brumberg, J. J. (1988). *Fasting girls: The emergence of anorexia nervosa as a modern disease*. Cambridge, Mass.: Harvard University Press.

Bullough, V. L., Shelton, B., & Slavin, S. (1988). *The subordinated sex: A history of attitudes toward women*. Athens: University of Georgia Press.

Butler, J. P. (1990). *Gender trouble: Feminism and the subversion of identity*. New York: Routledge.

Caplan, A. L. (Ed.). (1978). *The sociobiology debate: Readings on the ethical and scientific issues concerning sociobiology*. New York: Harper & Row.

Carey, S. (1985). *Conceptual change in childhood*. Cambridge, Mass.: MIT/Bradford Press.

Carter, D. B., & McCloskey, L. A. (1983–1984). Peers and the maintenance of sex-typed behavior: The development of children's conceptions of cross-gender behavior in their peers. *Social Cognition, 2,* 294–314.

Caspi, A., Bem, D. J., & Elder, G. H., Jr. (1989). Continuities and consequences of interactional styles across the life course. *Journal of Personality, 57,* 375–406.

Cass, V. C. (1979). Homosexual identity formation: A theoretical model. *Journal of Homosexuality, 4,* 219–235.

——— (1983–1984). Homosexual identity: A concept in need of definition. *Journal of Homosexuality, 9,* 105–126.

Chauncey, G. J. (1982–1983). From sexual inversion to homosexuality: Medicine and the changing conceptualization of female deviance. *Salmagundi: A Quarterly of the Humanities and Social Sciences, 58–59,* 114–146.

Chi, M. T. H. (1978). Knowledge structure and memory development. In R. S. Siegler (Ed.), *Children's thinking: What develops?* (pp. 73–96). Hillsdale, N.J.: Erlbaum.

Chodorow, N. J. (1978). *The reproduction of mothering: Psychoanalysis and the sociology of gender*. Berkeley: University of California Press.

——— (1989). *Feminism and psychoanalytic theory*. New Haven, Conn.: Yale University Press.

Clark, H. H. (1969). Linguistic processes in deductive reasoning. *Psychological Review, 76,* 387–404.

Clarke, E. H. (1873). *Sex in education; or, A fair chance for girls*. Boston: J. R. Osgood.

Cole, D. (1984). Strategies of difference: Litigating for women's rights in a man's world. *Law and Inequality: A Journal of Theory and Practice, 2,* 33–96.

REFERENCES

Coleman, E. (1982). Developmental stages of the coming-out process. *Journal of Homosexuality, 7*, 31–43.

Connell, R. W. (1987). *Gender and power*. Stanford, Calif.: Stanford University Press.

Constantinople, A. (1973). Masculinity-femininity: An exception to a famous dictum. *Psychological Bulletin, 80*, 389–407.

Cott, N. F. (1978). Passionlessness: A reinterpretation of Victorian sexual ideology, 1790–1850. *Signs: Journal of Women in Culture and Society, 4*, 219–236.

Crawford, M., & Maracek, J. (1989). Psychology reconstructs the female: 1968–1988. *Psychology of Women Quarterly, 13*, 147–165.

Crocker, P. (1985). The meaning of equality for battered women who kill men in self-defense. *Harvard Women's Law Journal, 8*, 121–153.

Daly, M. (1978). *Gyn/Ecology: The metaethics of radical feminism*. Boston: Beacon.

Darwin, C. (1859/1952). The origin of species by means of natural selection. In R. M. Hutchins (Ed.), *Great books of the Western world* (Vol. 49, pp. 1–251). Chicago: Encyclopaedia Britannica.

―――― (1871/1952). The descent of man and selection in relation to sex. In R. M. Hutchins (Ed.), *Great books of the Western world* (Vol. 49, pp. 253–600). Chicago: Encyclopaedia Britannica.

Davis, A. Y. (1981). *Women, race and class*. New York: Random House.

Dawkins, R. (1976). *The selfish gene*. New York: Oxford University Press.

Deaux, K. (1976). *The behavior of women and men*. Monterey, Calif.: Brooks/Cole.

―――― (1984). From individual differences to social categories: Analysis of a decade's research on gender. *American Psychologist, 39*, 105–116.

D'Emilio, J. (1983a). Capitalism and gay identity. In A. Snitow, C. Stansell & S. Thompson (Eds.), *Powers of desire: The politics of sexuality* (pp. 100–113). New York: Monthly Review Press.

―――― (1983b). *Sexual politics, sexual communities: The making of a homosexual minority in the United States, 1940–1970*. Chicago: University of Chicago Press.

D'Emilio, J., & Freedman, E. B. (1988). *Intimate matters: A history of sexuality in America*. New York: Harper & Row.

Donavan, J. (1988). *Feminist theory: The intellectual traditions of modern American feminism*. New York: Continuum.

Dornbusch, S. M., Carlsmith, J. M., Duncan, P. D., Gross, R. T., Martin, J. A., Ritter, P. L., & Siegel-Gorelick, B. (1984). Sexual maturation, social class, and the desire to be thin among adolescent females. *Developmental and Behavioral Pediatrics, 5*, 308–314.

REFERENCES

DSM. See American Psychiatric Association.

Duberman, M. B., Vicinus, M. B., & Chauncey, G., Jr. (Eds.). (1989). *Hidden from history: Reclaiming the gay and lesbian past*. New York: New American Library.

DuBois, E. C. (1978). *Feminism and suffrage: The emergence of an independent women's movement in America, 1848–1869*. Ithaca, N.Y.: Cornell University Press.

Eagly, A. H. (1987). *Sex differences in social behavior: A social-role interpretation*. Hillsdale, N.J.: Erlbaum.

Echols, A. (1983). *The new feminism of yin and yang*. New York: Monthly Review Press.

——— (1989). *Daring to be bad: Radical feminism in America, 1967–1975*. Minneapolis: University of Minnesota Press.

Edelstein, W. (1983). Cultural constraints on development and the vicissitudes of progress. In Kessel & Siegel, 1983, pp. 48–81.

Eisenstein, H. (1983). *Contemporary feminist thought*. Boston: G. K. Hall.

Eisenstein, H., & Jardine, A. (Eds.). (1980). *The future of difference*. Boston: G. K. Hall.

Eisenstein, Z. R. (1988). *The female body and the law*. Berkeley: University of California Press.

Ellis, H. (1928). *Studies in the psychology of sex*, Vol. 7: *Eonism and other supplementary studies*. Philadelphia: F. A. Davis.

Ellis, H., & Symonds, J. A. (1897/1975). *Sexual inversion*. New York: Arno Press.

Ember, C. (1973). Feminine task assignment and the social behavior of boys. *Ethos, 1*, 424–439.

Epstein, C. F. (1988). *Deceptive distinctions: Sex, gender, and the social order*. New Haven, Conn.: Yale University Press.

Erikson, E. H. (1968). Womanhood and the inner space. In E. H. Erikson (Ed.), *Identity: Youth and crisis* (pp. 261–294). New York: Norton.

Escoffier, J. (1990). Inside the ivory closet: The challenges facing lesbian and gay studies. *Out/Look*, Fall, pp. 40–48.

Estrich, S. (1987). *Real rape*. Cambridge, Mass.: Harvard University Press.

Faderman, L. (1978). The morbidification of love between women by nineteenth-century sexologists. *Journal of Homosexuality, 4*, 73–90.

——— (1981). *Surpassing the love of men: Romantic friendship and love between women from the Renaissance to the present*. New York: Morrow.

——— (1991). *Odd girls and twilight lovers: A history of lesbian life in twentieth-century America*. New York: Columbia University Press.

Fagot, B. I. (1977). Consequences of moderate cross-gender behavior in preschool children. *Child Development, 48,* 902–907.

——— (1985). Beyond the reinforcement principle: Another step toward understanding sex role development. *Developmental Psychology, 21,* 1097–1104.

Fagot, B. I., Hagen, R., Leinbach, M. D., & Kronsberg, S. (1985). Differential reactions to assertive and communicative acts of toddler boys and girls. *Child Development, 56,* 1499–1505.

Faludi, S. (1991). *Backlash: The undeclared war against American women.* New York: Crown.

Fausto-Sterling, A. (1985). *Myths of gender: Biological theories about women and men.* New York: Basic Books.

Feder, H. (1984). Hormones and sexual behavior. *Annual Review of Psychology, 35,* 165–200.

Ferguson, A. (1990). Is there a lesbian culture? In J. Allen (Ed.), *Lesbian philosophies and cultures* (pp. 63–88). Albany: State University of New York Press.

Feyerabend, P. K. (1976). *Against method.* New York: Humanities Press.

Figes, E. (1970). *Patriarchal attitudes.* London: Faber & Faber.

Fine, M. (1985). Reflections on a feminist psychology of women. *Psychology of Women Quarterly, 9,* 167–183.

Fine, M., & Gordon, S. M. (1989). Feminist transformations of/despite psychology. In M. Crawford & M. Gentry (Eds.) *Gender and thought: Psychological perspectives* (pp. 146–174). New York: Springer-Verlag.

Finnegan, D. G., & McNally, E. B. (1987). *Dual identities: Counseling chemically dependent gay men and lesbians.* Center City, Minn.: Hazelden.

Fiske, D. W., & Shweder, R. A. (Eds.). (1986). *Metatheory in social science: Pluralisms and subjectivities.* Chicago: University of Chicago Press.

Fitzhugh, G. (1854/1965). *Sociology for the South; or, The failure of free society.* New York: B. Franklin.

Flavell, J. H. (1963). *The developmental psychology of Jean Piaget.* New York: Van Nostrand.

Flax, J. (1987). Postmodernism and gender relations in feminist theory. *Signs: Journal of Women in Culture and Society, 12,* 621–643.

Fleming, A. S. (1989). Maternal responsiveness in human and animal mothers. In M. H. Bornstein (Ed.), *Maternal responsiveness: Characteristics and consequences. New directions for child development* (Vol. 43, pp. 31–47). San Francisco: Jossey-Bass.

Flexner, E. (1959). *Century of struggle: The woman's rights movement in the United States.* Cambridge, Mass.: Harvard University Press.

Fling, S., & Manosevitz, M. (1972). Sex typing in nursery school children's play interests. *Developmental Psychology, 7,* 146–152.

Ford, C. S., & Beach, F. A. (1951). *Patterns of sexual behavior*. New York: Harper.

Foucault, M. (1978). *The history of sexuality,* Vol. 1: *An introduction*. New York: Random House.

Frable, D. E. S. (1989). Sex-typing and gender ideology: Two facets of the individual's gender psychology that go together. *Journal of Personality and Social Psychology, 56,* 95–108.

——— (1990). Marginal and mindful: Deviants in social interactions. *Journal of Personality and Social Psychology, 59,* 140–149.

Frable, D. E. S., & Bem, S. L. (1985). If you're gender-schematic, all members of the opposite sex look alike. *Journal of Personality and Social Psychology, 49,* 459–468.

Frank, F. W., & Treichler, P. A. (Eds.). (1989). *Language, gender, and professional writing: Theoretical approaches and guidelines for nonsexist usage*. New York: Modern Language Association of America.

Fraser, N. (1989). *Unruly practices: Power, discourse, and gender in contemporary social theory*. Minneapolis: University of Minnesota Press.

Fredrickson, G. M. (1971). *The black image in the white mind: The debate on Afro-American character and destiny, 1817–1914*. New York: Harper & Row.

Freedman, E. B. (1990). Theoretical perspectives on sexual difference: An overview. In Rhode, 1990, pp. 257–261.

Freud, S. (1905/1962). *Three essays on the theory of sexuality*. New York: Basic Books.

——— (1920/1959). The psychogenesis of a case of homosexuality in a woman. In E. Jones (Ed.), *Sigmund Freud: Collected papers* (Vol. 2, pp. 202–231). New York: Basic Books.

——— (1924/1959). The passing of the Oedipus-complex. In E. Jones (Ed.), *Sigmund Freud: Collected papers* (Vol. 2, pp. 269–276). New York: Basic Books.

——— (1925/1959). Some psychological consequences of the anatomical distinction between the sexes. In E. Jones (Ed.), *Sigmund Freud: Collected papers* (Vol. 5, pp. 186–197). New York: Basic Books.

——— (1933/1964). Femininity. In J. Strachey (Ed.), *New introductory lectures on psychoanalysis* (pp. 99–119). New York: Norton.

Friedan, B. (1963). *The feminine mystique*. New York: Norton.

Friedman, R. C. (1988). *Male homosexuality: A contemporary psychoanalytic perspective*. New Haven, Conn.: Yale University Press.

Frodi, A., Macaulay, J., & Thome, P. R. (1977). Are women always less aggressive than men? A review of the experimental literature. *Psychological Bulletin, 84,* 634–660.

Fuchs, V. F. (1988). *Women's quest for economic equality.* Cambridge, Mass.: Harvard University Press.

Fuss, D. (1989). *Essentially speaking: Feminism, nature, and difference.* New York: Routledge.

Gallop, J. (1982). *The daughter's seduction: Feminism and psychoanalysis.* Ithaca, N.Y.: Cornell University Press.

———— (1985). *Reading Lacan.* Ithaca, N.Y.: Cornell University Press.

Garai, J. E., & Scheinfield, A. (1968). Sex differences in mental and behavioral traits. *Genetic Psychology Monographs, 77,* 169–299.

Garber, M. (1992). *Vested interests: Cross-dressing and cultural anxiety.* New York: Routledge.

Gardner, H. (1985). *The mind's new science: A history of the cognitive revolution.* New York: Basic Books.

Garfinkel, H. (1967). Passing and the managed achievement of sex status in an intersexed person, part 1. In H. Garfinkel (Ed.), *Studies in ethnomethodology* (pp. 116–185). Englewood Cliffs, N.J.: Prentice-Hall.

Geddes, P., & Thomson, J. A. (1890). *The evolution of sex.* New York: Scribner & Welford.

Geertz, C. (1973). *The interpretation of cultures.* New York: Basic Books.

———— (1983). From the native's point of view: On the nature of anthropological understanding. In C. Geertz (Ed.), *Local knowledge: Further essays in interpretive anthropology* (pp. 55–70). New York: Basic Books.

Gelman, R., & Baillargeon, R. (1983). A review of some Piagetian concepts. In J. H. Flavell & E. M. Markman (Eds.), *Handbook of child psychology: Cognitive development* (Vol. 3, pp. 167–230). New York: Wiley.

Gelman, R., & Gallistel, C. R. (1978). *The child's understanding of number.* Cambridge, Mass.: Harvard University Press.

Gelpi, B. C. (1974). The politics of androgyny. *Women's Studies, 2,* 151–160.

Gilligan, C. (1982). *In a different voice: Psychological theory and women's development.* Cambridge, Mass.: Harvard University Press.

Gilman, C. P. (1911/1971). *The man-made world; or, Our androcentric culture.* New York: Johnson Reprint.

Glass, A. L., & Holyoak, K. J. (1985). *Cognition.* New York: Random House.

Goddard, H. H. (1917). Mental tests and the immigrant. *Journal of Delinquency, 2,* 243–277.

REFERENCES

Goffman, E. (1963). *Stigma: Notes on the management of spoiled identity*. Englewood Cliffs, N.J.: Prentice-Hall.

Gold, M. E. (Ed.). (1983). *A dialogue on comparable worth*. Ithaca, N.Y.: Industrial and Labor Relations Press.

Goldfoot, D. A., & Neff, D. A. (1987). Assessment of behavioral sex differences in social contexts: Perspectives from primatology. In J. M. Reinisch, L. A. Rosenblum & S. A. Sanders (Eds.), *Masculinity/femininity: Basic perspectives* (pp. 179–195). New York: Oxford University Press.

Goldman, R. J., & Goldman, J. D. G. (1982). *Children's sexual thinking*. London: Routledge & Kegan Paul.

Gould, S. J. (1980). Women's brains. In S. J. Gould (Ed.), *The panda's thumb: More reflections in natural history* (pp. 152–159). New York: Norton.

——— (1981). *The mismeasure of man*. New York: Norton.

Goy, R., & Resko, J. A. (1972). Gonadal hormones and behavior of normal and pseudohermaphroditic nonhuman female primates. In E. B. Astwood (Ed.), *Recent progress in hormone research* (Vol. 28, pp. 707–754). New York: Academic Press.

Grant, M. (1922). *The passing of the great race; or, The racial basis of European history*. New York: Scribner's.

Green, R. (1974). *Sexual identity conflict in children and adults*. Baltimore, Md.: Penguin.

——— (1987). *The "sissy boy syndrome" and the development of homosexuality*. New Haven, Conn.: Yale University Press.

Green, R., & Money, J. (1969). *Transsexualism and sex reassignment*. Baltimore, Md.: Johns Hopkins University Press.

Greenberg, D. E. (1988). *The construction of homosexuality*. Chicago: University of Chicago Press.

Gurko, M. (1974). *The ladies of Seneca Falls: The birth of the woman's rights movement*. New York: Macmillan.

Hall, C. S. (1954). *A primer of Freudian psychology*. New York: World Publishing.

Hall, E. T. (1973). *The silent language*. Garden City, N.Y.: Anchor Press/ Doubleday.

Hall, G. S. (1904/1919). *Adolescence: Its psychology and its relations to physiology, anthropology, sociology, sex, crime, religion, and education* (Vol. 2). New York: Appleton.

Hall, R. (1928). *The well of loneliness*. London: J. Cape.

Haller, M. H. (1963). *Eugenics: Hereditarian attitudes in American thought*. New Brunswick, N.J.: Rutgers University Press.

REFERENCES

Halperin, D. M. (1990). *One hundred years of homosexuality and other essays on Greek love*. New York: Routledge.

Hamilton, W. D. (1964). The genetical evolution of social behavior. *Journal of Theoretical Biology, 7*, 1–52.

Haraway, D. J. (1981). In the beginning was the word: The genesis of biological theory. *Signs: Journal of Women in Culture and Society, 6*, 469–481.

——— (1989). *Primate visions: Gender, race, and nature in the world of modern science*. New York: Routledge.

Harding, S. (1986). *The science question in feminism*. Ithaca, N.Y.: Cornell University Press.

——— (Ed.). (1987). *Feminism and methodology: Social science issues*. Bloomington: Indiana University Press.

Harding, S., & O'Barr, J. F. (Eds.). (1987). *Sex and scientific inquiry*. Chicago: University of Chicago Press.

Hare-Mustin, R. T., & Maracek, J. (1988). The meaning of difference: Gender theory, postmodernism, and psychology. *American Psychologist, 43*, 455–464.

——— (Eds.). (1990). *Making a difference: Psychology and the construction of gender*. New Haven, Conn.: Yale University Press.

Hartsock, N. C. M. (1983). *Money, sex, and power: Toward a feminist historical materialism*. New York: Longman.

Hawkesworth, M. E. (1990). *Beyond oppression: Feminist theory and political strategy*. New York: Continuum.

Heilbrun, C. G. (1973). *Toward a recognition of androgyny*. New York: Norton.

——— (1980). Androgyny and the psychology of sex differences. In Eisenstein & Jardine, 1980, pp. 258–266.

Henley, N. M. (1977). *Body politics: Power, sex, and nonverbal communication*. Englewood Cliffs, N.J.: Prentice-Hall.

——— (1985). Review essay: Psychology and gender. *Signs: Journal of Women in Culture and Society, 11*, 101–119.

Herdt, G. H. (1981). *Guardians of the flutes: Idioms of masculinity; A study of ritualized homosexual behavior*. New York: McGraw-Hill.

Herdt, G. H., & Davidson, J. (1988). The Sambia "turnim-man": Sociocultural and clinical aspects of gender formation in male pseudohermaphrodites with 5-alpha-reductase deficiency in Papua New Guinea. *Archives of Sexual Behavior, 17*, 33–56.

Herek, G. M. (1988). Heterosexuals' attitudes toward lesbians and gay men: Correlates and gender differences. *Journal of Sex Research, 25*, 451–477.

Hochschild, A. (1973). A review of sex role research. In J. Huber (Ed.), *Changing women in a changing society* (pp. 249–267). Chicago: University of Chicago Press.

Hoffman, M. (1968). *The gay world: Male homosexuality and the social creation of evil*. New York: Basic Books.

Hofstadter, R. (1959). *Social Darwinism in American thought*. New York: Braziller.

Hooker, E. (1957). The adjustment of the male overt homosexual. *Journal of Projective Techniques, 21*, 18–31.

hooks, b. (1984). *Feminist theory: From margin to center*. Boston: South End Press.

Hsu, F. L. K. (1985). The self in cross-cultural perspective. In A. J. Marsella, G. DeVos & F. L. K. Hsu (Eds.), *Culture and self: Asian and Western perspectives* (pp. 24–55). New York: Tavistock.

Hubbard, R. (1979). Have only men evolved? In R. Hubbard, M. S. Henifin & B. Fried (Eds.), *Women look at biology looking at women* (pp. 7–35). Cambridge, Mass.: Schenkman.

Hull, G. T., Scott, P. B., & Smith, B. (Eds.). (1982). *All the women are white, all the blacks are men, but some of us are brave: Black women's studies*. New York: Feminist Press.

Huston, A. C. (1983). Sex-typing. In P. H. Mussen (Ed.), *Handbook of child psychology* (Vol. 4, pp. 387–467). New York: Wiley.

Huxley, J. (1943). *Evolution: The modern synthesis*. New York: Harper.

Hyde, J. S., & Linn, M. C. (Eds.). (1986). *The psychology of gender: Advances through meta-analysis*. Baltimore, Md.: Johns Hopkins University Press.

Imperato-McGinley, J., Peterson, R. E., Gautier, T., & Sturla, E. (1979a). Androgens and the evolution of male gender identity among male pseudohermaphrodites with a 5-alpha-reductase deficiency. *New England Journal of Medicine, 300*, 1236–1237.

——— (1979b). Male pseudohermaphroditism secondary to 5-alpha-reductase deficiency: A model for the role of androgens in both the development of the male phenotype and the evolution of a male gender identity. *Journal of Steroid Biochemistry, 11*, 637–645.

Irigaray, L. (1985). *This sex which is not one*. Ithaca, N.Y.: Cornell University Press.

——— (1991). *The Irigaray reader*. Cambridge, Mass.: Basil Blackwell.

Jacklin, C. N. (1989). Female and male: Issues of gender. *American Psychologist, 44*, 127–133.

Jaggar, A. M. (1983). *Feminist politics and human nature*. Totowa, N.J.: Rowman & Allanheld.

Jeffreys, S. (1985). *The spinster and her enemies: Feminism and sexuality, 1880–1930*. London: Pandora.

Jensen, A. R. (1969). How much can we boost IQ and scholastic achievement? *Harvard Educational Review, 39,* 1–123.

Jones, E. (1927/1961). The early development of female sexuality. In E. Jones (Ed.), *Papers on psycho-analysis* (pp. 438–451). Boston: Beacon.

―――― (1935/1961). Early female sexuality. In E. Jones (Ed.), *Papers on psycho-analysis* (pp. 485–495). Boston: Beacon.

―――― (1957). *The life and work of Sigmund Freud* (Vol. 3). New York: Basic Books.

Jordan, W. D. (1968). *White over black: American attitudes toward the Negro, 1550–1812*. Chapel Hill: University of North Carolina Press.

Jordanova, L. J. (1980). Natural facts: A historical perspective on science and sexuality. In C. P. MacCormack & M. Strathern (Eds.), *Nature, culture, and gender* (pp. 42–69). Cambridge, Eng.: Cambridge University Press.

―――― (1989). *Sexual visions: Images of gender in science and medicine between the eighteenth and twentieth centuries*. Madison: University of Wisconsin Press.

Joseph, G. I., & Lewis, J. (1981). *Common differences: Conflicts in black and white feminist perspectives*. Boston: South End Press.

Jost, A. (1953). Problems of fetal endocrinology: The gonadal and hypophyseal hormones. *Recent Progress in Hormone Research, 8,* 379–418.

―――― (1983). Genetic and hormonal factors in sex differentiation of the brain. *Psychoneuroendocrinology, 8,* 183–193.

Jung, C. G. (1953). Anima and animus. In C. G. Jung (Ed.), *Two essays in analytical psychology* (pp. 198–223). New York: Meridian.

Kamin, L. J. (1974). *The science and politics of I.Q.* New York: Wiley.

Kaminer, W. (1990). *A fearful freedom: Women's flight from equality*. Reading, Mass.: Addison-Wesley.

Kanter, R. M. (1977). *Men and women of the corporation*. New York: Basic Books.

Kardiner, A. (1954). *Sex and morality*. Indianapolis, Ind.: Bobbs-Merrill.

Karsch, F. J., Dierschke, D. J., & Knobil, E. (1973). Sexual differentiation of pituitary function: Apparent difference between primates and rodents. *Science, 179,* 484–486.

Katcher, A. (1955). The discrimination of sex differences by young children. *Journal of Genetic Psychology, 87,* 131–143.

Katz, J. (Ed.). (1976). *Gay American history: Lesbians and gay men in the U.S.A.* New York: Harper & Row.

REFERENCES

Keil, F. C. (1989). *Concepts, kinds, and cognitive development*. Cambridge, Mass.: MIT/Bradford Press.

Keller, E. F. (1985). *Reflections of gender and science*. New Haven, Conn.: Yale University Press.

Kelly, G. A. (1955). *The psychology of personal constructs*. New York: Norton.

Kessel, F. S., & Siegel, A. W. (Eds.). (1983). *The child and other cultural inventions*. New York: Praeger.

Kessen, W. (1979). The American child and other cultural inventions. *American Psychologist, 34*, 815–820.

Kessler, S. J., & McKenna, W. (1978). *Gender: An ethnomethodological approach*. New York: Wiley.

Kevles, D. J. (1985). *In the name of eugenics: Genetics and the uses of human heredity*. New York: Knopf.

King, D. (1981). Gender confusions: Psychological and psychiatric conceptions of transvestism and transsexualism. In Plummer, 1981b, pp. 155–183.

King, K. (1990). Producing sex, theory, and culture: Gay/straight remappings in contemporary feminism. In M. Hirsch & E. F. Keller (Eds.), *Conflicts in feminism* (pp. 82–101). New York: Routledge.

Kinsey, A. C., Pomeroy, W. B., & Martin, C. E. (1948). *Sexual behavior in the human male*. Philadelphia: W. B. Saunders.

Kinsey, A. C., Pomeroy, W. B., Martin, C. E., & Gebhard, P. H. (1953). *Sexual behavior in the human female*. Philadelphia: W. B. Saunders.

Kirp, D. L., Yudof, M. G., & Franks, M. S. (1986). *Gender justice*. Chicago: University of Chicago Press.

Kitzinger, C. (1987). *The social construction of lesbianism*. London: Sage.

Klein, M. (1932). *The psycho-analysis of children*. New York: Delacorte.

Knobil, E., Plant, T. M., Wildt, L., Belchetz, P. E., & Marshall, G. (1980). Control of the rhesus monkey menstrual cycle: Permissive role of hypothalamic gonadotropin-releasing hormone. *Science, 207*, 1371–1373.

Kohlberg, L. (1966). A cognitive-developmental analysis of children's sex-role concepts and attitudes. In E. E. Maccoby (Ed.), *The development of sex differences* (pp. 82–173). Stanford, Calif.: Stanford University Press.

Kuhlin, H., & Reiter, E. O. (1976). Gonadotropin and testosterone measurements after estrogen administration to adult men, prepubertal and pubertal boys, and men with hypogonadotropism: Evidence for positive feedback in the male. *Pediatric Research, 10*, 46–51.

Kuhn, T. S. (1962). *The structure of scientific revolutions*. Chicago: University of Chicago Press.

Kwawer, J. (1980). Transference and countertransference in homosexuality: Changing psychoanalytic views. *American Journal of Psychoanalytic Therapy, 34,* 72–80.

Lakoff, G. (1987). *Women, fire, and dangerous things: What categories reveal about the mind.* Chicago: University of Chicago Press.

Langlois, J. H., & Downs, A. C. (1980). Mothers, fathers, and peers as socialization agents of sex-typed play behaviors in young children. *Child Development, 51,* 1237–1247.

Leiderman, P. H. (1981). Human mother–infant bonding: Is there a sensitive phase? In K. Immelmann, G. W. Barlow, L. Petrinovich & M. Main (Eds.), *Behavioral development: The Bielefeld interdisciplinary project* (pp. 454–468). New York: Cambridge University Press.

Leifer, A. D., Leiderman, P. H., Barnett, C. R., & Williams, J. A. (1972). Effects of mother-infant separation on maternal attachment behavior. *Child Development, 43,* 1203–1218.

Lenney, E. (1991). Sex roles: The measurement of masculinity, femininity, and androgyny. In J. P. Robinson, P. R. Shaver & L. S. Wrightsman (Eds.), *Measures of personality and social psychological attitudes* (Vol. 1, pp. 573–660). San Diego, Calif.: Academic Press.

Lerner, G. (1986). *The creation of patriarchy.* New York: Oxford University Press.

Levin, S. M., Balistrieri, J., & Schukit, M. (1972). The development of sexual discrimination in children. *Journal of Child Psychology and Psychiatry, 13,* 47–53.

Levins, R., & Lewontin, R. C. (1985). *The dialectical biologist.* Cambridge, Mass.: Harvard University Press.

Lewes, K. (1988). *The psychoanalytic theory of male homosexuality.* New York: New American Library.

Lewin, M. (1984a). "Rather worse than folly?" Psychology measures femininity and masculinity, 1: From Terman and Miles to the Guilfords. In M. Lewin (Ed.), *In the shadow of the past: Psychology portrays the sexes; A social and intellectual history* (pp. 155–178). New York: Columbia University Press.

——— (1984b). Psychology measures femininity and masculinity, 2: From "thirteen gay men" to the instrumental-expressive distinction. In M. Lewin (Ed.), *In the shadow of the past: Psychology portrays the sexes; A social and intellectual history* (pp. 179–204). New York: Columbia University Press.

Lewis, M., & Brooks-Gunn, J. (1979). *Social cognition and the acquisition of self.* New York: Plenum.

Lewontin, R. C. (1977). Sociobiology—a caricature of Darwinism. In F. Suppe & P. D. Asquith (Eds.), *Proceedings of the 1976 biennial meeting of the Journal of*

Philosophy of Science Association (Vol. 2, pp. 22–31). East Lansing, Mich.: Philosophy of Science Association.

Lewontin, R. C., Rose, S., & Kamin, L. J. (1984). *Not in our genes: Biology, ideology, and human nature.* New York: Pantheon.

Lindgren, J. R., & Taub, N. (1988). *The law of sex discrimination.* St. Paul, Minn.: West.

Longino, H. E. (1987). Can there be a feminist science? *Hypatia, 2,* 51–64.

———— (1990). *Science as social knowledge: Values and objectivity in scientific inquiry.* Princeton, N.J.: Princeton University Press.

Longino, H. E., & Doell, R. (1983). Body, bias, and behavior: A comparative analysis of reasoning in two areas of biological science. *Signs: Journal of Women in Culture and Society, 9,* 206–227.

Lott, B. (1981). A feminist critique of androgyny: Toward the elimination of gender attributions for learned behavior. In Mayo & Henley, 1981, pp. 171–180.

———— (1987). *Women's lives: Themes and variations in gender learning.* Monterey, Calif.: Brooks/Cole.

Lykes, M. B., & Stewart, A. S. (1986). Evaluating the feminist challenge to research in personality and social psychology: 1963–1983. *Psychology of Women Quarterly, 10,* 393–412.

Lyons, J. (1977). *Semantics* (Vol. 1). Cambridge, Eng.: Cambridge University Press.

Maccoby, E. E., & Jacklin, C. N. (1974). *The psychology of sex differences.* Stanford, Calif.: Stanford University Press.

McIntosh, M. (1968). The homosexual role. *Social Problems, 16,* 182–192.

MacKinnon, C. A. (1987). Difference and dominance: On sex discrimination (1984). In C. A. MacKinnon (Ed.), *Feminism unmodified: Discourses on life and law* (pp. 32–45). Cambridge, Mass.: Harvard University Press.

MacKinnon, J. (1978). *The ape within us.* New York: Holt, Rinehart & Winston.

Malthus, T. R. (1798/1960). *On population.* New York: Modern Library.

Marcus, S. (1975). Introduction. In Freud, 1905/1962, pp. xix–xli.

Marcuse, H. (1955). *Eros and civilization.* New York: Random House.

Marshall, J. (1981). Pansies, perverts, and macho men: Changing conceptions of male homosexuality. In Plummer, 1981b, pp. 133–154.

Martin, C. L., & Halverson, C. F. (1981). A schematic processing model of sex typing and stereotyping in children. *Child Development, 52,* 1119–1134.

Martin, M. K., & Voorhies, B. (1975). *Female of the species*. New York: Columbia University Press.

Martyna, W. (1980). Beyond the he/man approach: The case for nonsexist language. *Signs: Journal of Women in Culture and Society, 5*, 492–493.

Matlin, M. W. (1987). *The psychology of women*. New York: Holt, Rinehart & Winston.

Mayo, C., & Henley, N. M. (Eds.). (1981). *Gender and nonverbal behavior*. New York: Springer-Verlag.

Mayr, E. (1982). *The growth of biological thought: Diversity, evolution, and inheritance*. Cambridge, Mass: Harvard University Press.

Meaney, M. J. (1988). The sexual differentiation of social play. *Trends in Neurosciences, 11*, 54–58.

Merchant, C. (1980). *The death of nature: Women, ecology, and the scientific revolution*. New York: Harper & Row.

Merton, R. K. (1948). The self-fulfilling prophecy. *Antioch Review, 8*, 193–210.

Meyer, J. K., & Reter, D. J. (1979). Sex reassignment. *Archives of General Psychiatry, 36*, 1010–1015.

Meyer-Bahlburg, H. F. L. (1984). Psychoendocrine research on sexual orientation. *Progress in Brain Research, 61*, 375–398.

Miller, J. B. (1976). *Toward a new psychology of women*. Boston: Beacon.

Millett, K. (1969). *Sexual politics*. New York: Ballantine Books.

Minow, M. (1990). *Making all the difference: Inclusion, exclusion, and American law*. Ithaca, N.Y.: Cornell University Press.

Mischel, W. (1970). Sex-typing and socialization. In P. H. Mussen (Ed.), *Carmichael's manual of child psychology* (Vol. 2, pp. 3–72). New York: Wiley.

Mitchell, J. (1974). *Psychoanalysis and feminism: Freud, Reich, Laing and women*. New York: Random House.

Moi, T. (1985). *Sexual/textual politics: Feminist literary theory*. New York: Routledge.

Money, J., & Ehrhardt, A. (1972). *Man and woman, boy and girl*. Baltimore, Md.: Johns Hopkins University Press.

Montrelay. M. (1977). *L'Ombre et le nom: Sur la féminité*. Paris: Minuit.

Moore, C. L. (1984). Maternal contributions to the development of masculine sexual behavior in laboratory rats. *Developmental Psychobiology, 17*, 347–356.

——— (1985). Another psychobiological view of sexual differentiation. *Developmental Review, 5*, 18–55.

REFERENCES

Moore, H. L. (1988). *Feminism and anthropology*. Minneapolis: University of Minnesota Press.

Morawski, J. G. (1985). The measurement of masculinity and femininity: Engendering categorical realities. *Journal of Personality, 53,* 196–223.

——— (1987). The troubled quest for masculinity, femininity, and androgyny. In P. Shaver & C. Hendrick (Eds.), *Review of personality and social psychology* (Vol. 7, pp. 44–69). Newbury Park, Calif.: Sage.

Morin, S. F., & Schultz, S. J. (1978). The gay movement and the rights of children. *Journal of Social Issues, 34,* 137–148.

Morris, J. (1974). *Conundrum*. New York: Signet.

Mussen, P. H. (1969). Early sex-role development. In D. A. Goslin (Ed.), *Handbook of socialization theory and research* (pp. 707–731). Chicago: Rand McNally.

Myers, B. J. (1984). Mother-infant bonding: The status of this critical-period hypothesis. *Developmental Review, 4,* 240–274.

Neisser, U. (1967). *Cognitive psychology*. New York: Appleton-Century-Crofts.

——— (1976). *Cognition and reality: Principles and implications of cognitive psychology*. San Francisco: Freeman.

Newman, L. M. (Ed.). (1985). *Men's ideas/Women's realities: Popular science, 1870–1915*. New York: Pergamon.

Newton, E. (1988). Of yams, grinders, and gays: The anthropology of homosexuality. *Out/Look,* Spring, pp. 28–50.

Newton, E., & Walton, S. (1984). The misunderstanding: Toward a more precise sexual vocabulary. In C. S. Vance (Ed.), *Pleasure and danger: Exploring female sexuality* (pp. 242–250). Boston: Routledge & Kegan Paul.

Nicholson, L. J. (1986). *Gender and history: The limits of social theory in the age of the family*. New York: Columbia University Press.

Norton, M. B. (1980). *Liberty's daughters: The revolutionary experience of American women*. Boston: Little, Brown.

Ochs, E., & Schieffelin, B. B. (1984). Language acquisition and socialization: Three developmental stories and their implications. In Shweder & LeVine, 1984, pp. 276–320.

Okin, S. M. (1979). *Women in Western political thought*. Princeton, N.J.: Princeton University Press.

——— (1989). *Justice, gender, and the family*. New York: Basic Books.

Pagels, E. (1976). What became of God the mother? Conflicting images of God in early Christianity. *Signs: Journal of Women in Culture and Society, 2,* 293–303.

——— (1977). *The Gnostic gospels*. New York: Random House.

——— (1988). *Adam, Eve, and the serpent*. New York: Random House.

Parlee, M. B. (1979). Psychology and women. *Signs: Journal of Women in Culture and Society, 5*, 121–133.

Parrot, A., & Bechhofer, L. (Eds.). (1991). *Acquaintance rape: The hidden crime*. New York: Wiley.

Parsons, T., & Bales, R. (1955). *Family, socialization, and inter-action process*. Glencoe, Ill.: Free Press.

Pateman, C. (1988). *The sexual contract*. Stanford, Calif.: Stanford University Press.

Phillips, J. A. (1984). *Eve: The history of an idea*. San Francisco: Harper & Row.

Phoenix, C. H., Goy, R. W., Gerall, A. A., & Young, W. C. (1959). Organizing action of prenatally administered testosterone propionate on the tissues mediating mating behavior in the female guinea pig. *Endocrinology , 65*, 369–382.

Piaget, J. (1932). *The moral judgment of the child*. London: Kegan Paul.

——— (1970). Piaget's theory. In P. H. Mussen (Ed.), *Carmichael's manual of child psychology* (Vol. 1, pp. 703–732). New York: Wiley.

Plaskow, J. (1990). *Standing against Sinai: Judaism from a feminist perspective*. San Francisco: Harper.

Plato (1952a). Laws. In R. M. Hutchins (Ed.), *Great books of the Western world* (Vol. 7, pp. 640–799). Chicago: Encyclopaedia Britannica.

——— (1952b). The Republic. In R. M. Hutchins (Ed.), *Great books of the Western world* (Vol. 7, pp. 295–441). Chicago: Encyclopaedia Britannica.

——— (1952c). Timaeus. In R. M. Hutchins (Ed.), *Great books of the Western world* (Vol. 7, pp. 442–477). Chicago: Encyclopaedia Britannica.

Pleck, E. (1987). *Domestic tyranny: The making of American social policy against family violence from colonial times to the present*. New York: Oxford University Press.

Plummer, K. (1981a). Building a sociology of homosexuality. In Plummer, 1981b, pp. 17–29.

——— (Ed.). (1981b). *The making of the modern homosexual*. Totowa, N.J.: Barnes & Noble.

Polanyi, M. (1967). *The tacit dimension*. London: Routledge & Kegan Paul.

Porter, N., & Geis, F. L. (1981). Women and nonverbal leadership cues: When seeing is not believing. In Mayo & Henley, 1981, pp. 39–61.

Porter, N., Geis, F. L., & Jennings, J. (1983). Are women invisible as leaders? *Sex Roles, 9*, 1035–1049.

Quadagno, D., Briscoe, R., & Quadagno, J. S. (1977). Effects of perinatal gonadal hormones on selected nonsexual behavior patterns: A critical assessment of the nonhuman and human literature. *Psychological Bulletin, 84,* 62–80.

Quadagno, J. S. (1979). Paradigms in evolutionary theory: The sociobiological model of natural selection. *American Sociological Review, 44,* 100–109.

Rado, S. (1940). A critical examination of the concept of bisexuality. *Psychosomatic Medicine, 2,* 459–467.

Raymond, J. G. (1979). *The transsexual empire: The making of the she-male.* Boston: Beacon.

Rekers, G. A. (1982a). *Growing up straight: What every family should know about homosexuality.* Chicago: Moody.

—— (1982b). *Shaping your child's sexual identity.* Grand Rapids, Mich.: Baker Book House.

Reskin, B. F. (Ed.). (1984). *Segregation in the workplace: Trends, explanations, remedies.* Washington, D.C.: National Academy Press.

Reskin, B. F., & Hartmann, H. I. (Eds.). (1986). *Women's work, men's work: Sex segregation on the job.* Washington, D.C.: National Research Council.

Reskin, B. F., & Roos, P. A. (1990). *Job queues, gender queues: Explaining women's inroads into male occupations.* Philadelphia: Temple University Press.

Reuther, R. R. (1985). *Womanguides: Readings toward a feminist theology.* Boston: Beacon.

Rhode, D. L. (1989). *Justice and gender: Sex discrimination and the law.* Cambridge, Mass.: Harvard University Press.

—— (Ed.). (1990). *Theoretical perspectives on sexual difference.* New Haven, Conn.: Yale University Press.

Rich, A. (1973). *Diving into the wreck: Poems, 1971–1972.* New York: Norton.

—— (1974). *Poems: Selected and new, 1950–1974.* New York: Norton.

—— (1976). *Of woman born: Motherhood as experience and institution.* New York: Norton.

—— (1978). *The dream of a common language: Poems, 1974–1977.* New York: Norton.

—— (1980). Compulsory heterosexuality and lesbian existence. *Signs: Journal of Women in Culture and Society, 5,* 631–660.

Robinson, P. (1976). *The modernization of sex: Havelock Ellis, Alfred Kinsey, William Masters and Virginia Johnson.* Ithaca, N.Y.: Cornell University Press.

Rodin, J., Silberstein, L., & Striegel-Moore , R. (1985). Women and weight: A normative discontent. In T. B. Sonderegger (Ed.), *Nebraska Symposium on Motivation, 1984: Psychology and gender* (pp. 197–221). Lincoln: University of Nebraska Press.

Rorty, R. (1979). *Philosophy and the mirror of nature*. Princeton, N.J.: Princeton University Press.

Rosch, E. H. (1973). Natural categories. *Cognitive Psychology, 4*, 328–350.

Rose, H. (1983). Hand, brain and heart: A feminist epistemology for the natural sciences. *Signs: Journal of Women in Culture and Society, 9*, 73–90.

Rosenberg, C. E. (1976). *No other gods: On science and American social thought*. Baltimore, Md.: Johns Hopkins University Press.

Rosenberg, R. (1982). *Beyond separate spheres: Intellectual roots of modern feminism*. New Haven, Conn.: Yale University Press.

Rosenblatt, J. S. (1967). Nonhormonal basis of maternal behavior in the rat. *Science, 156*, 1512–1513.

Rosenblatt, J. S., & Siegel, H. I. (1981). Factors governing the onset and maintenance of maternal behavior among nonprimate animals: The role of hormonal and nonhormonal factors. In D. J. Gubernick & P. H. Klopfer (Eds.), *Parental care in mammals* (pp. 13–76). New York: Plenum.

Rosenthal, R., & Jacobson, L. (1968). *Pygmalion in the classroom: Teacher expectation and pupils' intellectual development*. New York: Holt.

Rossi, A. S. (1977). A biosocial perspective on parenting. *Daedalus, 106*, 1–31.

———— (1985). Gender and parenthood. In A. S. Rossi (Ed.), *Gender and the life course* (pp. 161–191). New York: Aldine.

Rousseau, J. J. (1755/1952). On the origin of inequality. In R. M. Hutchins (Ed.), *Great books of the Western world* (Vol. 38, pp. 323–366). Chicago: Encyclopaedia Britannica.

Rubin, G. (1984). Thinking sex: Notes for a radical theory of the politics of sexuality. In C. S. Vance (Ed.), *Pleasure and danger: Exploring female sexuality* (pp. 267–319). Boston: Routledge & Kegan Paul.

Ruddick, S. (1989). *Maternal thinking: Toward a politics of peace*. Boston: Beacon.

Russell, D. E. H. (1982). *Rape in marriage*. New York: Macmillan.

Russett, C. E. (1989). *Sexual science: The Victorian construction of womanhood*. Cambridge, Mass.: Harvard University Press.

Sachs, A., & Wilson, J. H. (1978). *Sexism and the law: A study of male beliefs and legal bias in Britain and the United States*. New York: Free Press.

Sahlins, M. (1976). *The use and abuse of biology: An anthropological critique*. Ann Arbor: University of Michigan Press.

Sampson, E. E. (1977). Psychology and the American ideal. *Journal of Personality and Social Psychology, 35*, 767–782.

Sanday, P. R. (1981). *Female power and male dominance: On the origins of sexual inequality*. Cambridge, Eng.: Cambridge University Press.

REFERENCES

Saxonhouse, A. W. (1985). *Women in the history of political thought: Ancient Greece to Machiavelli*. New York: Praeger.

Sayers, J. (1982). *Biological politics: Feminist and anti-feminist perspectives*. New York: Tavistock.

Scales, A. C. (1980–81). Toward a feminist jurisprudence. *Indiana Law Journal, 56,* 375–444.

Schiebinger, L. L. (1987). The history and philosophy of women in science: A review essay. *Signs: Journal of Women in Culture and Society, 12,* 305–332.

——— (1989). *The mind has no sex? Women in the origins of modern science*. Cambridge, Mass.: Harvard University Press.

Schneider, E. M. (1980). Equal rights to trial for women: Sex bias in the law of self-defense. *Harvard Civil Rights–Civil Liberties Law Review, 15,* 623–647.

Schur, E. M. (1965). *Crimes without victims; Deviant behavior and public policy: Abortion, homosexuality, drug addiction*. Englewood Cliffs, N.J.: Prentice-Hall.

Secor, C. (1974). Androgyny: An early reappraisal. *Women's Studies, 2,* 161–169.

Sedgwick, E. K. (1990). *Epistemology of the closet*. Berkeley: University of California Press.

Segal, L. (1987). *Is the future female? Troubled thoughts on contemporary feminism*. London: Virago.

——— (1990). *Slow motion: Changing masculinities, changing men*. New Brunswick, N.J.: Rutgers University Press.

Seiwert, C. (1988). The brain as a reproductive organ: An analysis of the organizational theory of hormone action. Unpublished manuscript, Cornell University.

Sherif, C. W. (1979). Bias in psychology. In J. A. Sherman & E. T. Beck (Eds.), *The prism of sex: Essays in the sociology of knowledge* (pp. 93–133). Madison: University of Wisconsin Press.

Sherman, J. A. (1971). *On the psychology of women: A survey of empirical studies*. Springfield, Ill.: Charles C. Thomas.

Shields, S. A. (1975a). Functionalism, Darwinism, and the psychology of women. *American Psychologist, 30,* 739–754.

——— (1975b). Ms. Pilgrim's progress: The contributions of Leta Stetter Hollingworth to the psychology of women. *American Psychologist, 30,* 852–857.

——— (1982). The variability hypothesis: The history of a biological model of sex differences in intelligence. *Signs: Journal of Women in Culture and Society, 7,* 769–797.

Shweder, R. A. (1984). Anthropology's romantic rebellion against the enlightenment; or, There's more to thinking than reason and evidence. In Shweder & LeVine, 1984, pp. 27–66.

Shweder, R. A., & Bourne, E. J. (1984). Does the concept of the person vary cross-culturally? In Shweder & LeVine, 1984, pp. 158–199.

Shweder, R. A., & LeVine, R. A. (Eds.). (1984). *Culture theory: Essays on mind, self, and emotion.* Cambridge, Eng.: Cambridge University Press.

Simon, W., & Gagnon, J. H. (1967). Homosexuality: The formulation of a sociological perspective. *Journal of Health and Social Behavior, 8,* 177–184.

Sjoo, M., & Mor, B. (1987). *The great cosmic mother: Rediscovering the religion of the earth.* New York: Harper & Row.

Slijper, F. M. E. (1984). Androgens and gender role behaviour in girls with congenital adrenal hyperplasia (CAH). *Progress in Brain Research, 61,* 417–422.

Smith, D. E. (1987). *The everyday world as problematic: A feminist sociology.* Boston: Northeastern University Press.

Smith, E. E., & Medin, D. L. (1981). *Concepts and categories.* Cambridge, Mass.: Harvard University Press.

Smith-Rosenberg, C. (1975). The female world of love and ritual: Relations between women in nineteenth-century America. *Signs: Journal of Women in Culture and Society, 1,* 1–29.

Smith-Rosenberg, C., & Rosenberg, C. (1973). The female animal: Medical and biological views of woman and her role in nineteenth-century America. *Journal of American History, 60,* 332–356.

Snitow, A. (1989). Pages from a gender diary: Basic divisions in feminism. *Dissent, 36,* 205–224.

Snyder, M. (1981). On the self-perpetuating nature of social stereotypes. In D. L. Hamilton (Ed.), *Cognitive processes in stereotyping and intergroup behavior* (pp. 183–212). Hillsdale, N.J.: Erlbaum.

Snyderman, M., & Herrnstein, R. J. (1983). Intelligence tests and the Immigration Act of 1924. *American Psychologist, 38,* 986–995.

Socarides, C. (1968). *The overt homosexual.* New York: Grune & Stratton.

——— (1970). Homosexuality and medicine. *Journal of the American Medical Association, 212,* 1199–1202.

Spence, J. T. (1984). Masculinity, femininity, and gender-related traits: A conceptual analysis and critique of current research. In B. A. Maher & W. B. Maher (Eds.), *Progress in experimental research in personality* (Vol. 13, pp. 1–97). New York: Academic Press.

Spence, J. T., Helmreich, R. L., & Stapp, J. (1974). The Personal Attributes

Questionnaire: A measure of sex-role stereotypes and masculinity-femininity. *JSAS Catalog of Selected Documents in Psychology, 4,* 43–44.

Spencer, H. (1852). A theory of population deduced from the general law of animal fertility. *Westminster Review, 57,* 468–501.

—— (1873). Psychology of the sexes. *Popular Science Monthly, 4,* 30–38.

—— (1876). *The principles of sociology.* New York: Appleton.

Steiner, B. W. (Ed.). (1985). *Gender dysphoria: Development, research, management.* New York: Plenum.

Stimpson, C. R. (1974). The androgyne and the homosexual. *Women's Studies, 2,* 237–248.

—— (1980). The new scholarship about women: The state of the art. *Annals of Scholarship, 1,* 2–14.

Stoddard, L. (1920). *The rising tide of color against white world-supremacy.* New York: Scribner's.

Stoddart, T., & Turiel, E. (1985). Children's concepts of cross-gender activities. *Child Development, 56,* 1241–1252.

Stoller, R. J. (1968). *Sex and gender.* New York: Science House.

—— (1985). *Presentations of gender.* New Haven, Conn.: Yale University Press.

Sulloway, F. J. (1979). *Freud, biologist of the mind: Beyond the psychoanalytic legend.* New York: Basic Books.

Symons, D. (1979). *The evolution of human sexuality.* New York: Oxford University Press.

Szasz, T. S. (1961). *The myth of mental illness.* New York: Hoeber-Harper.

—— (1979). Review of Janice Raymond's "The transsexual empire." *New York Times Book Review,* June 10, 1979, pp. 11, 39.

Taub, N., & Schneider, E. M. (1982). Perspectives on women's subordination and the role of law. In D. Kairys (Ed.), *The politics of law: A progressive critique* (pp. 117–139). Boston: Pantheon.

Taylor, M. C., & Hall, J. A. (1982). Psychological androgyny: A review and reformulation of theories, methods, and conclusions. *Psychological Bulletin, 92,* 347–366.

Terman, L. M., & Miles, C. C. (1936). *Sex and personality: Studies in masculinity and femininity.* New York: McGraw-Hill.

Thompson, C. (1947). Changing concepts of homosexuality in psychoanalysis. *Psychiatry, 10,* 183–189.

Thompson, S. K., & Bentler, P. M. (1971). The priority of cues in sex discrimination by children and adults. *Developmental Psychology, 5,* 181–185.

Tiger, L. (1970). The possible biological origins of sex discrimination. *Impact of Science on Society, 20,* 29–44.

Tobin, J. J., Wu, D. Y. H., & Davidson, D. H. (1989). *Preschool in three cultures: Japan, China, and the United States.* New Haven, Conn.: Yale University Press.

Toulmin, S. E. (1972). *Human understanding.* Princeton, N.J.: Princeton University Press.

—— (1982). *The return to cosmology: Postmodern science and the theology of nature.* Berkeley: University of California Press.

Treiman, D. J., & Hartmann, H. I. (Eds.). (1981). *Women, work, and wages: Equal pay for jobs of equal value.* Washington, D.C.: National Academy Press.

Troiden, R. (1979). Becoming homosexual: A model of gay identity acquisition. *Psychiatry, 42,* 362–373.

Ullian, D. Z. (1981). The child's construction of gender: Anatomy as destiny. In E. K. Shapiro & E. Weber (Eds.), *Cognitive and affective growth: Developmental interaction* (pp. 171–184). Hillsdale, N.J.: Erlbaum.

Unger, R. K. (1983). Through the looking glass: No wonderland yet! (The reciprocal relationship between methodology and models of reality). *Psychology of Women Quarterly, 8,* 9–32.

Unger, R. K., & Crawford, M. (1992). *Women and gender: A feminist psychology.* New York: McGraw-Hill.

Valdés, E., del Castillo, C., Gutiérrez, R., Larrea, F., Medina, M., & Pérez-Palacios, G. (1979). Endocrine studies and successful treatment in a patient with true hermaphroditism. *Acta Endocrinologica, 91,* 184–192.

Veblen, T. (1899/1934). *The theory of the leisure class: An economic study of institutions.* New York: Random House/Modern Library.

Wallston, B. S. (1981). What are the questions in psychology of women: A feminist approach to research. *Psychology of Women Quarterly, 5,* 597–617.

Warshaw, R. (1988). *I never called it rape: The Ms. report on recognizing, fighting, and surviving date and acquaintance rape.* New York: Harper & Row.

Wartofsky, M. (1983). The child's construction of the world and the world's construction of the child: From historical epistemology to historical psychology. In Kessel & Siegel, 1983, pp. 188–215.

Weeks, J. (1977). *Coming out: Homosexual politics in Britain, from the nineteenth century to the present.* London: Quartet Books.

—— (1981). Discourse, desire and sexual deviance: Some problems in a history of homosexuality. In Plummer, 1981b, pp. 76–111.

—— (1986). *Sexuality.* London: Tavistock.

REFERENCES

Weitzman, L. J. (1985). *The divorce revolution: The unexpected social and economic consequences for women and children in America.* New York: Free Press.

Whalen, R. E. (1968). Differentiation of the neural mechanisms which control gonadotropin secretion and sexual behavior. In M. Diamond (Ed.), *Perspectives in reproduction and sexual behavior* (Vol. 15, pp. 325–376). Bloomington: Indiana University Press.

Whiting, B. B., & Edwards, C. P. (1988). *Children of different worlds: The formation of social behavior.* Cambridge, Mass.: Harvard University Press.

Wilson, E. O. (1975). *Sociobiology: The new synthesis.* Cambridge, Mass.: Harvard University Press.

——— (1978). *On human nature.* Cambridge, Mass.: Harvard University Press.

Wynne-Edwards, V. C. (1962). *Animal dispersion in relation to social behavior.* New York: Hafner.

Zucker, K. J. (1985). Cross-gender-identified children. In Steiner, 1985, pp. 75–174.

INDEX

Androcentric definition of a woman: as departure from male norm, 46–47, 50–52, 54, 59–60, 73–79, 144; in terms of male sexuality, 47, 48, 50, 55–56, 59, 144, 145, 166; in terms of domestic and reproductive functions, 47–48, 51–54, 59, 65, 67–70, 144, 145

Androcentrism: as defined by feminist theorists, 2, 39–43, 144–145; in Judeo-Christian theology, 43–49; in Greek philosophy, 49–56; in Freud's theory of male-female development, 56–62, 92; in U.S. law, 62–79, 184–185; as illuminated by woman-centered feminism, 130–132; process of transfer from culture to individual, 143–146; in structure of work and childhood in U.S., 143–146; in language, 145, 172; consequences once internalized by individual, 152–167; effects on heterosexuality, 163–164; analysis of how it transforms sexual difference into female disadvantage, 183–191. *See also* Internalized gender lenses

Androgyny: Greek roots of, viii; empirical work on, 118–120; as positively viewed by feminists, 120–122, 127, 153; feminist critiques of, 122–125; androcentrism in term itself, 123; inner tension in, 175

Aristotle, 50, 53–54, 201*n6*

Barash, David, 16, 17, 18–19

Beauvoir, Simone de, 41–42, 145, 199–200*n2*

Bem's enculturated lens theory: enculturation of lenses, 138–151; role of gender insecurity, 148–151; self-construction once lenses are internalized, 151–167. *See also* Enculturation; Individual gender formation, social constructionist theories of; Internalized gender lenses

Bem Sex Role Inventory (BSRI), 118–120, 126–127, 154–156, 206*n38*

Benbow, Camilla, 37

Bergler, Edmund, 93, 95–96

Bieber, Irving, 94–95

Biological essentialism: relation to religion, 2; definition, 2, 4; in nineteenth-century theorizing about race, class, national origin, and male-female difference, 6–13, 197–198*n4*; in sociobiology, 14–23; in prenatal hormone theory, 23–29; in Freud's theory of sexual object choice, 92; in woman-centered feminism, 131. *See also* Biology theorized in context

Biology theorized in context: 2–3, 6, 21–23, 26–29, 177; sexual universals of human social organization, 30–33; male-female differences in individual psychology, 33–38, 134; on diversity as human norm in sexuality and gender, 99–101, 167–169; and analysis of how androcentrism transforms sexual difference into female disadvantage, 183–191
Bleier, Ruth, 18, 20
Body, gendering of, 159–162
Brownmiller, Susan, 163

Chodorow, Nancy, 129, 136, 138
Clarke, Edward, 10
Class: applicability of lens analysis to, 3; biological theorizing about in nineteenth century, 6–9; in ancient Greek philosophy, 50; and definition of full-time work, 144; inclusiveness in feminist analysis, 188; hidden discrimination against the poor, 191
Comparable worth: 77–78, 79, 180
Cross-cultural universals: as theorized by sociobiology, 19–21; as theorized biohistorically, 20–23, 29–37, 134; anthropological debate on male political dominance, 30

Darwin, Charles, 11–13, 15, 59, 88
Diagnostic and Statistical Manual of Mental Disorders (DSM) of the American Psychiatric Association, 93, 94, 106–107, 109, 110, 111
Diversity among women: as source of conflict in feminism, 182, 210n4; and inclusive model of gender neutrality, 187–188
Divorce, 78–79, 179, 202n23
DSM. See Diagnostic and Statistical Manual of Mental Disorders (DSM) of the American Psychiatric Association

Eagly, Alice, 135

Ehrhardt, Anke, 25–27
Ellis, Havelock, 85–87, 91
Enculturation: of cultural natives, 139–143; of gendered cultural natives, 143–151
Epstein, Cynthia, 135
Equal protection clause: wording, 65–66; differential application to blacks and women, 66, 70–73; Supreme Court's refusal to apply in pregnancy discrimination, 74–77. *See also* Law; Supreme Court
Equal rights amendment: wording, 72; history and feminist reasoning on need for, 72–73, 178, 179, 181
Erikson, Erik, 60–61, 152

Fausto-Sterling, Anne, 18, 34–35
Feminist thought: racism in, 13; evolving concepts related to androcentrism, 40–42; reactions to Freud, 60–62; psychoanalytic feminism, 61–62, 129–130, 136, 138; recent historical shift from male-female similarity and gender neutrality to male-female difference and woman-centered benefits, 72–73, 127–128, 130, 177–182; about androgyny, 120–125; development of woman-centered feminism in *1970*s and critique thereof, 127–132; conflicts arising from focus on male-female difference, 176–182, 190–192; conflicts arising from focus on female-female difference, 182, 210n4; ambivalence about total dismantling of gender polarization, 192
Foucault, Michel, 99, 100
Freedman, Estelle, 81, 182
Freud, Sigmund, 56–62, 84, 86–93, 115, 136, 149
Friedan, Betty, 39, 61

Gay rights movement, 99, 169–174
Geddes, Patrick, 13
Gelpi, Barbara, 123

Gender depolarization, 115–122, 192–196

Gender development in childhood. *See* Individual gender formation, social constructionist theories of

Gender differences: biological theorizing about in nineteenth century, 9–13; in individual psychology, theorized biohistorically, 33–38; in physical aggression, 34–35; in parental responsiveness, 35–37, 134; in math ability, 37–38; empirical research on, 102, 204n22; in meaning of gender deviation, 86, 109, 114, 146, 149–151; in homophobia, 165–167; focus on, as paralyzing debate on sexual inequality, 176–182, 190–192; analysis of how they are transformed into female disadvantage by androcentrism, 183–191

Gender identity disorders: and homosexuality, 106, 109–10; gender polarization in discourse on, 106–11; as by-product of gender polarization in culture, 109, 111; critique of interventions with children as anti-gay, 110–111. *See also* Transsexuals

Gender identity formation. *See* Individual gender formation, social constructionist theories of

Gender insecurity, 147–151, 166–167

Gender neutrality: discussed in set-theory terms, 76–77; vs. special protection, 178–180; 190–191; traditional liberal vision of, as distorted by androcentrism, 183–191; as redefined to include female experience, 184–188, 190–191; and differences among women, 187–188; as requiring group rights for women, 190–191

Gender polarization: definition, 2, 80; of biological continuum into two sexes, 80; modes of operation, 80–81; relation to heterosexism, 81, 82;

in nineteenth-century discourse on sexual inversion, 81–87; in psychoanalytic theory of sexual orientation, 87–98; in masculinity-femininity assessment, 102–106; in discourse on gender identity disorders, 106–111, in discourse on "normal" gender development, 111–115; feminist challenges to, 115–127, 192–196; in woman-centered feminism, 130–131; in language, 146–147; process of transfer from culture to individual, 146–149; in U.S. social practice, 146–149; as fostering a social definition of male and female, 147–151; how resisted in Bem's rearing of own children, 149–151; consequences once internalized by individual, 152–167; empirical research on perception through lens of, 154–157. *See also* Gender depolarization; Internalized gender lenses

Gender schema theory, 125–127, 131, 138–139; empirical research on, 153–157

Genital difference between the sexes, children's knowledge of: as theorized by Freud, 57–60, 136; empirical data on, 114–117; as product of enculturation, 115, 147–149; legacy of gender insecurity, 148–151; as fostered in Bem's own family, 149

Gilligan, Carol, 128, 129

Gilman, Charlotte Perkins, 41

Green, Richard, 108–110

Heilbrun, Carolyn, 121, 124–125, 127, 206n40

Henley, Nancy, 135

Heterosexism: definition, 81; relation to gender polarization, 81, 82; Freud's challenge to, 88–89, 92; in U.S. social practices, 147; linked to male gender insecurity, 151; and identity construction of homosex-

Heterosexism (*continued*)
uals, 169–175; political resistance to, 172–174

Heterosexuality: Freud's de-privileging of, 88–90, 92; as a biohistorical construction, 98–101, 147, 167–169, 173, 192–193, 203n18; as socially constructed into the eroticizing of female inequality, 163–164

Hirschfeld, Magnus, 85, 87

Homophobia, 101, 165–167

Homosexuality: as differently conceptualized and expressed across time and place, 50, 81, 83, 85, 87, 98–101, 137, 165, 169–175, 209n28; nineteenth-century pathologizing of in language of sexual inversion, 81–87; twentieth-century pathologizing of by psychoanalytic theory, 87–98; abhorrence of, 95–97, 151, 165–167; political treatment of during McCarthy era, 97–98; social-constructionist perspectives on, 98–101, 147, 167–169, 173, 192–193, 203n18; and first masculinity-femininity scale, 103, 105; and transsexualism, 106, 109–110; U.S. social practices marginalizing, 147; changing meaning of homosexual identity over twentieth century, 167–175; stage theories of identity and critique thereof, 174–175

Hooker, Evelyn, 99

Hooks, bell, 130

Identity construction: Kohlberg's cognitive-developmental theory, 111–115; overview of theories, 136–138; by transsexuals, 137, 170–171; as related to identity politics, 137, 175; by gender-conforming males and females, 151–167; in Bem's enculturated-lens theory of gender formation, 151–175

—by gay men and lesbians: as compared to that of Jews, 169, 174; over course of twentieth century, 169–175; stage theories and critique thereof, 174–175

Identity politics, 137, 172–175

Imperato-McGinley, Julianne, 25, 27–29

Individual gender formation, social constructionist theories of: Freud's psychoanalytic theory, 56–62, 87–90; Kohlberg's cognitive-developmental theory, 111–115; Bem's gender schema theory, 125–127, 138–139; Chodorow's psychoanalytic object-relations theory, 129–130, 136; overview of socialization, social-structural, psychoanalytic, and identity-construction theories, 133–138; Bem's enculturated-lens theory, 138–167

Internalized gender lenses: as shaping perception and construction of identity and personality, 138, 152, 153–157, 158–159; empirical research on, 154–157; as shaping perception of others, 157; as responsible for self-construction of gendered body, 159–162; as responsible for eroticizing of female inequality, 163–164; and perception of male vs. female nudes, 164; as responsible for abhorrence of homosexuality, especially in men, 165–167; as needing to be resisted by otherized groups, 167–175

Jacklin, Carol, 34–35

Kanter, Rosabeth Moss, 135

Kardiner, Abram, 93, 96

Keller, Evelyn Fox, 129

Kinsey, Alfred, 98

Kohlberg, Lawrence, 112–115, 126, 137, 148

Lacan, Jacques, 62, 136

Language, 199–200n2: androcentrism in, 145, 172; gender polarization in, 146–147

Law: sterilization and immigration, 6–9; women's rights, androcentrism in history of, 62–79; self-defense, 184–185. *See also* Equal protection clause; Race; Supreme Court

Lewes, Kenneth, 95, 96

Maccoby, Eleanor, 34–35

MacKinnon, Catharine, 183, 184

Male-female dichotomy: two sexes as a social construction, 80

Male power: mechanisms of social reproduction, 3, 32–33, 79, 132, 152, 183–191; defined, 3, 191; theorized biohistorically, 29–33; anthropological debate over cross-cultural universality of, 30

Masculinity-femininity. *See* Gender depolarization; Internalized gender lenses

Masculinity-femininity development. *See* Individual gender formation, social constructionist theories of

M-F assessment, 102–106. *See also* Masculinity-femininity

Miller, Jean Baker, 128, 130

Millett, Kate, 40, 61

Mitchell, Juliet, 62

Money, John, 25–27

Oppositional consciousness, 130, 169, 174

Patriarchy. *See* Androcentrism

Personality, gendering of, 152–159

Phillips, John, 47, 48, 49

Piaget, Jean, 112–114

Plato, 50–53, 201n6

Pornography, and male nudes, 164

Preferential hiring, 180

Prenatal hormone theory, 23–29

Protective legislation, 68, 178–180, 190

Psychoanalytic perspectives. *See* Freud, Sigmund; Homosexuality; Individual gender formation, social constructionist theories of

Race: applicability of lens analysis to, 3; nineteenth-century biological theorizing about, 6–9, 13, 197–198n4; in history of equal rights law, 65, 66, 70; hidden discrimination against people of color, 191

Rape, 62, 163, 164; marital, as contested concept, 145

Rekers, George, 108, 110

Religion: relation to science, 1, 2, 6; androcentrism in, 43–49

Rich, Adrienne, 40, 99, 121–123, 129

Rose, Hilary, 128, 130

Rossi, Alice, 37

Rousseau, Jean Jacques, 55–56

Science: relation to religion, 1, 2, 6; feminist challenges to objectivity of, 6, 129–130; as affecting, and affected by, cultural and historical events, 6–10, 14, 81–82, 87, 97–98, 102–103, 118

Sexism, 1, 40–41

Sex typing. *See* Individual gender formation, social constructionist theories of

Sexual inequality: theorized biohistorically, 29–33; quagmires in historical debate on as produced by focus on male-female difference, 176–182; refocusing the debate on how androcentrism transforms sexual difference into female disadvantage, 183–191; historical quagmires transcended, 190–191

Sexual inversion, 81–87; and first masculinity-femininity test, 103, 105

Sexuality: inadequacy of available cultural categories, vii–viii; diversity as human norm, 167–168; as restruc-

Sexuality (*continued*)
  tured in absence of gender polarization, 192–193. *See also* Heterosexuality; Homosexuality
Soccarides, Charles, 93, 96
Sociobiology, 14–23
Special protection for women, 178–180
Spencer, Herbert, 10–11
Supreme Court: and women's rights,
  65–79; evolution of less than "strict
  scrutiny" standard for women, 70–
  73; similarly situated model of equal
  protection, 73–79, 179; decisions on
  insurance coverage for pregnancy,
  74–77, 79; decisions about women
  disadvantaged by laws preferring veterans, 77; and other Court decisions
  about women disadvantaged by gendered life experiences, 77–79. *See
  also* Equal protection clause; Law
Szasz, Thomas, 99, 111

Terman, Lewis, 8, 102–106, 119–120
Thomson, J. Arthur, 13

Transsexuals, 106–111; and identity-
  construction theories, 137; feelings
  about the body as not so different
  from those of non-transsexuals, 160;
  how "wrong" sex label might get attached to the self, 170–171

Violence: against women, 163–164;
  against homosexuals, 166–167, 173

Weeks, Jeffrey, 100–101
Weinberg, George, 101
Wilson, Edward O., 14–17, 21
Woman-centered feminism, 127–132;
  as gender polarizing, 130–131; as biologically essentialist, 131; as illuminating about androcentrism,
  131–132
Women's rights movement: pre-*1960*s,
  1, 9, 64–65, 69, 81; *1960*s and later,
  1–2, 39–40, 70, 72–73; racism in history of, 13. *See also* Feminist thought;
  Woman-centered feminism